Compiled just for you...

HOT POTATOES
The King of Vegetables
Cook Book

A Hot Item In Today's Menus

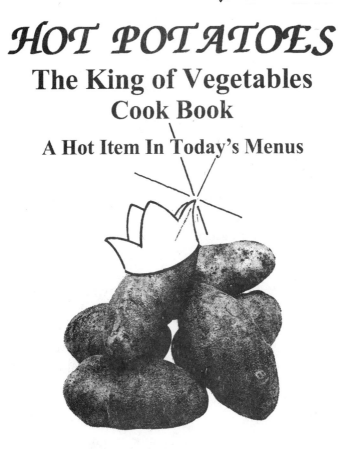

Summit Publications

1554 North 700 East   Shelley, Idaho 83274
Phone 208/357-5359   Fax 208/357-2302

Copyright protected 1994 © by Dorene Gomm
First Printing Sept. 1994   Second Printing Dec. 1994
Third Printing May 1995

Inside design and layout -- Dorene Gomm
Cover Design -- Lyle Gomm & Dorene Gomm
Editing -- Becky Pinkham & Annette Bohman

ISBN O-9643983-0-3

ACKNOWLEDGMENTS

My thanks to those who helped me locate and test the recipes for this potato cookbook. Many of the recipes are from family members who are all excellent cooks. Each recipe has been tested at least once. When the book was first compiled there were over 700 recipes. After testing and re-evaluating the number was narrowed down to 551. I'm sure many of these dishes will be used over and over again in your kitchen.

A special thanks to my husband, Ben, who on many occasions during the final 4 months of compiling this book found the time not only to get meals for himself but for me as well. He never complained, though I know he wished I would work faster. He has been my greatest help as well as my own personal cheerleader.

A thanks to our four children, Becky Pinkham, Sandee Lake, Ben Jr, and Annette Bohman who each offered encouragement when it was needed. They encouraged me to keep going when I wanted to quit. And, a special thanks to my daughters Becky and Annette who edited and re-edited the book.

Thank you Colleen Sloan, Arvella Stewart, Lyle Gomm, Veretta Jenkins, Carol McCabe, thank you friends, and especially thanks to each of you who have purchased my potato cookbook. Use it lots!

Here's to you *"Hot Potato"*.

This cookbook, one of a kind, has over 550 tested recipes all containing potatoes. It has been compiled especially for you...a potato lover. I'm sure all potato lovers already know that the potato has truly become the

"King of Vegetables"...

a title well deserved as the potato is a hot item in today's menus.

As popular as the potato is...and Americans eat four times more potatoes than any other vegetable...few of us realize that it's a near-perfect food. The Agricultural Research Department of the U.S.D.A. has declared that, "A diet of whole milk and potatoes would supply almost all the food elements for the maintenance of the human body." Add to this the fact that potatoes fit into a full range of dishes from appetizers to desserts and you'll understand why we're excited about this book of potato recipes.

Within these pages you will find recipes for salads, soups, breads, cakes, pancakes, toppings, crock-pot dishes, breakfast dishes and yes... main and side dishes containing potatoes from mashed, baked, fries, chips, flakes, to numerous other delicious ways of preparing satisfying, treats with your taste buds in mind.

Potatoes, like so many other favorite things, have picked up a few "nick-names". This is because the public loves them and usually "nick-names" are a way of showing affection. The most common potato nick-names are "Spuds" and "Taters". Call them whatever you like, but they are grown and loved world wide.

Recipes in this book will show you how to take one of the most inexpensive foods, the potato, and turn it into a

"Million Dollar Dish".

Norman & Carl Kelley's Farm Land & Equipment

Large expensive equipment is used to dig, windrow and load potatoes onto trucks. The ground is full of harvest ruts, it's bumpy, the load is heavy and the

drivers appreciate dry fields. Rain or snow is not welcomed by farmers during the harvest.

Potato farmers are gamblers in the sense they never know what the out-come of their harvest will be. Some years the gamble is very lucrative and other years it could mean financial ruin.

There is a variety of emotions the farmer goes through during harvest. But, the weather is the main concern. If storms or frost comes during harvest, the delay is sometimes disastrous. In 1993 many fields were lost to freezing weather.

The combine loading the potatoes onto the truck above is designed to filter out the majority of the dirt and vines prior to gently lowering the potatoes into the trucks bed. The potatoes can't be dropped over 18 inches or they may bruise, therefore great care is taken with the precious potatoes until they go into a dormant (sleeping) stage in the storage cellar.

Now that's a "heap" of potatoes headed for the cellar. This truck hauls about 30,000 pounds of potatoes. That translates to about 15 tons.

At the Kelly Brothers cellar a gate at the end of the truck is opened and the potatoes carefully drop onto a conveyer where hired hands assist their travel. Then a remote controlled piler will stack them 18' to 21' high, to be stored until sold to a processor.

Workers are always on the alert for potential problems such as equipment failure and debris, rocks and vines caught in the conveyer belt.

Excess dirt filters to the ground, but workers must remove rocks, vines and damaged potatoes. The conveyer moves at a fast pace, and hands are kept busy removing that which must be removed.

Oler Brothers Cellar

Designed and built in 1993 by my son, Ben Gomm Jr.

This modern cellar holds 8 million pounds of potatoes piled about 50' wide, 200' long and 20' high . It has a computer controlled atmospheric system. It can be connected to a large refrigerator system during the summer storage. This cellar will maintain the potatoes to within 1 degree accuracy. Temperature varies with the type of potatoes stored.

CONTENTS

Just Thought You'd Like To Know

When I was just a young girl growing up in Utah and my big brother was in the Navy, stationed in Idaho, he introduced me to the Idaho Potato by sending me the cutest 2 cent postcard I had ever seen. Pictured on the postcard was a big cartooned Idaho Russet potato. That potato and the little red wagon it filled was the entire card. The caption said: "Heave Ho From Idaho--Where The Big Potatoes Grow!"

I have since learned that not only are some of them big, but that caption could have said "Where The Best Potatoes Grow". At that time how could I have ever known that someday, I too would live in Idaho where the big potatoes grow---where the best potatoes grow.

By far the most versatile of the earthgrown foods is the POTATO. This vegetable has an old and honorable lineage. It was carried from Peru to Europe by 16th century conquistadors. At first it was met with suspicion and scorn, but went on to become one of the most used vegetables of all time. From a report dated in the early 1980's we can read; "Today it is produced in 130 of the world's 167 independent countries and has become the KING among vegetables. It is famous for its fruitfulness, hardiness, nutrition, and versatility."

Most of the world's crop of potatoes belong to the species Solanum tuberosum (a tuber which is part of the underground stem). The plant sprouts from an eye, or bud, of a sown piece of the tuber. Only the tuber of the potato plant is edible.

What could be more versatile than the potato? It even comes in five basic types...and numerous varieties.

● **RUSSETS:** These are the baking potatoes, long and oval with a netted surface and shallow-eyed. Their mealy texture is perfect for light and fluffy french frying or baking.

● **ALL-PURPOSE LONG WHITES:** The majority of marketed potatoes fall under this classification. Long, tan in color with fine speckles. The flesh can be waxy or mealy. The all-purpose variety is good for salads, creaming, scalloping, & baking.

- **ALL-PURPOSE ROUND WHITE:**
About the same uses as the long whites. The main difference is the shape.

- **RED POTATOES.**
Ranging in color from pink to vermillion, these waxy potatoes may be long or round. They are used for boiling and in salads.

- **NEW POTATOES:**
These are not a variety, but simply potatoes that come to market directly from the field and are not placed in storage. They are generally harvested smaller in size with a unique skin texture and are available all year in limited quantities. New potatoes are round red or long white with thin skins, usually waxy with high sugar content. Delicious boiled and served in their jackets with butter or creamed peas fresh out of the garden. Good for salads.

Potato maturity has three gradations; new, semi-early and late. New potatoes are simply washed and brushed with butter before baking. They are delicious, but do not keep long. Semi-early potatoes and late potatoes will keep longer and of course it is the late potato that can be stored all winter, even up until the new crop is harvested the following fall.

Potatoes are served often, and it's important to buy the best (Idaho Potatoes. Maybe I'm partial.) Idaho potatoes are the V.I.P. of the potatoes (Very Important Potato), and that's how Idaho farmers and cooks treat them. A great deal of care goes into raising the spuds. The care begins with certified Russet Burbank seed. Warm days in the high mountain valleys nourish the plant, and the cool nights send this nourishment down into the tuber where it is stored. Volcanic soil rich in minerals, and abundant mountain streams or deep wells for irrigation produce the finest potatoes in the land. In fact, Idaho grows more potatoes than any other state.

Idaho potatoes are held in scientifically ventilated storage facilities, graded by state & federal inspectors, then shipped in padded, temperature controlled train cars or semi-trucks to retain the flavor and fine texture.

Grades indicate appearance and physical qualities such as size and shape and are designed to provide protection against serious defects. Grades are established and controlled by the U.S. Department of Agriculture. U.S. No. 1 is the grade generally available to consumers. There are varying sizes in the grade. The baker size, is of course, the top grade.

If you are on a tight budget use lower grades, the nutritional value is about the same. The higher grades do look more attractive and are more uniform in size. But for everyday use, a lower grade will suffice. **Do** avoid potatoes with cuts, bruises, that are soft, shriveled or green in color.

No wonder these potatoes are known as the TIFFANY OF TUBERS. To make sure you've found the real thing at the store, look for the oblong label on the bag, showing a silhouette of the state and the words. "Grown in Idaho". Don't be fooled by the supermarkets.

HOW TO STORE IDAHO POTATOES PROPERLY:

Select a cool, dark, well-ventilated storage area--45 degrees is ideal. Don't refrigerate. At temperatures below 42 degrees potato starch turns to sugar and produces an uncharacteristic sweet flavor.

Protect from light to keep potatoes from turning green and acquiring a bitter flavor.

For a very inexpensive winter storage item purchase a large sack or two of potatoes each fall. I get mine fresh from the farmer at the same time he is putting them in his temperature and air controlled cellars. They keep very well in my basement storage area all winter.

POTATO EQUIVALENTS AND SUBSTITUTIONS:

Fresh Potatoes----1 pound of potatoes equals:
* about 3 medium potatoes
* 3 cups peeled & sliced
* 2¼ cups peeled, diced
* 2 cups mashed
* 2 cups french fries

Potato Salad----2 pounds of medium-sized equals:
* about 6 servings of potato salad (1 potato per serving).

Mashed Potatoes:
* main dish: 1 medium potato per serving.
* side dish or with gravy usually 1/2 to 3/4 cup.

Dehydrated Potatoes:
* Potato flakes and granules cannot always be used interchangeably in a recipe, because in dehydrated form they are not equal by volume measure. Substitutions may be made based on weight measure or on the amount of dehydrated potatoes needed to make equal amounts of mashed potatoes.

WHAT'S IN THE POTATO:

The potato is a nutrient-dense food. It provides good nutritional return for the calories. Our need for calories has probably decreased by one-third since the turn of the century because we aren't as active, but in general we still need about the same amount of nutrients as we did then. This means, in order to get the nutrition we need without consuming too many calories, we must include many nutrient-dense foods like potatoes in our diets.

A medium-size potato has only about 100 to 110 calories, four to five percent of the average adult's total daily intake of calories, but provides much higher percentages of our needs for many nutrients. For a big eater or a real potato eater, a medium-size potato may not be enough of a "good thing". But even a 250-gram potato (a little over one-half pound) has only about 160 calories, and a larger size gives you a real nutritional bonus.

The potato gives us a wide spectrum of valuable nutrients. For example, the potato is one of our most important sources of complex carbohydrates, often lacking in the American diet.

The potato is a good source of vitamin C and hard-to-get B6 and has long been known to be a storehouse of minerals. For example, potatoes contain valuable supplies of such essential trace elements as manganese, chromium, selenium and molybdenum. Exact mineral requirements for humans have not yet been established.

The starch content in potatoes is important whether they be Idaho potatoes of from other parts of the country. One way to determine the starch content of a potato is to rub two cut surfaces of a potato together. If a foam develops, this indicates a high starch content, and usually the two cut surfaces cling together. If the potato has a low starch content, the cut surface will be clean and moist and the two cut surfaces do not bond at all.

For baking and mashing and for potato soup, a potato with a high starch content is more desirable, because the potato tends to become mealy as it cooks. For potato salad or scalloped potatoes or even hash browns, a potato with a low starch content will hold its shape better as it cooks.

LOW SODIUM: A current nutritional goal is to reduce the amount of sodium consumed. While research is not complete, it indicates that the typical potato provides less than 10 mg. of sodium---compared to a typical daily intake of more than 4,000 mg.

HIGH POTASSIUM: We need to be concerned about adequate supplies of potassium. Here again, it appears that for the typical potato-eating

4

American, the potato supplies about 20 percent of the daily potassium needs.

FIBER: Fiber, almost entirely complex carbohydrates, has been the subject of renewed interest. Fiber is that part of the food we eat that is not digested, but travels through the digestive tract, some types holding water, and forming the bulk we need for eliminating solid waste. The potato has both soluble and non-soluble fiber, and both types are needed for proper bowel cleaning. While official recommendations for fiber haven't been established, about six grams daily is considered desirable. Most Americans fall far short. Overall fiber can be added by the consumption of potatoes. 10% of the daily intake of fiber can be had in one average potato.

PROTEIN: We usually consider protein to be an expensive food. That is not necessarily so. Potatoes contain small amounts of protein. Protein in potatoes is among the best to be found in vegetables, making it an inexpensive supplementary source of protein for your meals.   Eating potatoes along with a good source of a complete protein, helps the body utilize the protein from the potato.

IRON: Good sources of iron are not as easy to obtain in the diet as one may think. In fact, it's hard to get sufficient amounts of this mineral. Iron is lacking in many diets, particularly those of women, teen-age girls and young children.   Although few foods contain large amounts of iron, potatoes are a very good source. When consumed on a daily basis (5 ½ ounce average per person), potatoes furnish more iron than any other vegetable. Though not all the iron content in all foods is available for the body's use, iron in potatoes is highly usable by our bodies.

CARBOHYDRATES: The potato has been criticized for being "just a starch." There's a lot more to potatoes, of course, but the carbohydrates in potatoes are the most common form of complex carbohydrates and as such are important to a good diet. Carbohydrates are the body's primary source of energy fuel. Experts say at least 50 percent of our daily body fuel should come from carbohydrates.

Carbohydrates are of several types. Sugars are the most basic, the building blocks of complex carbohydrates. Contrary to the belief of many, gram for gram, carbohydrates have no more calories than protein and less than half that of fat. In fact, potatoes are virtually fat-free.

```
┌─────────────────────────────────────────────────────┐
│  NUTRITIONAL INFORMATION per serving in the raw      │
│  potato:                                             │
│  (A serving is one medium potato (150 grams) about 3 │
│  potatoes to the pound.                              │
│                                                      │
│  Calories ...................................... 100 to 110 │
│  Protein ............................................ 3 grams │
│  Carbohydrate .................................. 23 grams │
│  Fat .................................................... 0 │
│  Dietary Fiber ................................ 2710 mg │
│  Sodium ......................................... 10 mg │
│  Potassium ..................................... 750 mg │
│                                                      │
└─────────────────────────────────────────────────────┘
```

HOW TO COOK THE POTATO:

To clean gently scrub potatoes with a vegetable brush or cellulose sponge.

* Leaving skin on potatoes during cooking will conserve their nutrients. Many nutrients lie just beneath the tissue-thin skin.
* If potatoes are peeled before cooking, use a vegetable parer, keeping peelings as thin as possible.
* Potatoes retain nutrients better if cooked whole. However, half, slice or dice them if less cooking time is desired. Use as little water as possible and try to use the potato water.
* Peeled potatoes turn dark if not cooked right away. To protect their whiteness, toss them with ascorbic acid mixture or a little lemon juice. Prolonged soaking in cold water is not recommended as it can result in a soggy potato with some vitamin loss.

Steaming Potatoes: An excellent cooking method for preserving the nutrients in potatoes. Follow these instructions for a wonderful tasting steamed potato.

Place a wire rack in the bottom of a kettle or large saucepan and add water to just below the level of the rack. Bring water to a boil, add potatoes and cook, tightly covered, until fork-tender, whole for 30 to 45 minutes, cut up for 20 to 30 minutes. Additional water may be needed if lid is not tight-fitting. The secret is holding the potatoes above the water level.

If a rack isn't available use a few little wooden blocks or crumpled aluminum foil to make an elevated platform.

Oven-Steamed Potatoes: Clean potato, pierce the skin in a few well-distributed spots with a fork to allow the steam to escape from inside the potato, and wrap in aluminum foil. By using the foil the steam will stay in and around the potato, thus the steamed potato. Place in oven directly on the rack. Heat oven somewhere between 375 to 400 degrees. Test doneness with a fork deep within the potato or by squeezing the potato between the fingers, (it will feel soft to the squeeze if done).

Boiling Potatoes: Prepare by placing potatoes, with or without skins, whole or cut up, in a pan, covering it with about 2 inches of hot salted water. Bring to boiling, turn down heat keeping the water at the low boiling state. Boil until done. Test doneness by inserting a fork deep into the potato. If done the fork should penetrate the potato easily. Drain the water off as soon as the potato is done. Use the potato water as mashing and/or gravy liquid. If the lid is not tight fitting it may be necessary to add additional water during the cooking time. Whole potatoes 30 to 40 minutes, cut-up, 20 to 25 minutes.

Baked Potatoes: Wash, dry and pierce the skin in a few well-distributed spots with a fork. This allows the steam to escape while cooking. **Don't use foil wrap.** It holds in moisture, steaming rather than baking the potatoes. Many potato experts call foil baked potatoes, "Soggy Spuds". While cooking, turn the potatoes once or twice. The skin of the potato is wonderful tasting when baked a little crisp and browned. If a soft skin is desired, rub each potato with a little salad oil before baking.

Bake at 400 degrees for 40 to 45 minutes in a conventional oven. However, the oven temperatures can range from 325 to 450 degrees, so you can bake them along with whatever you have in the oven. Remember though, the higher the heat the closer you need to watch the browning of the skins, but the faster they bake.

Be careful not to overbake. Test with a fork that is easily inserted deep into the potato or by the squeezing method (it will squeeze easily).

Fried Potatoes: Place the fat of your choice in a skillet and on medium high heat place sliced, small chunked or grated potatoes in the pan. Cook until browned on both sides; turn heat down to low and cook until tender; stirring as needed to prevent scorching or burning. Serve while hot.

Steam-Fried Potatoes: Prepare and cook the same as Fried Potatoes above, except after turning down the heat add a small amount of water to the skillet; place a tight fitting lid on skillet and steam until tender; stirring only enough to prevent scorching or burning. Serve while hot.

Pan-Roasted Potatoes: Prepare boiled or steamed potatoes, but cook only 10 minutes; drain, peel, and cut-up if desired or leave whole. Arrange potatoes in a shallow pan. Brush with melted butter or margarine or salad oil. Bake uncovered at 400 degrees for 45 minutes or until fork-tender, turning occasionally and basting with more fat.

If roasting with meat, arrange peeled, raw, halved or quartered potatoes around meat in roasting pan about 1 ½ hours before serving. Baste with pan drippings. Turn and baste frequently to brown.

French-Fried Potatoes: Cut raw potatoes into strips about 1/4 inch thick. Toss strips into a bowl of ice and water to keep crisp and white while cutting the remainder. Don't soak. This lets the potato absorb water and prolongs the cooking time making the potatoes oily and soggy.

Pat the strips dry with paper towels. Heat about 4 inches of salad oil to 390 degrees in a deep fat fryer or large heavy saucepan. Place a layer of potato strips in a wire basket and immerse basket in hot fat; or place strips, a few at a time, directly into the hot oil. Cook about 5 minutes or until golden brown and tender. Drain well on paper towels; salt lightly and keep warm in 300 degree oven until ready to serve.

Double fry technique will assure crisp and hot french fries. In this instance repeat as above except cook 350 degrees until soft. Place on drain pan and then brown and crisp in oil at 400 degrees just before serving.

Note: Move center potatoes to outside edge of dish half-way through cooking to promote even cooking.

Home Freezing of Potatoes: The best potatoes for freezing are those that have been cooked such as mashed potato patties, baked stuffed potatoes, french fries, or hash browns.

Raw potatoes or potatoes in combination dishes such as soups and stews do not freeze well. Upon thawing and reheating, they tend to disintegrate, particularly if the potatoes are whole or cut in large cubes. If preparing a combination dish for freezing, omit the potatoes and add them, instead, during the thawing/reheating step before serving.

To freeze using the freezing styles mentioned above; prepare them according to your favorite recipe, cool quickly in the refrigerator, then freezer-wrap in moisture-vapor-proof packaging. Seal, label, date and freeze. Recommended maximum storage time is one month at 0 degrees. (I have however, kept oven blanched hash browns for up to 4 months without affecting the flavor.)

Processed Potatoes: So versatile for the busy person or for quick meals. The potato comes in many convenient processed forms....canned, dehydrated, frozen and chips.   Potatoes also are available in potato combination casseroles, soups and other dishes. All of these are convenient to store and prepare quickly.   In addition, these potato products are generally inexpensive on a per serving basis and the waste is zero.

Look in your supermarket for the following processed potatoes:

Dehydrated: Flakes, granules, slices, diced, hash browns shredded or Southern ranch-style, potato rounds.

Canned: Small whole.

Chips: Regular, ridged/ruffled, barbecue, sour cream, onion, snacks manufactured from dehydrated potatoes, shoestrings.

Frozen: French fries (regular or straight cut, crinkle cut, shoestring, ranch or country fries), tater tots, and hash browns.

To Rice Potatoes: Prepare boiled or steamed potatoes; drain and peel. Force potatoes through a potato ricer, a sieve or a food mill. Potatoes may be tossed with melted butter or margarine before or after ricing.

Mashed Potato: Prepare by boiling or steaming the potatoes. Using a potato masher, electric mixer or ricer, mash potatoes. Gradually add skim milk, (I like to use some of the water from steaming or boiling) salt and pepper to taste; beat until potatoes are smooth and fluffy. The amount of milk used determines the texture of the potatoes.   The more milk, the creamier and thinner the potatoes.

POTATOES FATTENING! ???:

Guilty until proven innocent, or innocent until proven guilty? All too often the potato is guilty by illusion and association. Actually, although the potato appears to be a bulky vegetable, it is 80% water, just a little less than in milk. Its association with high calorie toppings like butter, sour cream, gravy & mayonnaise dressings, put the low calorie potato at a disadvantage. Just one tablespoon of butter will double the number of calories in a baked potato. There are many low calorie ways to prepare potatoes deliciously. It does not have to be drowned in high calorie toppings.

Potatoes for Dieters:

Dieters, you don't have to give up all your favorite foods. The body must have good nutrition, dieting or not. Potatoes are chock-full of good nutrients for the body. Fad diets can wreck your health and vitality by robbing you of the very nutrients your body must have every day. When dieting it is best to use familiar foods, so as not to shock your body. Also, many diets force preparing separate meals for the rest of the family, thus giving you opportunities to break your diet.

The potato is a favorite vegetable. The taste is so satisfying. There is a humorous saying that goes: "If it tastes good...spit it out...it's not good for you." Not so, with the potato. The truth is that a medium-sized potato (3 per pound) is low in calories. Much lower than you would expect, yet it's high in good sound nutrition. For example a medium sized baked potato has about 100 to 110 calories, (depending on it's actual size). A serving (1/2 cup) of mashed potatoes using milk and one pat of butter is only 93 calories. It's strange, but many non-thinking dieters will eat steak and salad and skip the potato! The typical restaurant steak is close to 800 calories and 2 tablespoons of most salad dressings add another 175 calories.

Dieting experts suggest a dieter cut down on the main dish servings or desserts and add more variety of fruits and vegetables--including potatoes. The reward is fewer calories and **better nutrition.** For example; one third of your daily vitamin C can be obtained in one 90 calorie baked potato, plus contributing valuable vitamin B-1, niacin and iron. It also provides important carbohydrates which is the body's most important energy source. Potatoes are satisfying to the appetite. In addition, they're always a good buy in supermarkets. There are few foods that can compare with potatoes in nutritional value, flavor and versatility and still cost so little. The egg is one food that does come close. Put the two together and wow!!! Now that's nutritious, low-calorie, low-cost eating!

Dieting needn't mean giving up foods. Authorities are opposed to fad reducing diets that rule out whole categories of foods. Fad diets force us to make needless sacrifices of foods we like to eat and, perhaps above all, do nothing to teach a plan for eating for life that will prevent recurring bouts with excess weight. The best diet is one based on a variety of nutritious foods, and the potato offers a high return for relatively few calories.

NOW--A FEW GUIDELINES IN USING THIS COOKBOOK:

● Helpful bits of information and tips are not only found in this section of the book, but also at the beginning of all seven sections. Take the time to read them. I thought I knew potatoes, but I learned a lot more about them as I dug into my research project prior to compiling this book. For example, did you know.....soups and stew that have been over salted and are difficult to eat.....just add a raw potato, let it absorb the excess salt then throw it away.....they're inexpensive enough, to do that. It makes much more sense to throw away a potato than the soup or stew.

A real **"HOT"** tip for my **"HOT POTATO" COOK BOOK IS:** Always read through the entire recipe before starting to combine ingredients. Sometimes things are tucked in the body of the recipe that you don't expect. Reading the recipe first can eliminate little errors.

● Within the pages of this cookbook you will find recipes that appear to be similar to each other. Look a little closer. Seasoning and spices can totally change the taste and sometimes appearance of the dish being prepared.

● Many of the recipes will call for butter or for mayonnaise. These are generic terms. I personally believe butter to be the better food for the body, therefore I use that term. In most cases butter and margarine are interchangeable. The same thing applies to mayonnaise. It is often interchangeable with Miracle Whip or other brands of salad dressings. Mayonnaise is not as sweet as salad dressings.

● Whenever cooking or baking degrees are given they will always be in Fahrenheit, even though it will only read: 350 degrees.

Short-cut Methods:
● Short-cut methods have been used throughout the list of ingredients in each recipe. The most common of these are as follows:

Tb. or Tbs.	for tablespoon(s)	oz.	for ounces
tsp.	for teaspoons	ser.	for servings
C.	for cup	Am.	for American
lg.	for large	Evap.	for evaporated
sm.	for small	Cr.	for cream; as in
med.	for medium		creamed soups
lb. or lbs	for pound(s)	whl.	for whole
pkg.	for package	w/k	for whole kernel corn
grn.	for green	qt.	quart
veg.	for vegetable	bu.	for bunch
abt.	for about	ea.	for each
pt.	pint	opt.	optional

Potato Harvesting Time

I'm deep inside the dark cellar watching Julie Shumway remove vines, rocks or damaged potatoes off the conveyer belt while she is waiting for the truck she drives to be unloaded. A large percentage of drivers are housewives.

Farmers must wait until the soil warms up each morning before digging. There is such a short period of time suitable for harvesting it is not uncommon to see the fields being worked very late into the night and before the soil gets too cold. If potatoes are removed from cold soil the tubers can become damaged.

In this area, schools are closed for 2 weeks allowing students to help with the harvest. Some of the men also use part of their vacation time to work in the harvest. The social life as well as some church activities are canceled somewhat in the potato growing areas to help the farmers with their tight schedules.

SALADS

Parties, picnics, gatherings galore
That's precisely what salads are for.
You can eat them just about any time
But of course they're best eaten in their prime
--Carol Fielding McCabe

Information & Tips

Wash potatoes just before using, <u>not before storing.</u> They will keep longer with the dust and dirt left on them. Store them in a cool, dark place with plenty of air circulating around them. It is especially important to have nice firm potatoes for salad making.

To bake potatoes quickly for salads, boil them in salted water for ten minutes, then put them into the oven. The boiling water will heat them through more rapidly than if they were placed cold into the oven.

The term "mayonnaise" or "salad dressing" is a generic term. It can mean your favorite type of dressing, whether it is Mayonnaise, Miracle Whip or other favorite brands. Although a specific amount of "mayonnaise" has been suggested, you can use more or less depending upon the amount you prefer in your salads.

Any salad containing eggs or mayonnaise should **never** be left out of refrigeration for more than the average time it takes to serve a meal.

As a general rule, potato salads have better flavor if they are refrigerated at least four hours before serving. The best flavors are obtained if allowed to stand covered in the refrigerator overnight.

For better potato salads that hold their shape use potatoes with low starch content. To determine the starch content turn to the beginning of this book, it tells you how. (See page 4.)

Vegetables, including potatoes, can be added to many salads. Variety in vegetables is as important to taste as creative cuts are to the looks of any salad. Makes delightful looking and tasting salads.

An interesting twist to a potato salad is to add crushed potato chips on top of each individual serving of salad. Don't put them on the entire salad if there will be leftovers as the chips will be soggy before the salad is served again.

If by chance you have added too much mayonnaise mixture to a potato salad, yet the flavor is good, mix in a few potato flakes. They will absorb moisture from the mayonnaise mixture without changing the flavor to any great extent. They will also act as a thickening agent.

It is not a good idea to store potato salads in aluminum containers as they can cause discoloration, giving potatoes a grayish cast. The taste is also somewhat affected.

TRADITIONAL OR
BASIC POTATO SALADS:

"My mother in law loved my recipe!"

Famous Idaho Potato Salad

1 Tbs. salt	3/4 cup mayonnaise	2 diced dill pickles
1/4 cup lemon juice	1/8 tsp.ea.pepper & cayenne	1/4 cup thinly sliced celery
6 medium potatoes	6 hard cooked eggs,	and leaves
1/4 cup dill pickle juice	4 diced, 2 sliced	1/4 cup diced pimento
(& pickling seeds)	1 green pepper, diced	

Add salt, lemon juice and enough water to cover the potatoes. Cook until tender (do not over cook). Slightly cool potatoes with cold water. Peel and cut up into bite size cubes.

Mix together pickle juice, mayonnaise, 1 tsp. salt or salt to taste, and the peppers. Add this to the warm potatoes, and the remaining ingredients, except egg slices. Mix gently. Garnish with egg slices and if desired, paprika. Allow to set refrigerated for 6 to 8 hours before serving. This allows the flavors to mix together. Makes 6 to 8 servings.

Optional: Sprinkle fresh or dried parsley over top of salad.

Traditional Potato Salad

8 cups diced potatoes	1/4 tsp. dried thyme	1/2 cup mayonnaise
6 Tbs. white vinegar	1 tsp. ground rosemary	1/2 tsp. Dijon style mustard
1 cup vegetable oil	1/4 cup minced parsley	1/2 cup sour cream
1/4 cup diced onion	1/2 tsp. dried savory	4 hard-boiled eggs, quartered,
1/4 tsp. celery seeds	salt and pepper	sliced

Boil the potatoes until tender. In the meantime, whisk together the vinegar, oil, onion, and herbs for marinating. Season mixture to taste with salt and pepper.

Drain the potatoes and pour the marinade over the hot potatoes. Cover the bowl and marinate the potatoes for 20-30 minutes. Stir in the remaining ingredients. Chill the salad for 2 to 4 hours before serving. Garnish with fresh parsley and the sliced egg. Makes 8 to 10 servings.

Pesto Potato Salad

8 cups sliced potatoes	1 Tb. capers	1 cup diced sweet red pepper
4 Tbs. pesto (below)	1/3 cup olive oil	1/2 cup minced fresh parsley
5 Tbs. cider vinegar	2/3 cup sliced olives	

Boil the potatoes until just tender. Drain and place in large bowl to cool slightly, then dice. Whisk together the Pesto, vinegar, capers, and olive oil. Pour the dressing over the potatoes and toss to coat. Add the olives, pepper, and parsley. Season to taste with **salt** and **pepper.** Chill for 2 to 4 hours before serving. Makes 6 to 8 servings.

Pesto: Pesto is just about the best use of fresh basil I know. It will keep in the refrigerator for two months and in the freezer for one year. Replace the coating of olive oil after each use. The best time to harvest basil for quality Pesto is before the plant blossoms.

1/3 cup plus one Tbs. olive oil	1 cup chopped basil leaves
1/2 cup pine nuts (shelled)	3 garlic cloves, minced
2/3 cup grated parmesan cheese	salt and pepper

Combine 1/3 cup olive oil with the remaining ingredients in a food processor and process to make a thick paste. Transfer the Pesto to a container and smooth out the top. Cover with coating of olive oil.

Cover tightly and store any excess in fridge or freezer.

Baked Potato Salad

3 med. Idaho potatoes	1 Tbs. flour	2 Tbs. cider vinegar
1⅛ tsp. salt	1 tsp. prepared mustard	1/2 cup diced green pepper
2 Tbs. salad oil	1/4 tsp. celery seed	1/4 cup shredded carrot
1/2 cup chopped onions	1/2 cup water	1 cup shredded Cheddar cheese

Steam potatoes and 1 teaspoon salt in about one inch of water until tender; drain and cool. Peel potatoes and slice 1/4 inch thick; set aside.

Heat oil in skillet; saute onion until soft. Stir in flour, mustard, celery seed and 1/3 tsp. salt. Gradually add 1/2 cup water and vinegar; cook over low heat, stirring constantly, until mixture boils and thickens.

Combine potatoes, green pepper and carrots in a bowl; add sauce, mixing well. Spoon half the mixture into a shallow 8"x8" baking dish; sprinkle with 1/2 cup cheese. Cover with remaining potato mixture and cheese.

Bake, uncovered, in heated 350 degree oven 15 to 20 minutes or until cheese is melted and vegetables are hot. Serve hot or cold. Makes 4 servings.

Oven baked Potato Salad

4 cups red potatoes, quartered, unpeeled
1 cup Miracle Whip dressing
2 hard-cooked eggs, chopped
4 slices crisp bacon

1/4 cup sliced green onions including
   the green tops
1/4 tsp. salt and 1/4 tsp. pepper
1/2 cup shelled pinenuts or peanuts
1/2 cup crispy cereal (Rice Krispies or chex)

Heat oven to 425 degrees. Place potatoes on baking pan sprayed with no stick cooking spray. Bake 30-35 minutes or until potatoes are tender and golden brown, stirring once. Mix dressing, eggs, crumbled bacon, onions, salt and pepper in large bowl. Add potatoes; mix lightly. Serve warm or chilled. To keep nuts and cereal crisp, add just before serving. Makes 6 servings.

New Potato Salad

6 C. diced **new** potatoes
2 tsp. anchovy paste
1/4 cup sliced scallion

1/4 cup olive oil
1 Tb. lemon juice
1/8 tsp. ground rosemary

1/4 cup feta crumbled cheese
1/2 cup sour cream
1/4 cup minced fresh parsley
   salt and pepper

Boil the potatoes until just tender. In the meantime, whisk together the anchovy paste, scallion (or green onions), olive oil, lemon juice, and rosemary. Drain the cooked potatoes and place in a bowl. Pour the marinade mixture over the potatoes and cover. Let potatoes cool to room temperature in the marinade, about 1 hour. Then stir in the crumbled cheese, sour cream, and parsley. Season to taste with salt and pepper. Chill 2 to 4 hours before serving. Makes 6 or 7 servings.

Creamy Hard-Boiled Egg Potato Salad

2 lbs. red potatoes,
  peeled & cut-up
4 hard-boiled eggs,
  halved, separated

Egg Mayonnaise (pg. 16)
2 Tbs. warm water
4 tsp. prepared mustard

1½ tsp. salt; dash pepper
1/4 cup chopped onion
1/4 cup chopped grn. peppers

Boil potatoes until tender. Meanwhile, place the cooked egg yolks in medium-size bowl and mash well. Add mayonnaise, water, mustard, salt, and pepper, mixing well; set aside. Finely chop egg whites and set aside.

Drain cooked potatoes and place in a bowl. Add onions, bell peppers, egg whites, and mayonnaise mixture; mix well and breaking up some of the potatoes so the finished salad will be creamy textured with some lumps in it. Serve immediately or chill. Good either way. Makes 8 to 10 servings.

Egg Mayonnaise: This recipe makes 1¼ cups. Once you make home made mayonnaise it is hard to use the store bought kind again. You can make wonderful variations by adding stock of sea food or special seasonings. You must stir faster than fast to keep mayonnaise from getting too thick.

3 warm hard boiled egg yolks	1 raw egg yolk
1 Tb. white vinegar	1 cup salad oil

In a large mixing bowl, mash well the boiled egg yolks with a fork. Add raw egg yolk and vinegar; beat with whisk or blender until creamy. Gradually add oil in a thin stream, stirring briskly; making sure all the oil is incorporated before adding more. Refrigerate at least 20 minutes before serving.

Deluxe Caesar Potato Salad

8 cups diced potatoes	2 garlic cloves, minced	1/2 cup olive oil
1 egg	1/4 cup lemon juice	salt and pepper
2 anchovies	1/2 cup grated parmesan cheese	1/3 cup sliced scallions
		1/4 cup minced fresh parsley

Boil the potatoes until just tender, about 10 minutes. Drain and place in a large bowl to cool slightly.

In a food processor or blender, combine the egg, anchovies, garlic, lemon juice, and cheese. Process until smooth. With the processor running, slowly pour in the oil in a thin stream. The dressing will thicken slightly. Season to taste with salt and pepper. Pour the dressing over the potatoes, and add the scallions or green onions and parsley.

Toss to mix and coat. Chill the salad for at least 2 hours before serving. Makes 8 servings.

Caesar Potato Salad

1 egg	2 tsp. prepared mustard	4 peeled potatoes, cooked,
1/4 cup Italian dressing	1 tsp. salt	1/2 cup sliced black olives
1 Tbs. Worcestershire	1/4 cup grated Romano cheese	

In a large bowl, whisk together egg, oil & vinegar type Italian dressing, Worcestershire sauce, mustard and salt until well blended. Add hot cubed potatoes to this mixture. Mix well. Let stand until hot potatoes have cooked the egg, (about 10 to 15 minutes.) Refrigerate to chill. Mix cheese and olives, with the potato mixture.

VEGETABLE AND FRUIT SALADS:

"Oh darn, I was hoping we would have potatoes tonight."

Vegetable-Crouton Potato Salad

6 med. potatoes	1⅛ tsp. salt	2 celery stalks, sliced
1/4 cup bacon fat or oil	dash of pepper	1 cucumber, sliced, or 2
1½ Tbs. flour	sugar	cups cooked green beans
water for thickening	1 tsp. prepared mustard	"bacon bits" and croutons
1/3 cup vinegar	1 sm. head romaine lettuce	3 green onions

Boil or steam unpeeled potatoes just until tender. Meanwhile, in 10" skillet, over low heat, add bacon fat or oil, and stir in flour and water until smooth; add vinegar, salt, pepper, sugar, and mustard. Cook over low heat, stirring, until thickened; remove from heat. Drain potatoes; peel; slice. Put skillet back over low heat; add layer of potatoes, then celery, romaine (in bite-size pieces), cucumber, and onions; repeating until all are used. Cook until heated through, then toss gently. Top with bacon bits and croutons. Makes 6 servings.

Potato Beet Salad

2 16-oz. cans sliced potatoes drained (4 cups)	1/2 cup sliced celery
1 can cut green beans, drained	1/2 cup sliced green onion
8-oz. can tiny whole beets, drained	1/2 cup sliced radishes
	salt and pepper
	1/2 to 3/4 cup Horseradish Dressing

Thoroughly chill the sliced potatoes, green beans, and beets; toss with celery, onion, and radishes. Sprinkle with salt and pepper. Just before serving, toss with Horseradish Dressing or other dressing of your choice. Makes 6 to 8 servings.

Green Pepper Potato Salad

6 potatoes, boiled	1 small (inner) stalk celery cut
1 small onion, minced	into shreds (the size of peppers)
1/2 green pepper cut in long shreds	1/2 cup mayonnaise
1 pimento, chopped	1 tsp. salt
1 Tbs. lemon juice	lettuce
	10 sliced black olives

Peel potatoes and cut in 1/8 inch slices; slice carefully for an attractive salad. Mix onions, pepper, pimento, celery and lemon juice and combine gently with potatoes. Add mayonnaise and salt; chill for an hour or two before serving. Place on a bed of lettuce. Dot with sliced or chopped olives.

Hard-cooked eggs, minced parsley, sliced cucumber, or sliced radishes make an interesting addition.

Variation: Same ingredients and directions as the above recipe except reduce the mayonnaise to 1/3 cup and add 1/3 cup sour cream.

Stuffed Tomato-Potato Salad

4 lg. tomatoes, halved	1 med. carrot, peeled,	2 Tbs. chopped parsley
1 med. potato, peeled,	chopped	1/2 tsp. salt
cooked and diced	1/4 cup cottage cheese	

Cut tomatoes in half; scoop out centers to make cups. Strain pulp to remove excess liquid; reserve pulp. Pat insides of tomato cups with paper towels to dry. Combine reserved tomato pulp, potato, carrot, cottage cheese, parsley, and salt. Spoon mixture into tomato cups. Chill before serving. Grated cheese could be sprinkled on top of mixture if desired, giving this recipe more protein. Makes 4 servings.

Salad Musetta

1½ cups cooked potato	6 artichoke hearts, in oil	freshly ground pepper
1 diced celery heart	6 mushrooms, in oil	2 Tbs. wine vinegar
1 diced fennel heart	1 Tb. capers	1 Tb. mayonnaise
1/2 C. diced Swiss cheese	2 hard-cooked eggs	1/2 cup olive or salad oil
1 heart of chicory, cut-up	1/2 tsp. salt	Romaine lettuce

Dice and combine potato, celery, fennel, eggs and Swiss cheese. Add cut up pieces chicory, halved artichoke, sliced mushrooms, and capers. Season lightly with salt and pepper. Gradually blend vinegar into mayonnaise, then stir in olive oil. Pour over salad and toss lightly. Mound in a glass bowl rimmed with spears of romaine. Makes 4 to 6 servings.

Fruit/Veggie Vinaigrette Salad

5 med. potatoes
2 cups diced cooked beets
4 ribs celery, diced
1 lg. apple, pared, cored, diced
1 lg. diced dill pickle
salt and pepper

1 cup cooked green beans or peas
1/2 sm. can drained, crushed pineapple
3/4 cup vinaigrette dressing (below)
lettuce or chicory leaves
1 ½ cups mayonnaise (see below)

For Garnish: (Optional) Sliced dill pickle, celery curls, cooked, peeled shrimp, sliced salami.

Cook potatoes in skins in boiling salted water for 10 to 15 minutes; drain; peel and dice while still warm. Mix thoroughly with beets, celery, apple and dill pickle; season well. Stir in peas and pineapple with fork. Spoon the vinaigrette dressing on top of salad and lightly toss; chill 2-3 hours or overnight.

To serve, arrange lettuce or chicory leaves around a salad bowl, toss salad with mayonnaise and spoon into the salad bowl. Garnish.

Vinaigrette Dressing:

2 Tbs. vinegar, (any listed
    type below): red, white
    wine, cider or tarragon
1/2 tsp. fresh ground black
    pepper

1/2 tsp. salt
6 Tbs. oil, preferably olive or peanut
1 Tb. chopped fresh herbs, (thyme,
    marjoram, basil, or parsley)
pinch of sugar (optional)

Mix vinegar, salt and pepper together and gradually add the oil, whisking until the mixture thickens. Add the fresh herbs and sugar, and taste for seasoning. Makes 1/2 cup.

Mayonnaise:

2 egg yolks
pinch of dry mustard

2 Tbs. wine vinegar
salt and pepper

3/4 cup oil

In a bowl beat egg yolks and seasonings until thick with an electric mixer. Add the oil drop by drop, beating constantly. When 2 tablespoons of oil have been added, the mixture should be very thick. Stir in 1 teaspoon of vinegar.

The remaining oil can be added a little more quickly in a thin steady stream while the mixer is going. When all the oil has been mixed in, add remaining vinegar to taste, with extra salt and pepper if necessary.

To thin and lighten mayonnaise, add a little hot water. For a coating consistency, thin with cream or milk. If mayonnaise curdles, start with a fresh yolk in another bowl. Beat well with seasoning, then add the curdled mixture to it very slowly and carefully. When the curdled mixture is completely added, more oil can be beaten in if the mixture is too thin.

American Cheese Salad

8-oz. can sweet kernel corn	ground paprika	1 sweet red pepper
9-oz. aged Cheddar cheese	salt; celery salt; allspice	1 lb. cooked, sliced potatoes
8-oz. sour cream	Worcestershire sauce	1 grn. pepper, seeds removed
4 Tbs. mayonnaise	2 large onions, chopped	and finely chopped
		4 sweet pickles, chopped

Drain corn; cube cheese; blend with the sour cream, mayonnaise and seasonings, and mix with the other ingredients. Season to taste.

Potato, Celery And Apple Salad

This is a meatless salad, but it is good when served with cold, cooked meats.

3 medium potatoes	1/4 cup vinaigrette	bunch celery, sliced
1 lg. tart apple	dressing (pg. 19)	1 cup lemon cream dressing
		(see recipe below

Cook potatoes in skins in boiling salted water for 10-15 minutes or until just tender. Drain, peel, slice while still hot. Toss potatoes with vinaigrette dressing and cool.

Pare, core and slice the apple and mix with celery and potatoes and half the lemon cream dressing, (see below). Pile the salad in a bowl; spoon the remaining dressing on top and serve cold, within 1 hour.

Lemon Cream Dressing:

1/2 cup heavy cream, whipped	grated rind and juice of lemon
until it holds soft shape	salt and pepper
1/2 cup mayonnaise	1/2 tsp. prepared mustard

Fold whipped cream into the mayonnaise. Gradually stir in lemon rind and juice, season well and add mustard to taste. Add 1 tablespoon water to thin the dressing, if necessary. Makes 1 cup.

Dilled Potato-Beet Salad

2 16-oz. cans new potatoes	1/2 cup chopped dill pickles	1 Tb. chopped fresh dill or
drained, cut-up	1/2 cup mayonnaise	1/2 tsp. dill weed
16-oz. can diced beets,	1/4 cup chopped onion	1 tsp. dry mustard
drained	1 Tb. sugar	3/4 tsp. salt
8-oz. can peas/carrots,	1 Tb. cider vinegar	Romaine leaves
drained		

In a large bowl, gently toss all the ingredients except romaine; cover and refrigerate for several hours before serving.

Just before serving lightly toss the mixture and serve in a romaine-lined salad bowl. Makes 8 servings.

Red Onion Potato Salad

1/4 cup oil & vinegar type Italian dressing
3 Tbs. wine or cider vinegar
2 tsp. salt; dash cayenne pepper

1 cup thinly sliced red onion
1/4 cup chopped parsley
1 cup sliced celery
6 potatoes peeled, cooked, sliced

In a small dish mix together the Italian dressing, vinegar, salt and pepper. Place remaining ingredients in large serving bowl. Pour dressing mixture over vegetable mixture. Mix until evenly coated. Chill in the refrigerator. Makes 6 to 7 servings.

Green Beans--New Potatoes And Pesto

6 golf ball-size new potatoes
1/2 lb. fresh green beans
2 ½ cup tightly packed fresh basil leaves
2 Tbs. chopped fresh parsley

6 Tbs. olive oil
1 lg. clove garlic, halved
1/2 cup pine nuts, shelled
1/4 cup grated Parmesan cheese

Scrub small potatoes until jackets are a lighter color. Do not peel, rather cook in jackets until tender. Drain. If you like smaller pieces of potatoes, cut each potato in half or quarters.

Bring water to boil in steamer for the green beans. Trim and wash beans. Steam for about 7 to 9 minutes, until they are crisp-tender; drain and run under cold water. Cut in small pieces about 1 ½ inches long.

Pesto: In a food processor or blender, combine basil with parsley, oil, garlic, pine nuts, and Parmesan cheese. Process until rough paste is formed. This is called pesto. Add this mixture to potatoes and beans. Toss together.

Just A Good Salad

1 egg plant
1 egg, whipped
salt and pepper
flour
salad oil for frying

3/4 C. Creamy French dressing
1/4 cup mayonnaise
1 head lettuce
15 ½-oz. can kidney beans,
    drained

1 diced dill pickle
1 minced onion
2 diced boiled potatoes
1 sliced dill pickle

Clean and slice egg plant. Dip in a whipped seasoned egg. Coat each side with flour. Place in an oiled fry pan and fry until coating is browned. Combine French dressing and mayonnaise.

Line salad bowl with lettuce leaves. Mix all other ingredients except sliced pickle, and egg plant. Mix in dressing, and mound in center of bowl. Decorate with sliced pickle, and fried egg plant.

DAIRY-BASED SALADS

"Kids, you WILL eat every potato and pea on your plate."

Pink Potato Salad

3/4 cup cottage cheese	1 tsp. salt; dash pepper	1 cup sliced celery
3 Tbs. French dressing	1 tsp. paprika	1/4 cup pimento
1 Tb. vinegar	4 cup cooked potatoes	

In a blender combine cottage cheese, creamy type French dressing, vinegar, salt, dash of pepper, and paprika until fairly smooth. In large bowl, combine cubed potatoes, celery, pimento. Toss together with cottage cheese mixture. Chill in the refrigerator until time to serve.

Potato & Cottage Cheese Salad

6 med. potatoes, cooked, diced	2 Tbs. chopped parsley	1 tsp. Worcestershire sauce
	1/2 lb. cottage cheese	3/4 cup milk
1 medium onion, grated	2 tsp. salt	1/4 cup shredded process
dash of cayenne		American cheese ·

Put potatoes in a greased shallow baking dish. Mix remaining ingredients except American cheese; pour over potatoes. Top with shredded American cheese; bake in preheated 400 degree oven 15 minutes. Makes 4 servings.

Mushroom Potato Salad

3 Tbs. wine or cider vinegar	2 potatoes, peeled, cooked, cubed
1 Tb. catsup	1 pkg. Ramen Noodles with flavor pkt.
1/2 tsp. prepared mustard	1/4 cup sliced fresh mushrooms
2 Tbs. brown sugar	1/4 cup plain yogurt
	lettuce leaves

In a large bowl, combine vinegar, catsup, mustard, and sugar. Add potatoes, Ramen noodles and contents from packet, mushrooms, and yogurt. Toss gently, mix well. Chill, and serve on lettuce leaves immediately.

New Generation Potato Salad

10-12 small peeled red potatoes
1/2 cup sliced green onions
3/4 tsp. garlic salt, divided

1/4 tsp. fresh ground black pepper
2 cups plain yogurt
3 Tbs. buttermilk
1 cup Blue cheese, crumbled

Cut potatoes into 3/4 inch pieces. Cook in boiling water to cover 15 to 20 minutes or until tender; drain. Combine potatoes, onions, 1/2 teaspoon garlic salt and the pepper; toss gently to combine. Stir together yogurt, buttermilk, Blue cheese and remaining 1/4 teaspoon garlic salt. Add to potatoes; toss gently to coat. Cover and chill at least 2 hours.

TIP: When cleaning celery put it in a quart jar; add 3/4 inch cold water, put on the lid and refrigerate. It will last several days longer than expected and it will stay crisp.

Cottage-Rice Chex Salad

2 cups cubed, cooked,
  potatoes
1/2 cup sliced celery
1/2 cup shredded carrot
1 boiled egg, chopped

1/4 cup chopped green
  onion with tops
2 Tbs. milk
1/2 cup mayonnaise
1 tsp. dried dill weed

1/4 tsp. salt
1 Tb. vinegar
1 cup cream-style
  cottage cheese
1 ½ cup Rice Chex

Mix, potatoes, celery, carrots, onions and eggs together. Blend together a dash of pepper and the remaining ingredients except cereal and cottage cheese. Toss to coat. Just before serving mix a little milk to thin the cottage cheese. Mix thinned sour cream with Rice Chex (breakfast cereal) and mix into the salad.

Chill. Serve on green pepper rings and trim with carrot curls and green pepper, if desired. Makes 6 servings.

Optional: Add an Italian salad dressing instead of mayonnaise.

Swiss Potato Salad

4 cups cubed, peeled,
  cooked potatoes
1 tsp. salt

4 slices Swiss Cheese
  cut in narrow strips
1 cup dairy sour cream

3 Tbs. milk
2 Tbs. snipped chives
1/2 tsp. dry mustard

Sprinkle potatoes with salt; combine with cheese strips. In small bowl blend together sour cream, milk, chives, and mustard; pour over potato mixture. Toss lightly. Serve at room temperature. Makes 4 or 5 servings.

A Super Salad

1/2 cup chopped onions	1/2 cup sour cream	3 cups cooked, cubed potatoes
1 Tb. butter	1/4 tsp. caraway seed	1/2 cup shelled peanuts
1 can Cr. Celery Soup	1/8 tsp. pepper	1 Tb. chopped parsley

In skillet, cook onion in butter until tender. Blend in soup, sour cream, caraway seeds and pepper. Blend in potatoes, heating and stirring gently. Just before serving add peanuts and garnish with parsley. Makes 4 servings.

Optional: Use bread croutons instead of nuts.

SALADS WITH MEATS:

"I'm sure I put the onions in here somewhere."

French Beef Salad

3 C. cubed,cooked,potatoes	1/2 cup mayonnaise	2 Tbs. sliced green onions
1/4 cup French dressing	1/2 cup sliced radishes	1 Tb. lemon juice
1 ½ cubs cubed,cooked,beef	1/3 cup chili sauce	1/2 tsp. salt
1 cup sliced celery	1/4 cup dairy sour cream	lettuce cups

In bowl combine potatoes and creamy type French dressing. Mix beef, celery, mayonnaise, radishes, chili sauce, sour cream, onion, lemon juice, and salt; stir into potatoes. Cover and chill. Serve in lettuce cups. Makes 6 servings.

Beefy Potato Salad

1 lb. cooked beef round, well-trimmed (or left-over roast beef, chopped)		
3 Tbs. wine or cider	1/2 tsp. prepared mustard	1/4 cup sliced mushrooms
vinegar	2 Tbs. brown sugar	1/4 cup plain yogurt
1 Tb. catsup	2 cooked, peeled potatoes	lettuce leaves

Cut beef into 1/2 inch cubes. In large bowl, combine beef, vinegar, catsup, mustard, and sugar. Marinate for two hours in the refrigerator; stirring occasionally. Add peeled, cooked, cubed potatoes, mushrooms, and yogurt. Toss gently to mix well; chill; serve on lettuce leaves.

Souper Salad

1 cup diced cooked ham	1 can Cr. celery soup	1/8 tsp. pepper
1/2 cup chopped onions	1/2 cup sour cream	3 cups cooked, cubed potatoes
1 Tb. butter	1/4 tsp. caraway seed	1 Tb. chopped parsley

In skillet, heat ham and onion in butter until onion is tender. Blend in soup, sour cream, caraway seeds and pepper. Blend in cubed potatoes, heating and stirring gently. Garnish with parsley. Makes 4 servings.

TIP: Keep potato peelings thin. Precious nutrients are found just under the thin layer of skin. Don't throw these nutrients down the disposal with thick potato peelings.

Neapolitan Salad

3 Tbs. olive oil	white part of 1 leek	3-oz. aged cheese
juice of one lemon	1/2 tsp. crushed sage	3-oz. ham
salt and pepper	3-oz. salami	1 small jar sweet gherkins
2 shallots, finely chopped	1 large apple	lettuce leaves

Make a dressing with olive oil, lemon juice, salt, pepper, shallots or green onions, finely sliced leek and crushed sage. Cut the rest of the ingredients, except lettuce into thin strips and mix with the dressing (reserve a little of the ingredients for a garnish). Chill the salad for several hours, stirring once or twice. Serve on a bed of lettuce; garnish with the remaining ingredients. Chill before serving.

Optional: The use of sprouts is a nice accent to many salads. There is a variety of excellent sprouts available. Radish, peas, or alfalfa sprouts would be very good with this salad.

Ham And Potato Salad Loaf

1 Tb. plain gelatin	1 cup diced ham	6 cups diced cooked potatoes
1/4 cup hot water	1 cup mayonnaise	2 stalks celery, chopped
1 pimento, minced	3 sprigs parsley, minced	1/2 lb. thinly sliced baked ham
1 ½ tsp. salt		1 small chopped onion

Mix together gelatin and hot water until gelatin is dissolved. Add remaining ingredients except sliced ham.

Line loaf pan with wax paper (extend the wax paper up over the sides). Cover bottom and sides of pan with sliced baked ham. Add gelatin mixture. Chill mixture for about 1 hour. Turn contents of loaf pan out on platter and remove paper. Cut in thick slices to serve. Makes 8 servings.

Party Salad

1 head lettuce	1 cup diced apple	1 pkg. frozen artichoke hearts,
1/4 cup mayonnaise	1 chopped dill pickle	cooked
3/4 cup French dressing	2 chopped pimentos	2 chopped hard-boiled eggs
2 cups diced ham	3 Tbs. chopped parsley	1 Tb prepared mustard
	1 lg. boiled potato	1/4 cup chopped onion

Line salad bowl with lettuce; mix the mayonnaise and Creamy French dressings. Mix all remaining ingredients with dressing mixture and mound in center of bowl. Chill and serve.

Variation: Substitute sour cream for mayonnaise. Add 3 chopped cooked beets to salad mound and sprinkle with 1 tablespoon fresh chopped dill.
Note: Add drained, dry beets at last minute so juice won't color salad.

Hot Sweet-And-Sour Potato Salad

8 med. Idaho potatoes	2 eggs	1/4 tsp. dry mustard
salt	1/2 cup sugar	1/2 cup chopped bread-and-
4 slices diced bacon	1/2 cup cider vinegar	butter pickles
	pepper	1 cup sliced celery

In 5 quart Dutch oven over high heat, in 1 inch boiling water, heat unpeeled potatoes and **2 teaspoons salt** to boiling. Reduce heat to low; cover and simmer 30 minutes or until potatoes are tender. Drain; peel and cut in cubes.

In 3-quart saucepan over medium-low heat, cook bacon until browned. Meanwhile, in small bowl, with spoon, mix well the eggs, sugar, vinegar, pepper, mustard and salt to taste.

With slotted spoon, remove bacon to paper towels. Into bacon drippings in saucepan, stir egg mixture; cook, stirring constantly, until sauce is just thickened but not boiling. Add potatoes, pickles, celery and bacon; gently toss to coat well. Makes 6 servings.

German Winter Potato Salad

6 cups diced potatoes	1/2 cup diced dill pickle	1 tsp. caraway seeds
1/4 lb. diced bacon	1/4 cup cider or	1/4 cup dill pickle juice
3/4 cup diced scallions	wine vinegar	1 tsp. sugar
or green onions	1/2 tsp. celery seeds	salt and pepper

Boil potatoes until tender. While cooking, brown the bacon and remove it from the pan. Drain off the bacon fat, reserving 1/4 cup. Combine the bacon fat, scallions, pickle, vinegar, celery, caraway seeds, pickle juice, and sugar in the pan. Simmer for 3 minutes. Drain potatoes and place in a large bowl. Pour the dressing over the potatoes and toss to coat. Add the bacon. Season to taste with salt and pepper. Serve immediately. Makes 6 to 8 servings. (Extra bacon, dried parsley, and cayenne pepper can be added to the top as a garnish.)

Optional: Grate cheese and sprinkle on top of finished salad. The heat from the salad should melt the cheese a bit.

Winter Hot Salad (German)

1 pkg. Idahoan® Scallop potatoes (save sauce)
2¼ cups boiling water
2 tsp. mustard seed

1 tsp. dry mustard
2 Tbs. sugar
1/2 cup boiling water
1/4 cup cider vinegar
4 full strips bacon

6 scallions or green onions, tops included, sliced
1/4 cup chopped parsley
4 eggs, riced or diced

In 3-quart saucepan combine potatoes, 2¼ cups water and mustard seed. Bring to boil; simmer for 20 minutes, or until potatoes are tender. Set aside.

In small bowl combine reserved sauce packet, dry mustard, sugar, 1/2 cup water and vinegar. Set aside. Fry bacon until crisp; crumble and set aside. Discard all but 4 tablespoons fat. Quickly saute onions just to heat through. Add mustard-vinegar mixture; mix well. Carefully fold in potatoes including liquid and crumbled bacon. Simmer for 5 minutes. Garnish with parsley and riced eggs or diced eggs. Makes 6 servings

Skillet Potato Salad

6 medium potatoes
6 to 8 bacon slices
1/4 cup bacon fat
1½ Tbs. flour
water (mix with flour)
1/3 cup vinegar

1⅛ tsp. salt
dash of pepper
Sugar to taste
1 tsp. prepared mustard
2 celery stalks, sliced

1 small head romaine lettuce
1 cucumber, sliced, or 2 cups cooked green beans
3 gm. or 1 yellow onion, chop'd
6 red radishes, sliced

Boil unpeeled potatoes just until tender. Meanwhile, in 10" skillet, over low heat, fry bacon until crisp. Reserve and set aside bacon fat. Remove skillet from heat; drain bacon on paper towels; crumble bacon.

Return 1/4 cup bacon fat to skillet; stir in flour, then water; mix until smooth; add vinegar, salt, pepper, sugar, mustard. Cook over low heat, stirring, until thickened; remove from heat.

Drain potatoes; peel; slice. Put skillet back over low heat; add layer of potatoes, then celery, romaine (in bite-size pieces), cucumber, and onions, repeating until all are used. Toss gently. Top with radishes and bacon. Makes 6 servings.

Sour Cream & Bacon Potato Salad

Cook **5 slices of bacon**; crumble. Cook **8 medium potatoes**, slice. In a skillet, combine: **1 can Cream of Celery Soup** and **1 cup sour cream**. Add the potatoes, part of the bacon and **2 tablespoons sliced green onions**. Heat and garnish with remaining bacon. Add parsley flakes and paprika.

Hot Sausage And Potato Salad

4 slices crisp bacon	1/2 cup chopped onion	2 Tbs. sweet pickle relish
5 smoked sausage links, cooked sliced	1 can Cr. Celery Soup	1/4 tsp. salt
2 Tbs. bacon drippings	1/4 cup water	16-oz. pkg. frozen
	2 Tbs. vinegar	French-fried potatoes

Cook sausage and onions in bacon drippings until meat is browned and onion is tender, about 5 minutes. Stir in soup, water, pickle relish, vinegar, and salt; bring to boiling. Cut French-fried potatoes in half; add to skillet and cook, covered, for 10 minutes, stirring once or twice. Place mixture in a serving bowl.

Potato-Sausage Salad

6 med. new potatoes	1 Tb. garlic-wine or cider vinegar	lettuce
4 hot Italian sausages	1 Tb. crushed dill weed	4 hard-cooked eggs, quartered
1/4 cup dry red wine	1/2 tsp. salt	2 ripe tomatoes, peeled,
1 cup plain yogurt	1/4 tsp. pepper	sliced and drained
1 sm. onion, minced		

Cook potatoes in skins in boiling salted water in large saucepan until tender, about 20 minutes. Drain; return to saucepan; shake over very low heat to dry. Peel; cut into 1/4 inch thick slices into a medium-size bowl.

Prick the sausages in several places to keep skins from bursting. Poach, covered, in wine in a small saucepan for about 10 minutes, turning at least once. Uncover pan; let sausage brown. Drain; cool; cut into 1/4 inch thick slices.

Blend the yogurt, onion, vinegar, dill weed, salt and pepper in a small bowl. Pour dressing over the potatoes, tossing gently to coat.

Line a salad bowl with lettuce leaves; arrange the potato and sausage on them. Garnish with eggs and tomatoes.

Italian Sausage Potato Salad

1 cup plain yogurt	1/2 cup sliced celery	1/4 cup sliced onions
2 tsp. prepared mustard	2 cups cooked cubed potatoes	1 Tb. chopped chives
2 Tbs. horseradish	1 med. cucumber, sliced	1/4 cup cubed Italian Sausage
		1/2 cup Rice Krispies

In large bowl, combine yogurt, mustard, and horseradish. Add remaining ingredients, except Rice Krispies; toss to mix. Chill. Scatter Rice Krispies on top just before serving. Makes 4 servings.

Hot Curried Potato Salad

6 medium potatoes
1/3 cup butter
2 Tbs. chopped onions
1 cup cooked, cubed chicken

3 Tbs. flour
1 tsp. curry powder
1/2 tsp. salt
1¼ cups chicken broth

2 Tbs. vinegar
1 apple, cored; cut in wedges
1/2 cup sliced celery
1/2 cup seeded grapes; halved

Cook unpeeled potatoes until just tender. Drain and cool slightly. Peel and cut into 1/4 inch slices. In a large skillet heat butter; add onion and chicken; cook until onion is transparent and chicken is heated through. Blend in flour, curry powder and salt; cook, stirring constantly, for 1 or 2 minutes. Slowly stir in chicken broth and vinegar; cook, stirring constantly until thickened. Add potatoes, apple, celery and grapes. Heat about 5 minutes. Serve immediately. Serves 4 - 6.

TIP: When celery loses its crispness, place it in a pan of cold water with slices of potato. Let it stand a few hours then remove it from the water and it will have become crisp again.

Oriental Hot Chicken Salad

2 lg. chicken breasts,
   cooked, pulled apart
2 Tbs. mayonnaise
3/4 C. slivered almonds

2 Tbs. minced onion
1 cup sliced water chestnuts,
1 cup chopped celery
   sliced thin

1 can Cr. Chicken Soup
1 Tb. lemon juice
1/2 cup grated cheese
1 small pkg. potato
   chips, crushed

Toss all ingredients into casserole except cheese and 1/2 of the potato chips. Sprinkle remaining chips on top. Bake 1 hour at 300 degrees. Remove from oven and sprinkle cheese on top. Makes 6 servings.

Optional: As a topping, shoestring potatoes also works very well, and so does Tater-tots.

Winter Chicken Salad

White meat, carrots and celery team up in a warm salad for cold weather.
3 chicken breasts (abt.12-oz. ea.)
2 cups carrots, peeled, sliced thin
2 cups sliced celery
1 lg. onion, chopped (1/2 cup)
1/2 cup mayonnaise

1/4 cup water
1 envelope instant chicken
   broth or bouillon cube
2 tsp. salt
potato chips

Pull skin from chicken breasts, then cut meat from bones; dice meat. Combine with carrots, celery, onion, water, chicken broth and salt in a large frying pan; heat to boiling; cover. Simmer 30 minutes, or until chicken is tender. Drain off any broth, save and refrigerate to add to a soup or stew. Fold mayonnaise into chicken mixture. Spoon onto a large serving platter; frame with potato chips and garnish with parsley if you wish.

Vinaigrette Salad

This salad is ideal for using leftovers of meat and fish. Unless seafood is added, this salad is best made a day ahead.

5 med. potatoes
2 cups diced cooked beets
4 ribs celery, diced
1 lg. apple, pared, cored, diced
1 lg. diced dill pickle
salt and pepper

1 cup cooked green beans or peas
1/2 cup cooked meat, chicken, fish,
    shellfish, cut in strips or flaked
3/4 cup vinaigrette dressing (pg. 19
lettuce or chicory leaves
1 ¼ cups mayonnaise

For Garnish: (Optional) Sliced dill pickle, celery curls, cooked, peeled shrimps, sliced salami.

Cook potatoes in skins in boiling salted water for 10 to 15 minutes; drain; peel and dice while still warm. Mix thoroughly with beets, celery, apple and dill pickle; season well. Stir in peas, meat, chicken, shellfish or fish with fork. Spoon over the vinaigrette dressing; chill 2-3 hours or overnight.
    To serve, arrange lettuce or chicory leaves around a salad bowl, toss salad with mayonnaise and spoon into bowl. Garnish.

TIP: Raw foods in the vegetable and fruit groups yield more nutrients than their processed counterparts. Use fresh vegetables and fruits whenever possible for most recipes.

Frankfurter Salad

3/4 cup French dressing
1/4 cup mayonnaise
1 head lettuce

2 diced boiled potatoes
1 minced onion
1 sliced dill pickle

15½-oz. can kidney beans
4 thinly sliced frankfurters
1 diced dill pickle

Combine creamy type French dressing and mayonnaise. Line salad bowl with lettuce leaves. Drain kidney beans. Mix all other ingredients but sliced pickle; mix in dressing, and mound in center of bowl. Decorate with sliced pickle.

***** ***** ***** ***** *****

**Cleaning your house while your kids are still growing
Is like shoveling the walk before it stops snowing.**

***** ***** ***** ***** *****

SEAFOOD SALADS:

"Yes! I lured my fisherman home with his favorite Chip crab Salad!"

"Yeh!"

Tuna And Cheese Potato Salad

2 med. cooked, peeled, cubed, potatoes
2 Tbs. oil & vinegar type Italian dressing
1 Tb. snipped parsley
5 cups torn lettuce
9¼-oz. can tuna, drained and flaked

3 hard cooked eggs, quartered
3-oz. Swiss cheese, cut in strips
1/2 cup sliced black olives
2 Tbs. finely chopped onion
1/2 cup oil & vinegar Italian dressing

Place potatoes in salad bowl; sprinkle with 2 tablespoons Italian dressing and the parsley. Layer lettuce, tuna, hard-cooked eggs, Swiss cheese, olives, and onion atop potatoes. Chill. At serving time, pour the 1/2 cup Italian dressing over salad; toss gently to coat. Makes 8 servings.

California Carrot Salad

4 cups diced carrots
2 cups diced potatoes
1½ cups sliced black olives
1/2 cup chopped scallions, or onions with green tops

2 Tbs. minced fresh dill
13-oz. can flaked tuna
2 Tbs. lemon juice
1 tsp. paprika
salt and pepper

3/4 cup olive oil
1/3 cup wine vinegar
1 C. cherry tomatoes, quartered
1/4 cup tomato catsup
1 tsp. honey or sugar
lettuce leaves

In separate pans parboil the carrots and potatoes until just chewy tender. Plunge into cold water. Drain. Combine the carrots, potatoes, olives, scallions, dill, and tuna in a large salad bowl. Toss to mix.

In blender or food processor, combine all remaining ingredients except the lettuce leaves and quartered cherry tomatoes, and blend until smooth. Pour the dressing over the salad and toss to coat. Pack the salad into a 5-cup ring mold. Chill for at least 2 hours. Invert the mold onto a serving plate lined with lettuce leaves. Fill the center with quartered cherry tomatoes and serve. A very attractive dish!

Portuguese Potato and Sardine Salad

Sardines blended in the dressing are a hearty and flavorful touch to this salad that makes 6 servings.

6 med. new potatoes	1/4 cup mayonnaise	1/4 tsp. pepper
2 chopped celery ribs	2 Tbs. lemon juice	Romaine lettuce
2 cans sardines, drained	1/2 tsp. Dijon-style	1 lg. red thin sliced onion
1/4 cup dairy sour cream	mustard	2 Tbs. chopped broadleaf
	1/2 tsp. salt	parsley

Cook potatoes in their skins in boiling salted water in a large saucepan until tender, about 20 minutes. Drain; return to saucepan; shake over very low heat to dry. Peel and cube potatoes into a large bowl. Add the celery.

Mash one can of the sardines into a small bowl. Add the sour cream, mayonnaise, lemon juice, mustard, salt and pepper; mix well.

Add the sardine mixture to the potatoes and celery, tossing gently but well. Line a salad bowl with the Romaine leaves; spoon in the salad. Garnish with remaining sardines like spokes in a wheel, and rim the salad with onion slices. Sprinkle parsley over all.

Chip-Crab Salad

1 ½ cup cut-up crab meat	1/2 cup sliced celery
or imitation crab	1/2 cup chopped green pepper
2 tsp. minced green onion	1/3 cup mayonnaise
	1 cup crushed potato chips

Toss together all ingredients except chips; chill. Toss in chips; serve on crisp lettuce. Garnish with slices of honeydew melon and/or strawberries. Makes 4 servings.

Cottage-Salmon Salad

16-oz. can salmon, drained, boned,	1 boiled egg, chopped
skinned, and broken in chunks	1 cup cream-style cottage cheese
2 cups cubed, cooked, potatoes	1/2 cup mayonnaise
1/2 cup sliced celery	1 tsp. dried dill weed
1/2 cup shredded carrot	2 Tbs. milk
1/4 C. chopped green onion with tops	1 Tbs. vinegar
	1/4 tsp. salt

Mix salmon, potatoes, celery, carrots, onions and eggs together. Blend together remaining ingredients and dash of pepper; add to salmon mixture. Toss to coat. Chill. Serve on green pepper rings and trim with carrot curls and green pepper. Makes 6 servings.

Optional: Reduce cottage cheese to 1/2 cup and add 1/2 cup sour cream. Add an creamy type Italian salad dressing instead of mayonnaise. Add sliced radishes and sliced olives.

Crab Stuffed Potato Salad

7-oz. can crab meat, or equal amount of imitation crab meat from your supermarket.

2 hard cooked eggs, coarsely chopped	1/4 cup mayonnaise	4 medium baked potatoes
	1 tsp. lemon juice	lettuce leaves
1/4 cup chopped celery	2 tsp. grated onion	lemon slices

Break crab meat into bite sized pieces. Combine with eggs, celery, mayonnaise, 1 teaspoon lemon juice and onion. Let chill in refrigerator. Cut potatoes in halves. Scoop out about half the potato in each of the potato halves. Set this aside. Fill potato halves with crab meat mixture. Serve on lettuce lined plates garnished with lemon slices. Makes about 6 to 8 servings.

For a more creamy salad, scoop out entire potato. Set 1/2 aside. With other half mash and whip in a little butter, milk, and salt. Spoon mixture back into potato shells. Finish filling with crab mixture

Note: Refrigerate remaining potatoes and use the next morning for breakfast by heating in a skillet with butter; adding salt & pepper. Heat through then sprinkle grated cheese on top. Let cheese slightly melt. Serve hot. Makes 4 servings.

TIP: Lemon juice is so versatile. It's used in cooking as well as laundry, cleaning and skin care. Cut it into slices and boil with stained white clothes to remove stains and keep them white. It also remove stains from hands, yet at the same time it enhances food flavors and makes wonderful lemonade.

Potato Crisp Salad

salad greens	1/2 cup mayonnaise	1/4 tsp. Worcestershire
2 to 4 tomatoes, peeled	1 Tb. cider or wine vinegar	6 to 8 radishes, sliced
1 clove garlic, mashed	1 lb. can salmon, or 7-oz.	1 pkg. shoestring potatoes
3/4 tsp. salt	can tuna drain	

Tear crisp cold salad greens into bite-size pieces in salad bowl. Slice peeled tomatoes vertically, with stem ends down. (Will lose less juices and salad doesn't get watery). Cut half of tomato slices into chunks; then add them to greens. With fork, mash garlic and salt until garlic disintegrates. Combine with mayonnaise, vinegar, Worcestershire; set aside.

Break salmon or tuna into large chunks over greens; also scatter on radish slices and a small package of shoestring potatoes. Pour on dressing; toss to coat well. Garnish with remaining tomato slices. Makes 4 big servings.

Idaho Salmon And Potato Salad

1 can salmon, chilled. (In Idaho we can get fresh salmon. If you can, it tastes wonderful---but so does the canned.)

lettuce	1 cup fresh peas	salt and pepper
4 med. cooked potatoes	1 cup cucumber, sliced	Caraway Dressing (see below)
(warm)	2 Tbs. minced grn. onions	2 Tbs. parsley
1 cup sliced squash	1/4 cup chopped celery	

Drain salmon; break into chunks. Arrange on lettuce-lined platter a mixture of slightly undercooked chewy potatoes and squash. Add peas, cucumber, celery, green onions. Sprinkle with salt and pepper. Pour Caraway dressing over mixture.

Place the drained salmon on top of the vegetable mixture. Add some Caraway dressing over the salmon.

Vegetable additions could include: Pea pods, sliced zucchini, sliced carrots, broccoli floweretts, cherry tomatoes, sliced green beans and sweet red or green pepper strips. Also consider adding olives (black or green).

Caraway Dressing:

1/2 cup oil	1/4 tsp. sugar	1/4 tsp. salt
1/2 tsp. dry mustard	1/3 cup white vinegar	1/4 tsp. caraway seeds
dash of pepper	(or wine vinegar)	chopped or crushed

Mix well. Makes about 1 cup.

> *TIP: Use romaine lettuce leaves to dress up a salad, but be sure to eat the leaves. Romaine has more nutritional value than the more popular iceberg lettuce.*

Italian Potato-Shrimp Salad

Hearts of romaine lettuce	4 anchovy fillets	1/4 cup mayonnaise
4 sm. potatoes, cooked,	2 Tbs. capers	salt
peeled and sliced	3 Tbs. olive oil	freshly ground black pepper
2 cups cooked shrimp	2 Tbs. lemon juice	minced parsley

Stand spears of romaine all around sides of shallow glass salad bowl. Fill in bottom with cut-up small pieces of romaine. Cover with sliced potatoes, shrimp, chopped anchovy fillets and capers. Mix next 3 ingredients, pour over salad and mix gently, taking care not to break potato slices. Season to taste with salt and pepper and top with parsley. Makes 6 servings.

MISCELLANEOUS SALADS:

"Oops!
I didn't know we
were out of
potatoes."

Mexican Potato Salad

2 Tbs. wine vinegar
1 Tb. oil
1/2 tsp. seasoned salt
2 lg. cooked potatoes, chopped

1 med. onion, chopped
2 Tbs. green chilies, chopped
2 Tbs. chopped parsley
2 hard cooked eggs, diced

1/2 cup mayonnaise
2 Tbs. hot chili sauce
1/2 cup coarsely chopped salted nuts

Mix vinegar, oil and seasoned salt; pour over potatoes and onion. Toss lightly; cool. Add chilies, parsley and eggs. Blend mayonnaise and chili sauce; toss with potato mixture and then stir in peanuts. Serve at once or chill. If made ahead, add salted peanuts just before serving, to keep them crisp. Makes 2 or 3 servings

Potato Salad & Sauerkraut Dressing

5 cups cooked, diced potatoes
1½ Tbs. chopped onion
1/4 cup chopped pimento
1/3 cup snipped parsley

1/3 cup canned sauerkraut juice
1/3 tsp. salt
1/3 cup skim or mixed powdered milk
1/3 cup mayonnaise

Combine potatoes, onion, pimento, and parsley. Place in the refrigerator. In small bowl, combine sauerkraut juice, salt, milk, and mayonnaise. With mixer, mix until smooth; refrigerate. At serving time pour dressing over potato mixture; toss gently. Makes 8 servings.

Chinese Potato Salad

2 Tbs. wine or cider vinegar
1 Tb. soy sauce
1/2 tsp. salt
sugar
1/4 tsp. dry mustard

1/4 tsp. garlic powder
1/4 tsp. ginger
1/3 cup oil
4 lg. cooked potatoes, cooled, pared, cubed
3/4 cup celery, sliced

4 green onions, sliced, white part only
2 Tbs. chopped/slivered almonds
salad greens (optional)

To make dressing, mix well and shake in jar; vinegar, soy sauce, salt, sugar, mustard, garlic powder, ginger and oil. Chill. Combine potatoes, celery and onions in serving bowl. Pour dressing over salad and toss well. Chill; then toss again. Sprinkle with almonds and parsley; serve with greens. Makes 8 servings.

Sweet & Seasoned Potato Salad

2 lbs. red potatoes, peeled,
1/4 cup slightly drained
   sweet pickle relish
1 tsp. prepared mustard
2 C. "Seasoned Mayonnaise "(below)

1 tsp. salt; 1/4 tsp. pepper
4 hard-boiled eggs, chopped
   cut into bite-size cubes
1/2 tsp. cayenne

Boil the cubed potatoes until tender. Drain well and while still hot place in large bowl. Add remaining ingredients and mix well. Serve warm or cold. Makes 8-10 servings.

Variation: Christmas Salad
Boil potatoes and beets together, while still hot dice and add onions which have been sauteed with pork fat, vinegar, salt and black pepper. A pretty red salad. Add chopped green bell peppers or green pickle relish for a delightful Christmas Salad.

Seasoned Mayonnaise:
Makes 2½ cups. All-purpose mayonnaise with a nice little zing.

1 Tb. white vinegar
1 tsp. dry mustard
3 egg yolks

1 Tb. lemon juice
1 tsp. cayenne pepper
1 egg

1 tsp. salt
2 cups vegetable oil

Place all ingredients except oil in food processor and process about 30 seconds. With machine still running, add oil in a thin steady stream; blend until mixed, pushing sides down once or twice with a spatula, until well mixed. Refrigerate at least 30 minutes before serving.

Mixed Potato Salad

Sweet potatoes cook faster than white potatoes, do not cook together.

4 C. cubed sweet potatoes
4 C. cubed white potatoes
1 Tb. white vinegar
1 tsp. cardamom

1/2 cup vegetable oil
3 Tbs. lemon juice
3 Tbs. honey
1/2 tsp. salt

1/2 tsp. white pepper
2 Tbs. minced fresh chives
1 tsp. curry powder

Parboil the sweet potatoes until just chewy tender. Plunge into cold water. Drain, peel, and set aside. Parboil the white potatoes until just chewy tender. Plunge into cold water. Drain and peel. Combine with the sweet potatoes.

Mix the remaining ingredients and pour over the potatoes. Toss gently to coat. Marinate for at least 1 hour to let flavors mingle. Serve cold, garnished with alfalfa sprouts and halved cherry tomatoes. Makes 8 servings.

SOUPS, STEWS, CHOWDERS, & CROCK POT DISHES

Families love to meet and eat,
It's lots of fun t'is true.
So hopefully this soup section
Will be of help to you.
--by Carol Fielding McCabe

Information & Tips

Potatoes are one of the most popular vegetables in the world. They offer high mineral and vitamin content and are easily digested. There are almost endless methods of preparing and serving potatoes and they are also excellent "go-alongs" with meat, fish, fowl, and a wide variety of vegetables.

The starch content of a potato plays an important role as to how the potato is best used. High starch content makes the potato more suitable for baking and mashing and for potato-type soups. A potato with a high starch content tends to become mealy as it cooks. (See 5th. paragraph, page 4.)

One of the secrets of a good stew is in the browning of the meat and wise use of seasonings. Experiment with seasonings. It is usually best to not salt meat until later in the cooking process.

Left over beef, chicken or vegetables are excellent additions to many soups and stews. Place in freezer containers and freeze to use later for a quick vegetable soup or stew.

Before scraping new potatoes, soak them for half an hour in cold water which has been salted. Not only do the skins peel off easily, but the hands are not stained. Remember you do not soak potatoes for long periods of time because they will lose some of their nutritional value.

There are many interpretations of different cooking methods. Following are the interpretation we have used in this book:

Broth: These are clear flavorful liquids made from meat or vegetables. They need long simmering over gentle heat to extract the maximum flavor from the ingredients.

Creamed Soups: These are usually made from vegetables cooked in milk. They are sieved or blended until smooth and thickened with egg yolk and cream. They have a velvety, creamy consistency.

Puree Soups: These have a flour, root vegetable or meat base and after cooking they, too, are sieved or pureed in a blender. Both cream and puree soups are cooked for a relatively short time - 20 to 40 minutes. They should be sieved or pureed as soon as cooked because standing or prolonged cooking ruins their flavor and contributes to nutrient loss. It can also spoil their consistency. However, puree soups based on dried vegetables need long, slow cooking so the vegetables are really soft and almost fall apart before they are sieved or blended.

Soups:

MEATLESS SOUPS:

"...You can leave the peelings on,
It doesn't matter."

Cream of Potato Soup

2 tsp. salt	1 small sliced onion	2 Tbs. flour
2 cups water	3 Tbs. butter	3 cups milk
4 cups sliced potatoes	4 or 5 sprigs parsley	salt, pepper, & cayenne

Add salt to water and cook potatoes until tender. Saute onion in butter. Place potatoes, cooking water, onion, parsley and flour in blender container and blend until smooth. Return to saucepan and add milk. Stir and heat to summering. Season to taste with salt and peppers.

Swiss Potato Soup

Put **1 unopened can frozen Cream-of-Potato Soup** in **warm water** for 2 to 3 minutes; open and empty into saucepan. Add **1 cup light cream, 3/4 cup milk, 1/8 teaspoon each of nutmeg and paprika and 1/4 cup grated Swiss cheese**; heat, stirring occasionally. Garnish with **watercress or alfalfa sprouts**. Makes 4 servings.

Carrot And Potato Soup

6 medium sized carrots	2 cups milk	salt and pepper to taste
3 small potatoes		

Cook carrots and potatoes until tender in small amount of water; mash through a strainer with remaining liquid. Add milk, salt, and pepper; heat to the boiling point, but do not boil. Serves 6.

Soups:

Quick Potato Soup

1 Tb. grated onion	2 cups milk	1 tsp. salt; 1/4 tsp. pepper
1½ cups chicken broth	1/2 cup instant mashed potatoes	

Add onion to chicken broth; bring to boiling. Slowly add milk, potato, and seasonings. For thicker soup add more potato flakes. Heat to boiling, but do not boil. Top each individual serving bowl with cut chives from that pot in your window (or dried chives). Makes 4 servings.

Soup Crecy

1 lb. carrots, sliced	4 lg. potatoes, peeled,	1 tsp. sugar
3 Tb. butter	quartered	4 slices French bread,
salt	6 cups water	diced, fried
		1 Tb. chopped parsley

In kettle, combine carrots, and 2 tablespoons butter. Cover; cook over low heat for 20 minutes. Add potatoes, salt, 6 cups water, and sugar. Bring to boil; cover, simmer for 45 minutes. Strain, reserving liquid. Mash vegetables. Stir cooking liquid into mashed vegetables and return to pan. Bring to boil; simmer 15 minutes Add bread pieces; mix well and serve; top with parsley.

Cream Of Leek & Potato Soup

Saute lightly **2 chopped leeks or sweet onions and 4 diced potatoes** in **margarine or butter**. When onion is transparent, add **3 cups fresh milk, 1/4 tsp. freshly ground black peppercorns, 1 tsp. Worcestershire, 1½ tsp salt and 1 to 4 drops Tabasco**. Place in a covered container and heat to simmering. When milk is hot, add the following and blend until smooth them simmer 3 to 6 minutes: **1 to 2 cups shredded, liquified, or grated vegetables** of your choice and **1 or 2 pimentos**, if needed.

Five minutes before serving add 1 cup fresh milk and 1/3 to 1/2 cup instant powdered milk. Serve as soon as these last ingredients have heated through; <u>do not boil.</u>; taste for seasoning and add if necessary. Stir in 2 Tbs. chopped parsley, and garnish with paprika or chives.

---

* * * * * * * * * * * * * *

Begin the day with friendliness,
And only friends you'll find.
Yes, greet the dawn with happiness;
Keep happy thoughts in mind.

* * * * * * * * * * * * * *

Soups:

Cream Of Onion Soup

2 med. onion	1 sm. can tomato puree	lemon juice
3 Tbs. butter	salt	1 egg yolk
2 med. cubed potatoes	nutmeg	1/2 cup cream

Cut the peeled onions with a course slicing disc or knife and saute in butter until done. Boil potatoes and blend with the onions, add the tomato puree and simmer again. Flavor with salt, nutmeg and lemon juice, adding egg yolk and cream. One shredded carrot is also very good with this favorite soup.

Cream Of Greens Soup

1 Tb. butter	1½ tsp.fresh thyme or	1-2 cups roughly chopped
1 Tb. vegetable oil	1/2 tsp. dried	greens (any type)
1½ cup diced onion	1½ tsp.fresh marjoram	6 cups water
2 garlic cloves, minced	or 1/2 tsp. dried	1 cup cream, milk or yogurt
	4 C. peeled, diced potatoes	salt and pepper

In pot, heat butter and oil; saute onion, garlic, thyme, and marjoram until onion is limp, about 5 min. Let soup cool slightly, then puree in a blender or food processor onion mixture, other vegetables, and water. Return the soup to the pot and reheat. Add the cream, and heat through. Season to taste with salt and pepper. Serve at once. (This delicious soup must be enjoyed fresh; the greens turn a nasty olive color overnight.) Makes 6 servings.

Cream Of Artichoke Soup

1 lb. Jerusalem artichokes	2 onions, sliced thin	1/4 tsp. ground nutmeg
juice of 1/2 lemon	1 C. potatoes, chopped sm.	1 whole clove
2 Tbs. butter	4 cups stock	salt and pepper
		1 cup milk

Peel; thinly slice artichokes; drop in water with lemon juice (to prevent them from turning brown). In kettle melt butter and add onion. Add dry artichokes, and potatoes to onion; cover; cook gently 10-15 minutes, stirring occasionally, until vegetables are tender. Add stock, spices, and seasoning; bring to boil; cover; simmer 10-15 min. Discard clove; puree mixture in a blender. Reheat it with the milk. Do not boil.

For liaison: 2 egg yolks and 1/2 cup heavy cream
Preparing the liaison: In bowl mix egg yolks and cream; stir in a little hot soup. Add this mixture to remaining soup, heat gently, stirring until soup thickens slightly. Do not let soup boil or it will curdle. Taste soup for seasoning and serve with cheese croissants

Soups:

Ben's (Idaho) Potato Soup
(Ben is my husband and his soup is the best!)

In a four qt. saucepan just cover with water the ingredients in the first 2 columns.

2 cups cut bite-size Idaho Potato	3/4 cup chopped celery	4 eggs
diced onion (1 ¼ cup)	1/2 cup pearl barley	1 ½ cans evap. milk
1/2 cup shredded carrots	1/2 tsp. seasoning salt	bacon bits
	1 tsp. salt, dash pepper	grated cheese

Peel; cut-up; cover and boil until potatoes, onions, carrots, celery, and barley are just soft. Stir occasionally to prevent barley from sticking; then add salt, seasoning salt, and pepper. TURN OFF HEAT!!! As soon as boiling stops add 4 eggs. Break yolks and whites with fork and swish fork several times through the eggs. Don't over stir. Eggs should be in chunks when poached about five minutes, or until whites are cooked. Add 1 ½ cans evaporated milk and stir. Taste for seasoning.

Note: Do not over cook if re-heated in the microwave or stove. Heat only until potatoes are warmed through.) To each serving add bacon bits or crisp cooked bacon chunks. Serve hot or cold. The barley has a tendency to settle to the bottom. Stir before putting soup into individual soup bowls. Grated cheese can be added to the individual servings. Makes 8 to 10 medium servings.

Mushroom Potato Soup

1/2 lb. mushrooms, chopped	3 Tbs. flour	chopped olives
1 small onion, minced	5 cups water	2 potatoes cubed
1 Tb. margarine	2 tsp. salt, dash pepper,	2 tsp. Worcestershire sauce
	1 Tb. lemon juice	

In large kettle, cook mushrooms and onion in margarine for 5 minutes. Stir in flour and cook 2 more minutes. Gradually add the water; cook, stirring until mixture thickens and boils. Add remaining ingredients. Cover and simmer 45 minutes or until potatoes are tender.

Cabbage Soup

1 med. head cabbage	1 lg. peeled, potato	2 Tbs. butter
1 large onion	3 cups skim milk	salt & pepper to taste

Shred cabbage; thinly slice onion and potato. Place vegetables in heavy saucepan with a small amount of water. Cover; cook slowly until tender. Mash to a pulp, leaving some texture. Add milk, butter, salt, and pepper. Simmer 10 to 15 minutes. Serve hot. (Makes 1 ½ quarts.)

Soups:

French Potage Bonne Femme

6-8 med. leeks	salt and pepper	2/3 cup light cream
5 Tbs. butter	2 cups milk	2 tsp. chopped parsley
3 med. potatoes,	2 cups water	croutons for garnish
peeled, sliced	2 egg yolks	(See below)

Reserve 1 leek for garnish, split the remainder lengthwise, wash well and slice the white parts. Melt butter in large saucepan, add leeks, potatoes and seasoning; cook over low heat, stirring until almost soft. Cover with foil and lid, cook 10 minutes or until very soft. Pour in milk, water and stir until mixture comes to a boil. Half cover with lid, simmer 15 minutes. Puree in a blender or food mill. Cut reserved leek into fine slices, put in cold water, bring to boil and boil 2 minutes, drain, pat dry.

Reheat soup; mix the egg yolks and cream in bowl, stir in a little of the hot soup. Add to remaining soup; stir over low heat until it thickens slightly. **Do not let the soup boil or it will curdle.**

Garnish soup with a little sliced leek and chopped parsley. Serve the croutons separately.

Croutons: Cut several slices of bread into cubes, removing the crusts. Fry the cubes in 3 or 4 tablespoons hot shallow fat or in deep fat until golden brown; drain on paper towels. Sprinkle lightly with salt.

The Best "Cheese Soup"

4 Tbs. butter	1 cup chopped grn. pepper	2 Tb. flour
1 cup chopped onion	1 cup sliced celery	1 tsp. salt; pepper to taste
1 cup sliced carrots	1-2 C. potatoes, sm. cubed	8-oz. Cheddar cheese

Take **4 chicken bouillon cubes** and dissolved in **1 can light beer** (room temp.) and **2 cups evaporated milk**. Melt butter or margarine in large skillet. Add vegetables and cook until tender crisp. Sprinkle in flour, stir, then add beer broth and cook for 2 minutes. Add salt, pepper and a little more milk if needed. Grate cheese and add to soup. Cook only until cheese melts. Makes 4 servings.

*** *** *** *** *** *** *** ***
We need not pray for great opportunities, but rather
the willingness to do little things in a great way.

41

Soups:

Idahoan® Minestrone

2 cups water	15¼-oz. can dark red	salt and pepper to taste
1 can beef booth	kidney beans, drained	1 Tb. oregano
1 pkg. Idahoan® Western	15¼-oz. can Northern	2 tsp. thyme
Style Potatoes	white beans, drained	1/2 tsp. red pepper flakes
1 sm. onion, chopped	10-oz.pkg.frozen chopped	1/2 cup butter (optional)
2 clove garlic, minced	spinach	1/4 cup chopped fresh parsley
16-oz. can Italian style	10-oz. pkg.mixed veggies,	1/4 C. grated Parmesan cheese
stewed tomatoes	peas, carrots, corn	

In a large kettle boil water and broth. Add potatoes with sauce packet, onion, garlic and stewed tomatoes; boil for 10 minutes. Stir in kidney beans, white beans, spinach and mixed vegetables; cook for 10 minutes. Mix in salt, pepper, oregano, thyme and red pepper flakes. Continue cooking for 10 minutes; stirring frequently.

Just before serving, garnish bowl with butter (optional) and a sprinkle each of parsley and Parmesan cheese. This soup freezes well and can be reheated in the microwave. Serves 8 as a main course.

French Garbure Paysanne

3 Tbs. butter	1/3 cup dried navy or Great Northern
1 med. white turnip, sliced	beans soaked overnight & cooked
2 med. carrots, sliced	2½ qts. water or stock
2 med. onions, sliced	1 long crusty roll, sliced,
1/2 head cabbage, sliced	fried in butter
white part of 2 leeks, sliced	1/2 cup grated Gruyere cheese
5 stalks celery, sliced	salt and pepper

In large kettle melt 2 tablespoons. butter; add turnip, carrot, cabbage, onion, leek, celery and potato. Press piece of buttered foil on top; add the lid; cook gently 15-20 minutes until vegetables are tender; don't let them brown. Add beans, seasoning and 5 cups water or stock or to cover. Cover, simmer 20-30 minutes or until very tender. Fry the crusty roll and drain on paper towels. (The garnish of croutes is the roll slices fried in butter.)

Lift 2 heaping tablespoons. vegetables from the soup, drain, work them through sieve. Put in small pan with remaining tablespoons. butter; cook, stirring, to the consistency of mashed potato. Spread this puree over the croutes, coating it well, and sprinkle with grated cheese. Bake the croutes in moderately hot oven 375 degrees for 10-12 minutes or until browned.

Puree the remaining soup in a blender; add the remaining water or stock, simmer 10-15 minutes longer or until soup is smooth, the thickness of light cream. Season and stir in 2 tablespoons butter in small pieces.

Serve soup hot with croutes floating in each bowl or serve separately.

Soups:

Spartan Soup

1 lb. carrot	2 lb. potatoes	a few slices celery
8-oz. onion	1 qt. stock	6-oz. aged cheese
1½-oz. butter	2 cups milk	salt and pepper
		seasoning salt

Combine finely chopped carrots & onions. Saute in butter 10 minutes. Cube potatoes and add to stock & vegetables. Simmer gently 30 minutes. Stir in milk and chopped celery. Cook a bit longer; remove from heat. Add cubed cheese & season to taste.

Pumpkin Soup

1½ to 2 lb. pumpkin, peeled	5 cups cold water	little milk (optional)
3 med. potatoes, peeled	salt and pepper	1 Tb. butter
3 tomatoes, halved, seeded	1½ Tbs. rice	1/4 cup heavy cream

Cut the pumpkin (or fresh or frozen yellow winter squash) into chunks, discarding seeds and fibers. In kettle combine pumpkin, potatoes and tomatoes with cold water and season. Cover, bring to a boil, simmer gently for 25-30 minutes or until the vegetables are tender.

Boil the rice in salted water for 12 minutes or until tender. Drain; rinse with hot water to separate the grains and set aside.

Puree the soup and return to the pan. Adjust the seasoning and add a little milk if the soup is too thick. Reheat it; add rice, butter and cream. Stir well and serve. Makes 6-8 servings.

Southern Bean Dip Soup

3 10½-oz. cans Fritos brand	3 med. potatoes, peeled, cut
jalapeno bean dip	1 cup chopped onion
1 can beef broth	1 cup chopped celery, 1" cubes
1 broth can water	1 can whl. kernel corn, undrained
	1/2 cup chopped green pepper

Mix the dip, broth and water. Simmer uncovered 30 minutes. Add potatoes, onion, celery, corn and pepper; simmer for 1 hour. Serve hot. Serves 8 to 10.

TIP: Green pepper is an excellent source of vitamin C. In addition to using green peppers in recipes, cut it into strips to serve with meals, or as nibblers.

Soups:

Vegetable Medley

1 cauliflower, cut unto flowerettes	2 carrots sliced in 1/4 inch slices
1 small onion, minced	2 yellow squash, sliced in 1/4 inch slices
2 zucchini, sliced in 1/4 inch slices	1 can Condensed Tomato Soup
2 potatoes, cubed	1 tsp. Italian salad dressing mix (unprepared)

In a large kettle boil vegetables until tender, add tomato soup; stir to blend. Sprinkle Italian salad dressing on top of soup just before serving.

Irish Cabbage And Potato Soup

Blender chop or chop separately, then combine in saucepan;
1/4 head firm cabbage   1 medium onion   2 medium potatoes, peeled
2 cups beef broth

Add **2 cups well-seasoned beef, ham , or corned beef stock**. **2 tablespoons salt** (to taste), and **1/4 teaspoon pepper**. Cover, and simmer, until vegetables are soft. Add **2 cups milk**. Heat again, adjust seasoning to taste, and serve in bowls. Top each portion with; **1/2 slice crisp cooked, crumbled bacon** and a sprinkle of fresh **chopped parsley**.

> *TIP: If parsley is washed with nearly hot water instead of cold or luke warm it will retain it's flavor better and it is much easier to chop. In addition, it retains a greener color longer.*

Lentil Porridge

1 cup lentils	2 med. diced potatoes	2 Tbs. oil
4 cups water	1 cup carrots, grated	1 Tb. flour
		salt and pepper

Cover lentils with 4 cups of water in a large pot. Bring to a boil and cook 1 hour. Add potatoes and carrots. Cook 20 minutes more, or until vegetables are tender.

Blend oil and flour over medium heat. Cook, stirring until smooth. Pour into the lentils; mix well, and bring to a boil. Season to taste.

Imitation bacon bits or cubes of lean canadian bacon may be used for additional flavoring. Yields about 1 quart.

Soups:

BEEF AND PREPARED MEATS SOUP:

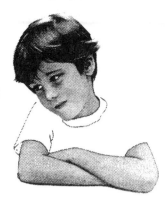

"seems to me a guy ought to be able to call them "spuds" if he wants too!"

Swiss Cream-Of-Potato Soup

4 med. potatoes, peeled	1 Tb. snipped parsley	3 cups milk
2 bacon slices, diced	2 tsp. salt; dash cayenne	2 tsp. Worcestershire sauce
1/4 cup minced onion	1/2 tsp. nutmeg	1/2 cup grated Swiss
2 Tbs. butter	1/4 tsp. dried mustard	or process Cheddar cheese

Cook potatoes until tender; drain. Meanwhile, saute bacon and onion over low heat, stirring until brown and tender. Mash potatoes; add bacon, onion, butter, parsley, salt, nutmeg, cayenne, mustard, and Worcestershire. Stir in milk. Heat over low heat, stirring; do not boil. Sprinkle with cheese. Serve at once. Makes 4 servings.

Leftover ham is a nice addition to this soup. You could saute the ham in a little fat and replace the bacon. I like both ham and bacon.

Creamy Potato Soup

6 slices bacon	1 cup water	2 soup cans milk
1 cup chopped onions	2 cans Cr. Chicken	1 tsp. salt
2 cups cubed potatoes	Soup (undiluted)	2 Tbs. cut parsley

In saucepan, cook bacon until crisp; set aside. Pour off all but 3 tablespoons drippings from saucepan; add onions; brown a bit. Add potatoes and water. Cook, covered, about 15 minutes, or until potatoes are tender. Blend in chicken soup, milk, and salt; heat, but do not boil. To serve, garnish with crisp bacon slices and parsley. Makes 4 servings.

Beef-Corn Soup

In large saucepan combine **2 lbs. beef shank cross cuts, 6 cups water, 1 cup chopped onion, 1 cup chopped celery, 1 cup chopped carrot, 1 cup chopped peeled potato, 1 tablespoon salt, and dash pepper**. Bring to boiling. Cover; simmer until beef is very tender, about 1½ hours.

When cool, remove meat from bones; chop meat and return to soup. Discard bones. Add **1 undrained 16-oz. can cut green beans, 1 undrained 16-oz. can whole kernel corn**, and **1/2 cup uncooked macaroni**. Cover and simmer about 20 minutes. Season to taste. 12 servings.

Soups:

Italian Tiny Meat Ball Soup

Mix in a soup kettle:

3 cups Condensed Beef Bouillon	1/4 cup canned tomatoes	1/4 tsp. pepper
1/4 tsp. oregano	1 C. chopped celery w/tops	2 cups cubed raw potatoes
	1 carrot, chopped fine	1/4 tsp. salt

Simmer for 30 minutes. In the meantime, soak 2 slices bread in water and squeeze out. Mix bread with:

1 lb. hamburger	1 egg, slightly beaten	1 tsp. salt
1 crushed clove garlic	1/4 tsp. pepper	

Form into tiny balls; saute in 2 tablespoons butter. Drop the meat balls and **1/2 cup fine soup pasta** into soup and cook about 3 more minutes. Serve in bowls and sprinkle with Parmesan cheese. Makes 4 servings.

Garden Patch Meatball Soup

3 medium potatoes, peeled, cubed	1 can tomatoes
1/2 cup chopped green peppers	2 tsp. salt
2 medium carrots, peeled, cubed	1 lb. lean ground beef
1 medium chopped onion	1 egg
4 celery stalks, coarsely chopped	1/4 cup chopped parsley

In a large pot, combine potatoes, peppers, carrots, onion, celery, tomatoes, salt and **3 cups water**. Cover and simmer 30 minutes. Meanwhile, combine ground beef, egg and parsley. Shape meat into 1 inch balls. Add to soup. Simmer, covered, 15 minutes or longer until meatballs are tender.

Italian Beef Minestrone Soup

In **2 tablespoons cooking fat**, in a large kettle, saute **1 cup chopped onions and 1 pound ground beef** until meat is brown. Add:

1 # 303 can tomatoes	1 cup chopped cabbage	3/4 cup sliced celery
1 cup raw cubed potatoes	1 cup sliced raw carrots	1/4 cup chopped grn. pepper

Bring to a boil and add:

1 ½ qts. water	1/4 cup uncooked rice	2 bay leaves
1/2 tsp. thyme	1/4 tsp. oregano	3/4 cup sliced celery
	salt and pepper	1/4 cup chopped green pepper

Cover and simmer for 1 hour. Serve sprinkled with grated Parmesan cheese. Makes 6 servings.

Variation: For a richer tomato taste, replace 1/2 the water with tomato juice.

Soups:

Potato Beef Soup

1 cup milk	1 cup chicken bouillon	evaporated milk
2 Tbs. flour	1 tsp. salt & dash pepper	1/2 lb. browned ground beef
		3 cooked, diced potatoes

Put all ingredients except potatoes and beef in a blender and blend for 30-45 seconds. Pour into saucepan with potatoes and meat and heat until hot, about 5 minutes. Makes 4 small servings.

Note: You can also use frozen hash browns instead of cooked potatoes and brown with beef a few minutes to cook.

Grandpa Ben's Vegetable Soup

1 ½ lbs. stew meat	1 cup pearl barley	3 C. potatoes, bite-size cubes
small amount oil	1 16-oz. can tomatoes	2 C. carrots, slice 1/2" thick
4 cups tomato juice	1 C. celery,cut bite-size	11 ½-oz. spicy hot V-8 juice
2 lg. onions, chopped	salt and pepper to taste	1/4 head cabbage, chunked

Brown meat on all sides in vegetable oil. Remove from pan; place in large kettle or crock pot; add all remaining ingredients; stir, mixing well.

Cook on high heat until it boils. Turn down heat and cook covered, just below the boiling point for about 1 hour; turn heat to low and cook until meat is tender. (In crock pot cook for about 2-3 hour on high and 3-4 hours on low.) Serves our son, Ben Jr's family of 7 until full.

TIP: When a recipe calls for 'pepper', try using fresh ground peppercorns ground in a pepper mill. The flavor is greatly improved. Take care in purchasing a good pepper mill.

Kartoffelsuppe
German Potato Soup

1/2 lb. diagonal sliced franks	2 Tbs. butter or margarine
1/2 cup chopped celery	2 10-oz Cr. Potato Soup
1/4 cup chopped onion	1 ½ cans milk
1/4 tsp. celery seed	1/4 cup chopped parsley

In large saucepan, brown franks and cook celery and onion with celery seed in butter until tender. Blend in soup, milk and parsley. Heat; stir occasionally. Makes 5 ½ cups.

Soups:

SOUPS WITH LAMB AND PORK:

"How's my little Tater Tot?
Want some potato soup?"

Swedish Cabbage Soup

1 Tb. whole allspice	2 qts. water	1/4 cup cut parsley
2 lamb shanks (3 lb.)	1 C. chopped leeks or onions	1/2 cup sliced celery
2 beef bouillon cubes	1/2 C. diced, peeled parsnips	2 med. cabbage shredded
1/2 tsp.pepper; 2 Tbs.salt	1 cup peeled, sliced carrots	2 cups, diced potatoes

Day before: Tie allspice in cheesecloth; place in kettle with shanks, bouillon cubes, pepper, salt, water. Simmer, covered 2 hrs. Refrigerate overnight. **About 1/2 hr. before dinner** skim fat from soup. Remove meat from bones; cube. Bring broth to boil; remove allspice bag; add leeks, parsnips, carrots, parsley, celery. Simmer, covered, 10 minutes. Add cabbage, potatoes, meat; cook covered 20 minutes. 6 hearty servings.

Potato And Avocado Soup

5 slices bacon, cut in small pieces	2 avocados peeled, seeded & cubed
1 cup minced onion	1/2 cup dairy sour cream
2 med. potatoes, peeled, cubed	salt and pepper to taste
3 cups chicken broth	

Fry bacon until crisp. Remove bacon and add minced onion to hot fat; saute until tender. Add potatoes to chicken broth. Heat to boiling; reduce heat and simmer until potatoes are tender.

Remove from heat, add avocado. Puree mixture in blender. Return puree to pan and heat to boiling. Remove from heat and stir in sour cream. Salt and pepper to taste. Garnish with bacon and avocado.

TIP: When making soup remember the maxim: 'Soup boiled is soup spoiled.' Soup should be cooked gently and evenly.

Soups:

Snowmobile Soup

1 round steak, pork or beef
2 Tbs. vegetable oil
2 cups carrots
1 cup celery

2 lg. onions, chopped
3 cups potatoes
1 can tomato soup
1 soup can water

1/4 tsp. pepper
3 Tbs. tapioca
1 tsp. salt

Cut up meat and lightly brown in vegetable oil. Remove from pan and cut into small chunks. Put meat and all remaining ingredients into a large kettle. Add more water if soup is too thick. Cook on high heat until it starts to boil. Turn heat down and cook several hours on med/low heat until tender. (It could be put in a crock-pot.) Excellent for those cold, fun days in the snow with your snowmobile.

Nacho Potato Soup

4 slices bacon, cut up
1/2 cup chopped grn. pepper
3 cups water

1 pkg. Au Gratin potatoes
12-oz. can whl./kernel corn
16-oz. can tomatoes, cut up

salt; pepper to taste
2 cups milk

Cook bacon and green pepper in large pan until bacon is crisp. Pour off excess fat. Add water, potatoes, and seasoning mix from package, corn, tomatoes, salt and pepper. Cover and simmer 30 minutes, stirring occasionally. Add milk; heat gently. Do not boil.

Green String Bean Soup

8 slices bacon (or equivalent ham)
savory, fresh or dried
4 cups potatoes, peeled, cubed
salt to taste

4 C. cooked, cut-up green beans
1 cup sour cream
2 cups buttermilk
4 cups yellow wax beans (for color, & variety)

Simmer bacon and savory with 2 cups water for 15 minutes, or until nearly done. Savory is a must for this soup. Add potatoes, salt and water to cover; simmer until potatoes are tender. Add green and yellow beans, heat until nearly to boiling. Remove from heat. Blend sour cream and buttermilk, add slowly to potato, bacon and bean mixture. Cook until thoroughly heated.

Harvest Soup

1 cup ham, chopped
4 Tbs. butter
1 cup potatoes, cubed
1 cup zucchini, sliced

2 ribs celery, sliced
1 cup broccoli, chopped
1 cup carrots, sliced
1/2 onion, chopped
1 cup cauliflower pieces

2 cups chicken broth
1/2 cup flour
1 cup half & half
1 cup milk
2 C. Velveeta cheese, cubed

Melt butter, add ham and vegetables. Saute until tender. Add broth; simmer 30 minutes, covered. Mix flour, half & half and milk. Add to soup. Add cheese, cook until melted and soup is thick.

Soups:

Senate Bean Soup

3 qts. water	2 cups minced onion	1/2 bay leaf
1½ lbs. dried navy beans	1 cup minced celery	1/4 tsp. ground pepper
2 1" ham slices	1 cup mashed potatoes	1 Tbs. chopped parsley
2 smoked pork chops	1 cup carrots	salt to taste
1 ham bone or hock	2 cloves garlic, minced	

Put water & beans in pot; bring to boil; boil 5 minutes. Cover; remove from heat; steep 1 hour. Add meats; simmer 1 hour. Add onions, celery, carrots, potatoes, garlic, bay leaf, and pepper. Simmer 2 hours. Remove meats from pot; chop; return meat to soup; add parsley and salt. Makes 8 to 12 servings.

Soup Of The Day

Use leftover green salad -- it cannot be served again because the dressing wilts the leaves. But with the addition of a little milk or stock it makes delicious soup. The dressing gives it an unusual tang.

2 Tbs. butter	1½ cups leftover cooked vegetables, such
1 med. onion, chopped fine	as, potatoes in white sauce, or carrots,
leftover green salad, with dressing	onions from ham, etc. coarsely chopped
2 cups milk	salt and pepper
2 cups liquid from cooked ham or use bouillon	

In large pan, melt butter and saute onion until soft. Add leftover salad and continue cooking, covered, over very low heat for 10 minutes. Add vegetables with ham liquid, simmer 10 minutes more. Puree in blender. Return to pan with milk, bring just to a boil and taste for seasoning.

Jamboree Ham Bone Soup

1 ham bone with meat or 1/2 lb. ham steak, cut in narrow 2" strips	
2 qts. water	1 cup black-eyed peas, cooked
1 cup onion, diced	1½ cups tomatoes, peeled, diced
1 cup celery, diced	1 corn kernels, fresh or frozen
1½ cups green beans, cut 2"length	1 tsp. salt
1 cup turnip, diced	1/2 tsp. black pepper
2 cups potato, diced	sugar
1/2 cup green peas, fresh or frozen	

Add ham bone or ham strips to water, bring to boil, simmer 15 minutes. Add onion, celery, green beans, turnip, black-eyed peas and potato. Simmer until vegetables are barely tender. Add remaining ingredients, simmer 5 minutes. Adjust seasonings to taste. Makes 8 to 10 servings.

Soups:

All-Day Split Pea Soup

16-oz. split green peas	7 cups water	1 tsp. salt
1/2 lb. smoked pork hock	2 cups potatoes, diced	1/4 tsp. pepper
1 ½ cup chopped onion	1 cup cubed celery	1 clove garlic, crushed
1/4 tsp. red pepper sauce	1 cup sliced carrots	

Rinse split peas under cold water; drain. In large bowl, combine all ingredients. Place in slow cooker.

Just before serving, remove hock or ham and cut into bite-size pieces. Return to soup. Makes 10-11 cups of soup.

Basque Potato Soup

1 lb. Italian sausage, sliced	2 cans tomatoes	1/4 cup chopped parsley
1/2 cup chopped onion	4 potatoes, pared, diced	1 cup sliced celery
1 ½ cups water	1 bay leaf	2 Tbs. chopped celery leaves
1/2 tsp. dried leaf thyme	2 beef bouillon cubes	1 Tb. lemon juice
1 Tb. salt; 1/4 tsp. pepper		

In large saucepan, brown sausage over medium heat. Add onion; cook 5 minutes. Add remaining ingredients; bring to a boil, reduce heat, simmer uncovered 40 minutes, or until potatoes are tender. Makes 6 servings.

CHICKEN AND SEAFOOD SOUP:

"Wow! That must've been cayenne, not paprika."

Potato Cheese Soup

In a large pot, melt **2 tablespoons butter**, and saute **2 cups diced onions**, until limp, 3-5 minutes. Add **5 cups peeled, diced potatoes** and **4 cups chicken broth**. Simmer until the potatoes are tender, about 15 minutes. Cool the soup slightly. Puree in a blender or food processor until smooth.

Return to the pot. Stir in **1 cup heavy cream, 2 cups grated cheese**, and **2 teaspoons Dijon-style mustard**. Reheat until the cheese is melted. Serve warm. Makes 6 to 8 servings.

Soups:

Iced Soup Vichyssoise

This classic French soup must be made with well-flavored stock and heavy cream. If leeks aren't available, use mild or Bermuda onions.

2 Tbs. butter
6 leeks, finely sliced, (white part)
1 celery stalk, sliced fine
2 med. potatoes, peeled, sliced

2/3 cup heavy cream
5 cups chicken stock
1 Tb. chopped chives
salt and pepper

In large pan, melt butter, add leeks, celery and potatoes. Sweat them by placing foil on top, cover with lid, cook over very low heat 10-15 minutes, stirring occasionally, or until very soft but not brown.

Stir in the stock, bring to a boil; season; simmer 12-15 minutes. Puree in a blender. Stir in cream and season to taste. Cover soup and cool. Whisk a few seconds; cover and chill. Soup should have the consistency of cream and be smooth and delicate. Sprinkle a few chives over each bowl before serving cold.

Soup Divine From Left Overs

1 thin sliced onion
1 ½ cups chicken broth or
   2 bouillon cubes and
   1 ½ cup water

1 cup left over potatoes
   or thawed hash browns
1/4 cup fresh parsley
1 cup half and half or evap. milk

1/2 tsp. celery salt
1 cup leftover cooked veggies
   (any kind except leaf)

Put onion, 1/2 cup broth and cooked potatoes in blender; cover; blend 10 seconds. Add remaining broth, vegetables, parsley and celery salt; cover; blend 10 seconds. Add half and half and blend an additional 5 seconds. Heat mixture in saucepan just to boiling, do nor overheat. Add salt and pepper to taste. Makes 4 to 6 servings.

Dilly Potato Soup

10 ½-oz. can chicken broth
1/2 cup chopped onions
3 cups cubed potatoes
1/2 cup chopped carrot
1 cup sliced celery

2 Tbs. cut parsley
1 tsp. salt
1/8 tsp. pepper
1/4 tsp. dried dill weed
3 ½ cups milk

3 Tbs. butter
1/4 cup all-purpose flour
1 Tb. chopped, canned
   pimento

In a 3-quart saucepan combine first 9 ingredients. Cover; simmer until veggies are tender, about 25 minutes. Add milk and remaining ingredients except 1/2 cup milk and the flour. Mix 1/2 cup milk and flour together; blend until smooth; stir blended mixture into the soup; cook and stir no longer than necessary until slightly thickened and bubbly. Males 8 servings.

Soups:

Potato Cauliflower Soup

1 can chicken broth
1 lb. potatoes, peeled and sliced
1/2 med. cauliflower (2 C. flowerets)

1 medium carrot, diced
1½ cups milk
2 Tbs. chopped fresh chives

In a saucepan, combine chicken broth, potatoes, cauliflower, and carrot; heat to boiling. Reduce heat to low; cover; simmer 10-15 minutes, until vegetables are tender. Ladle about 1 cup of vegetable mixture into food processor or blender. Process or blend until smooth and creamy.

Pour mixture into medium bowl. Repeat with remaining vegetables. Return pureed mixture to saucepan; stir in milk and cook until heated through. Garnish with chives, if desired.

Pink Swirl Soup

When it comes to appearance, this soup has no equal. It is a beautiful white potato soup with a beet puree marbled in.

3 Tbs. butter
4 cups leeks,quartered,diced

5 cups finely diced, potatoes
6 cups chicken broth
3/4 cup cream

3/4 cup milk
salt and pepper
2 cups cooked beets

In a soup pot, melt the butter and saute the leeks until they are wilted, about 3 minutes. Add the potatoes and broth. Cook the soup until the potatoes are tender. Cool soup slightly and process in a blender or food processor until smooth. Add cream and milk. Season to taste with salt and pepper. Blend and puree the diced, cooked beets until smooth. Add 2 cups of the soup and process until smooth.

Ladle hot soup into individual bowls. Pour a little beet and potato puree into each bowl and swirl it with a spoon. Beautiful. If you would like to serve cold soup, chill soup and beet mixtures separately and swirl together at the last minute. For a shocking pink soup mix beets and potatoes together until totally blended. Makes 6 to 8 servings.

Potato Broccoli Soup

3 cups thin sliced potatoes
3 cups chopped broccoli

1 lg. onions
1 tsp.crushed clove garlic
3 cups chicken stock

2 cups milk
1 cup cream
1 tsp. salt; 1 tsp. pepper

Boil potatoes, broccoli, onions and garlic in stock. Cover and simmer gently for 30 minutes. Puree in blender; return to pot. Add milk, cream, salt and pepper and reheat, but do not boil. If soup is too thick, thin with a little more milk. If you like a chunk type soup do not blend, rather cut potatoes and onions in small cubes instead of slices

Soups:

TIP: *Egg drop noodles are so easy and good. Make a soft sticky dough by mixing eggs, flour and a little salt. You can also add a little milk if you want too. With a spoon scoop up some of the mix. With your finger scoop small droplets off the end of the spoon into the nearly boiling soup.*

Chicken And Dumplings Or Noodles

3 ½ to 4 lb. stewing chicken
1 carrot sliced thin
4-6 cups water
1 lg. onion, diced

1 cup chopped celery
2 tsp. salt
1/2 tsp. pepper

2 Tbs.parsley flakes
4 lg. potatoes, quartered
Dumplings or Noodles
(see below and page 55)

In a large covered Dutch oven, combine all ingredients except potatoes. Bring to a boil; simmer, covered 1 ½ hours or until chicken is fork tender. Remove chicken and 1 cup broth to cool for dumpling recipe. Add potatoes. Cook in broth 20 minutes.

Prepare dumplings or noodles while potatoes are cooking using recipe below. Drop dumplings into rapidly boiling chicken broth and cover. Cook 20 minutes or until dumplings or noodles are firm. Shake pot often so dumplings will not stick together. While dumplings or noodles are cooking, remove chicken bones. Discard skin and bones. To serve, pour broth, dumplings or noodles and potatoes over cooked chicken.

Egg Dumplings:

Mix together: **2 cups flour, 4 teaspoons baking powder** and **1/2 teaspoon salt**. Mix together **1 beaten egg** and **3/4 cup milk**; stir into flour mixture. Drop into nearly boiling stew and cover container, steam until done, about 15 minutes. Don't peek! That makes doughy dumplings.

Easy Noodles:

about 3 cups sifted flour
1 tsp. salt

4 Tbs. shortening
1/2 cup chicken broth

1 egg

Sift dry ingredients together; cut in shortening using knives or a pastry blender until the mixture resembles coarse corn meal. Gradually with a fork stir in enough cooled chicken broth and egg to make a soft dough.

Knead two minutes or until all the flour is mixed into dough, adding more or less flour if necessary to make a soft dough. Turn dough onto a floured surface. With a floured rolling pin, roll dough to about 1/8 inch thickness. Cut into thin strips. Continue with recipe for "Chicken and Dumplings".

Soups:

Grandma's Homemade Noodles:

So good in soups or stews. Exceptional when mixed with chicken for a chicken noodle soup or stew.

2 eggs   1/4 cup milk   salt and pepper   flour

Mix eggs, milk, salt, pepper, and enough flour to make a semi-sticky dough. Place dough on a floured board for kneading. Knead additional flour into the dough until it is barely stiff enough to prevent sticking. Do not use too much flour. If dough becomes too stiff, add another egg or a little more milk. Additional egg is better than additional milk unless only a spoonful or two of liquid is needed.

Cover and place in the fridge for 2-3 hours. Remove and place on a floured board. Roll dough out flat, about 1/8 inch thick. Sprinkle the top of the rolled out dough generously with flour, but do not work it in. Starting at one end, roll the dough into a long roll.

With a sharp knife cut the rolled dough into thin, thin slices, almost like slivering. After several slices have been cut off, unroll the strips and place on a bed of flour--coat the strips with flour to prevent sticking together. Continue cutting until all the dough has been made into thin noodles. Lay the noodles out on the floured board or on floured wax paper to dry at room temperature for several hours. Run your fingers through them, mixing them up and turning them over every so often.

After noodles have formed a dried outer covering they are ready to mix with the soup or stew. They should cook for 10 to 15 minutes.

Potato And Chicken Soup

4 slices bacon, cut in small pieces	1 cup water	1 pat butter
	2 cans Cr. Chicken soup	crackers
1/2 cup chopped onion	1 cup milk	chopped chives or
1 ½ cup cubed potatoes	1/2 tsp. salt	parsley

Place bacon in saucepan, cook until crisp. Remove bacon. Retain about 2 tablespoons fat, pour off the remainder. Saute onions in fat until tender.

Add potatoes and water, cook covered until the potatoes are tender. Add soup, milk, bacon, and salt. Heat to blend. Add butter. Garnish soup with crackers, chopped chives or parsley. Makes 4 servings.

This recipe is enhanced with the addition of small chunks of left over or fresh cooked chicken.

Soups:

Chicken N' Vegetables

An easy to make soup that is ready to serve in about 30 minutes.

1 medium-sized onion, chopped
16-oz. can whl. kernel corn, drained
10-oz. pkg. frozen lima beans,
  cooked, and drained
2 cans chicken broth
1 Tb. butter or margarine
1 Tb. Worcestershire sauce

2 med. potatoes, peeled, and
  chopped
10-oz. can tomato juice
1 cup cooked chicken
1 ½ tsp. salt
1/4 tsp. pepper

Combine all ingredients in large kettle or Dutch oven; simmer about 30 minutes or until vegetables are done. Serve hot. Makes 6 hearty servings.

Variation: This same recipe is excellent when made with beef and beef broth instead of chicken. Use cut up round or stew meat or meat from a roast. Prepare according to above directions.

> *TIP: If using a lot of fresh corn in a recipe or for canning, cut the corn over an angel food pan, using the center of the pan to support the ear. Cut the corn off the cob with a sharp knife and let the kernels fall into the pan.*

Chicken In The Pot

1 broiler-fryer (3 pounds)
8 sm. new potatoes, washed
4 carrots, pared and diced
2 turnips, pared and diced
2 stalks celery with tops, diced
1 leek, or onion trimmed, washed, chopped

1 Tb. salt
5 to 6 cups water
2 sprigs parsley
6 peppercorns
1 bay leaf

Cut chicken into serving-size pieces: 2 legs, 2 thighs and 2 wings. Cut each side of breast crosswise into 3 pieces. Layer chicken, halved potatoes, carrots, turnips, celery and leek in a 3-quart flameproof casserole or Dutch oven; sprinkle salt between layers. Add water almost to cover.

Tie tops from celery, parsley, peppercorns and bay leaf in a piece of cheesecloth; push under liquid; bring to boil; reduce heat; cover. Simmer about 1 hour, or until meat and vegetables are tender. Discard bag.

Ladle into soup bowls, spooning 2 pieces of chicken into each bowl. Good served with crusty bread. Makes 6 servings. Try adding some chopped green onion and a little cayenne. Good!

56

Soups:

Turkey Frame Soup

5 quarts water	4 tsp. salt	16-oz. can tomatoes,
1 meaty turkey frame	1 cup raw,cubed potatoes,	1 tsp. dried thyme, crushed
1 onion, quartered	cut up	1/2 tsp. dried oregano,
*7 cups fresh vegetables	Homemade Noodles (page 61)	crushed

In Dutch oven combine water, turkey frame, onion, and salt. Simmer, covered, 1 ½ hours. Remove frame and onion; cool frame. Remove meat from bones. Discard bones and onion. Add the turkey meat, potatoes, fresh vegetables, undrained tomatoes, thyme, and oregano to the broth.
Bring mixture to boiling; cover. Simmer 45 minutes. Add homemade noodles; boil 15 minutes longer. Makes 4 quarts.

* Any combination of sliced celery or carrot, chopped onion or rutabaga, sliced mushrooms, chopped broccoli, or cauliflowerets.

Cucumber Salmon Soup

1 Tb. butter	1/2 tsp. dried dill weed	1 soup can of milk
1/2 cup shredded carrots	2 cans Cr. potato soup	2 cups chopped cucumber
2 Tbs. chopped onions	1 soup can of water	8 oz can salmon, drained and flaked

In 2 qt. saucepan over medium heat, in hot butter, cook carrots and onions with dill until tender. Stir in soup, milk, water and cucumber. Add salmon Heat thoroughly, stirring occasionally. 6-7 1 cup servings.

School Cooks Honored In Guinness Book Of World Record

The "Russette Chief" potato peeling team breaks all records.
Manager Cleone Winder and the five team peelers, Marj Killian, Marilyn Small, Barbara Paulson, Terry Anderson and Janene Utkins earned the title in 1992 by peeling 1,064.6 pounds of Idaho potatoes in 45 minutes.

After great effort and two years later the event was documented and the Shelley School Cooks were placed in the Guinness Book Of World Records as the world champion potato peelers.

The manager and team members appeared on the Regis and Kathie Lee show in July, 1994. The 4 day expense paid trip took them to New Your City where they were treated like royalty, staying in the finest hotel, eating the greatest meals and traveling in limousines. They met and had pictures taken with Arnold Schwarzenegger and Dom Deluise. Their sight-seeing highlight of the trip was the specular Statue of Liberty.

Congratulation "Russette Chief" Shelley School Cooks (manager and team members) from the great state of Idaho in the heart of potato country, Shelley, Idaho. You have made us proud. What an experience!

STEWS WITH BEEF OR PREPARED MEATS:

Thanks mom!
You're the goodest cook.

Beef Oven Stew

1 beaten egg	1/2 lb. ground beef	salt and pepper
2 Tbs. cornmeal	2 Tbs. cooking oil	8-oz. can tomatoes
2 tsp. instant minced onion	2 small potatoes	2 tsp. all-purpose flour
1/2 tsp. dry mustard	2 small carrots, sliced	1 beef bouillon cube
1/4 tsp. chili powder	1 small onion, quartered	2 Tbs. water
1 tsp. salt		

Heat oven to 350 degrees. Combine egg, cornmeal, instant onion, mustard, chili powder, and 1/2 tsp. salt. Add beef; mix well. Shape into 6 balls; brown in hot oil. Place meatballs in 1½ quart casserole. Add peeled and quartered potatoes, carrots, and quartered onion. Sprinkle with salt and pepper. Blend flour into drippings in skillet. Add tomatoes, bouillon cube, and 2 tablespoons water.

Cook and stir until bubbly. Pour over meat and vegetables. Cover. Bake until vegetables are tender, about 1 hour. Makes 2 servings.

Stew With Cheese

4 Tbs. butter	1/2 cup broth	9-oz. beets
1 medium diced onion	instant mashed potatoes	2 large cucumbers
1 lb. ground beef	2 cups water	3 Bismark herring
dash of nutmeg	1 cup milk	1 cup aged Gouda cheese,
salt, pepper, paprika		grated

Heat butter; saute diced onions until glazed. Add ground beef and slowly begin to braise. Use seasonings to create a mild taste, and add 1/2 cup broth. Continue to braise for 8 minutes. Prepare mashed potatoes as package directs. Cube the beets, cucumbers, herring and cheese and blend, along with the ground beef, into the mashed potatoes.

Round-Up Stew

1½ lbs. ground beef	6 potatoes, cut in chunks	1 can Tomato Soup
1 lg. onion, chopped	1 cup sliced carrots	water as desired
1/2 cup celery, chopped	1 can Cr. Mushroom Soup	

Brown meat, onion and celery in fry pan and season to taste. Boil potatoes and carrots together. Drain; add seasoned meat mixture and the soups. Add water as desired from potatoes and carrots. Put in casserole or small roaster and bake about 45 minutes at 350 degrees. Makes 6 servings.

Chili Stew With Egg Dumplings

1 can red kidney beans	1 Tb. shortening	1 can Tomato Soup
2½ cups raw potatoes	1/2 cup chopped onions	Egg Dumplings or Grandma's
salt and pepper	1 lb. ground beef	Noodles (See pg. 54 & 55)
4 cups water	2 tsp. chili powder	1 cup dairy sour cream

Combine undrained beans, cubed potatoes, 1 teaspoon salt, 1/2 teaspoon pepper, and water in saucepan; bring to a boil. While mixture boils, heat shortening in skillet; saute onion until tender; add beef, chili powder and 1 teaspoon salt. Cook until meat is browned. Add meat and tomato soup; stir well; simmer, covered, for 1 hour.

Return to boil; drop egg dumplings by spoonful into boiling stew. Cover tightly, steam, 12-15 minutes. Remove to warm plate. Add sour cream to stew and stir well and serve immediately. Makes 12 servings.

Meat Ball Stew

1 lb. ground beef	1/2 tsp. salt	1 can Condensed Tomato Soup
1 egg, slightly beaten	8-oz. can undrained peas	16-oz. can sm. potatoes,
1/2 cup sm. bread cubes	2 Tbs. shortening	drained, cut up
3/4 cup chopped onion	1 can beef broth	1/8 tsp. thyme, crushed

Mix thoroughly beef, eggs, bread cubes, 1/4 cup chopped onion, and salt. Shape firmly into about 36 meat balls; brown in shortening; pour off fat. Add remaining ingredients. Heat; stir occasionally. Makes about 6½ cups.

TIP: When thickening stew, flour is good for soups served hot while cornstarch is better for soups served cold.

Burgundy Meat Ball Stew

Mix Together:

2 lbs. ground beef	2 eggs, beaten	1 crushed clove garlic
1 C bread crumbs	2 Tbs. minced parsley	1/2 tsp. pepper
2 tsp. salt	1/4 cup minced onions	1/2 cup Burgundy

Form meat mixture into 32 balls, roll in flour and brown on all sides in skillet with 1/3 cup butter. Add 3 cups boiling water, 5 cloves, and 1 cup Burgundy. Cover and simmer for 20 minutes. Add:

4 cups cubed potatoes	16 small white onions	2 cups chunked cabbage
2 cups sliced celery	2 cups thick sliced carrots	

Cover; simmer; 30 minutes until done; Remove cloves. Makes 8 servings.

Beef Stew With Dumplings

1 lb. boneless beef chuck, cut 1" cubes	1 sm. bay leaf, crumbled	1/8 tsp. pepper
1/2 tsp. Worcestershire	1/2 tsp. lemon juice	3 carrots, cut 1" pieces
1/2 clove garlic, minced	pinch of allspice	1 sm. onion, sliced
4 small onions	1/2 tsp. sugar	2 potatoes, peeled, cubed
1 tsp. salt	2 cups water	large dumplings (see below)

Brown meat thoroughly on all sides in heavy saucepan. Add all ingredients except carrots, whole onions, potatoes, and dumplings. Cover tightly. Cook 1 hour, 45 minutes. Add vegetables; cook 10 min. Add dumplings; finish cooking stew with dumplings Makes 4 servings.

Dumplings:

Mix **3 tablespoon milk** with **1/2 cup buttermilk baking mix**. Spoon batter lightly onto bubbling stew. Cook 10 minutes uncovered and 10 minutes covered. Remove. Top stew with dumpling on warm plates.

Potato Dumplings

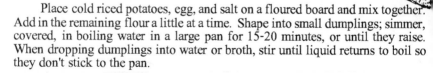

4 lg. boiled potatoes , riced	1 egg
2½ tsp. salt	1 cup flour

Place cold riced potatoes, egg, and salt on a floured board and mix together. Add in the remaining flour a little at a time. Shape into small dumplings; simmer, covered, in boiling water in a large pan for 15-20 minutes, or until they raise. When dropping dumplings into water or broth, stir until liquid returns to boil so they don't stick to the pan.

Stews:

Cabbage Patch Stew

1/2 lb. ground beef	1/2 cup diced celery	salt and pepper
2 Tbs. fat	#1 can red kidney beans	1 tsp. chili powder
2 med. onions, sliced thin	1 cup cooked tomatoes	hot mashed potatoes
1 cup shredded cabbage		

Brown ground beef in hot fat over medium heat; add onions, cabbage and celery; cook until cabbage is yellow. Add water to cover (about 2 cups); simmer 15 minutes. Add beans, tomatoes and seasonings; cook 15 to 25 minutes. Serve in bowls topped with spoonfuls of mashed potatoes. Makes 6 servings.

Potato-Topped Stew
(Freeze For A Busy Day)

2 Tbs. all-purpose flour	1 Tb. instant minced onion
salt and pepper	1/4 tsp. dried crushed basil
1 lb. beef stew meat, cut in	10-oz. pkg. frozen mixed vegetables
3/4" cubes	1/3 cup dry red wine
2 Tbs. shortening	4 servings instant mashed potatoes
1 can Golden Mushroom Soup	1/2 cup shredded process American cheese

Advance preparation: Combine flour, 1 teaspoon salt, and dash pepper in plastic or paper bag. Shake meat cubes with flour mixture to coat. In heavy pot or Dutch oven brown the meat in hot shortening. Stir in soup, instant minced onion, basil, and **3/4 cup water.** Cover; cook, stirring occasionally, for 30 minutes. Add mixed vegetables; continue cooking until meat is tender, about 30 minutes more. Stir in wine (optional--the alcohol is destroyed with heat.) Spoon into 12-quart casserole. Cover tightly. Seal, label, and freeze up to 2 months.

Before serving: Bake frozen casserole; covered; at 400; 1¼ hours. Prepare potatoes, following package direction. Spoon around edge; sprinkle with cheese. Bake, uncovered, 15 min. more. Makes 4 servings.

Quick Potato-Beef Stew

1 large cubed potato	1/4 cup flour	1 can cut green beans
1 lb. sliced carrots	1 pkg. dry onion soup mix	3 cups, chunked, cooked beef

Cook potato and carrots in enough water to cover until tender; drain, reserving the liquid. Combine flour and soup mix in large skillet; add water and reserved liquid to measure 3 cups; stir into mixture in skillet. Heat to boiling, stirring constantly. Boil and stir for 1 minute. Stir in veggies and beef. Cover; cook over low heat about 10 minutes or until heated through.

Paniola
(Hawaiian Cowboy Stew)

2 lbs. beef (1 ½ " cubes)	1 tsp. garlic powder	6 carrots
soy sauce to cover cubes	1/2 cup chopped onions	1 ½ cup cut green beans
2 Tbs. bacon fat	2/3 tsp. salt	4 medium potatoes
4 cups boiling water	1/2 tsp. pepper	2 Tbs. flour
1 tsp. Worcestershire	1 tsp. brown sugar	4 Tbs. cold water

Soak beef in soy sauce for 1 or 2 hours. Brown well in bacon fat, (or cooking oil); add water, Worcestershire sauce, garlic, onion, salt, pepper and brown sugar. Allow it to simmer for 1 ½ hours, stirring occasionally. Cut carrots, beans, and potatoes into 1 inch pieces and add vegetables to meat; cook until done. Mix flour in water and add to stew. Cook until gravy is thickened.

Beefed, Beef Stew

1¾ lbs. beef, 1 ½ inch	3 Tbs. fat or drippings	1/2 tsp. salt
thick, chuck or round	1/4 cup diced onion	1/2 tsp. Worcestershire
1/3 cup flour	1 minced clove of garlic	4 med. potatoes, quartered
1/2 tsp. salt	2¾ cups boiling water	12 small white onions
1/4 tsp. pepper	1 cup canned tomatoes	12 peeled, carrots, 2" pieces
2 bay leaves	2 Tbs. tomato paste	1 ½ cup frozen peas

Trim excess fat from meat; cut-up. Combine flour, pepper, salt in paper bag; add meat; shake until pieces are coated. Melt fat in heavy pot or Dutch Oven; add meat; brown on all sides. Add diced onion, garlic, boiling water, canned tomatoes, tomato paste, 1/2 tsp. salt, bay leaves, and Worcestershire Sauce.

Cover; reduce heat to low; simmer 2 hrs. or until meat is tender. Add potatoes, onions, carrots; cook 20 minutes. Add peas; cook 15 minutes longer. Makes 4 servings.

Green Pepper Stew

1 ½ lb. cubed beef	3 peeled, diced tomatoes	salt and pepper
2 Tbs. shortening	1 cup water or bouillon	1 diced green pepper
1 minced onion	1/2 tsp. basil	1 lb. can potatoes or cook
		your own sm. potatoes

Brown beef in hot shortening, add onion, cook until onion is soft. Add tomatoes, water, basil, salt, pepper, and simmer, covered, for 1 ½ hours. Add green pepper, cook for 15 minutes more; add drained potatoes, cook for final 15 minutes.

Stews:

Devilish Beef Stew

1 ½ lb. beef stew meat	1 Tbs. dry mustard	1/4 tsp. pepper
cut 1" cubes	1 ½ tsp. salt	1/2 cup water
1/3 cup flour	1 minced clove of garlic	4 med. potatoes,
2 Tbs. cooking oil	1 tsp. chili powder	6 small onions, quartered
2 cups water	1 tsp. Worcestershire sauce	2 cups bias-sliced carrots

Coat beef with flour, reserving remaining flour. In a saucepan or Dutch oven brown the beef, half at a time, in hot oil. Add the 2 cups water, mustard, salt, garlic, chili powder, Worcestershire, and pepper. Simmer, covered, until meat is almost tender, 1 to 1 ½ hours. Add the 1 1/2 cups water, peeled, quartered potatoes, onions, and carrots. Simmer, covered, until vegetables are tender, about 25 minutes.

For gravy, remove vegetables and skim fat from liquid, if necessary. Slowly blend in **1/4 cup cold water** into the reserved flour until smooth. Stir slowly into hot liquid. Cook and stir till bubbly, Season to taste with **salt and pepper**. Return vegetable to gravy mixture. Heat through. Makes 8 servings.

Variegated Stew

2/3 lbs. beef	1 small head cauliflower	1 bunch chives
1 quart water	1 red pepper; 1 grn. pepper	2/3 cup young Gouda cheese
1 ½ lbs. potatoes	1 bunch parsley	salt, pepper, and paprika

Boil the meat in cold water for 1 hour. Peel, cube and cook potatoes in broth; boil for 10 minutes. Separate the rosettes of cauliflower; set them in cold salt water. Quarter peppers, remove ribs and seeds, cut into strips. Add these to the cooked potatoes and boil 15 min. more. Blend in the chopped herbs and cubed cheese and season to taste.

Chili Beef With Vegetables

2 Tbs. flour	1 ½ lbs. cubed beef chuck	2 sliced carrots
salt and pepper	oil	1 sliced parsnip or turnip
1 tsp. chili powder (to taste)	12 small peeled onions	4 cubed potatoes

Season flour with salt, pepper and chili powder. Coat meat in flour. Heat oil in saucepan and fry meat until brown. Add onions, carrots, parsnip or turnip, potatoes, and **stock**. Bring to a boil, stirring occasionally. Pour mixture into a baking dish and cook in a 325 degree oven for 2 hours or until the meat and vegetables are tender. Makes 4 to 6 servings.

Old Time Beef Stew

2 lbs. beef chuck, cut in 1½" cubes	1 clove garlic	1/2 tsp. paprika
2 Tbs. shortening	1 med. onion, sliced	6 carrots, peeled, quartered
2 cups hot water	2 bay leaves	4 potatoes, peeled, cut-up
1 tsp. Worcestershire sauce	1 Tb. salt	1 lb. sm. white onions
dash ground allspice	1 tsp. sugar	Gravy
	1/4 tsp. pepper	

In Dutch oven thoroughly brown meat in 2 tablespoons hot shortening, turning often. Add 2 cups hot water, Worcestershire sauce, allspice, garlic, onion, bay leaves, salt, sugar, pepper, and paprika. Cover; simmer for 1½ hours, stirring occasionally to keep from sticking. Remove bay leaves and garlic. Add carrots, potatoes, and onions. Cover and cook 30 to 45 minutes or until vegetables are tender.

Gravy: Skim fat from liquid; measure **1¾ cups liquid**. Combine **1/4 cup water** and **2 tablespoons all-purpose flour** until smooth. Stir slowly into hot liquid. Cook and stir until bubbly. Cook and stir 3 minutes. Makes 6 to 8 servings.

Oven Beef Stew

1 Tb. flour	1 Tb. shortening	1/4 tsp. dried basil, crushed
3/4 tsp. salt; dash pepper	1 can Tomato Soup	2 med. potatoes, peeled,
1¾ lbs. beef chuck, cut 1" cubes	1 soup can water	2 med carrots, cut 1" pieces
	3/4 cup chopped onion	1/4 cup dry red wine or water

Combine flour, salt, and pepper; coat meat cubes in seasoned flour. Brown in hot shortening in small oven proof container or Dutch oven; add soup, water, onion, and basil.

Cover; bake at 375 about 1 hr. Add potatoes, carrots, and wine or water; cover; bake 1 hour longer or until tender. Makes 2 or 3 servings.

Note: The alcohol from wine is destroyed in cooking, but the flavor remains.

TIP: If you over salt a soup or stew, add a few pieces of raw potato or turnip, or a teaspoon each of vinegar and sugar; simmer a little longer. These items will absorb or neutralize the salty flavor.

Spicy Apricot Stew

1¼ lb. beef	salt and black pepper	1 lb. peeled, potatoes
1 onion, diced	6 cups water	1/2 lb. tomatoes
clove	1/3 cup dried apricots	1 tsp. butter
bay leaf	4 medium onions	1 cup aged Gouda cheese
pimento	3½ Tbs. butter	

Add the beef and spices (onion, clove, bay leaf, pimento and salt) into boiling water, and simmer over low heat for 30 minutes. Set the apricots in 1 cup of lukewarm water and let simmer for 1 hour. Saute 2 finely diced onions in hot butter until glazed. Add **4 cups of the beef broth** to the onions.

Peel the potatoes, cut into small cubes and boil for 10 minutes in the broth. Then add the apricots along with the remaining soaking water and skinned and halved tomatoes. Cook the stew for 15 minutes, or until done. Remove the meat, cut into cubes and put back into the pan. Season with pepper.

Cut the remaining 2 onions in half, saute in butter until glazed. Add them to the stew and sprinkle heavily with grated cheese. Bake in a pre-heated oven at 400 degrees for 5 minutes until cheese begins to melt.

> *TIP: New potatoes can be used in most recipes. Before scraping them, soak for 1/2 hour in cold salted water. The skins will rub off easily and you will not stain your hands.*

Spice Box Stew

1½ lbs. beef cubes	1/2 cup burgundy or	3 med. potatoes, quartered
2 Tbs. shortening	other dry wine	8 sm. whole white onions
2 cans Tomato Soup	1 small bay leaf	10-oz. pkg. frozen peas
1/2 cup water	1/4 tsp. thyme leaves	

In a large heavy pan, brown beef in shortening; pour off fat. Add soup, water, burgundy, bay leaf, and thyme. Cover; cook over low heat 1½ hours.

Add potatoes and onions. Cook 45 minutes; add peas. Cook 15 minutes longer or until done. Stir occasionally. Remove bay leaf. Makes about 8 cups.

Cowpuncher Stew

1 ½ lbs. beef stew meat cut in 1" cubes	2 Tbs. molasses	1 ½ cup cold water
2 Tbs. all-purpose flour	1 clove garlic, minced	4 carrots, cut 1/2" slices
1 tsp. salt	1 tsp. salt	2 sm. onions, quartered
2 Tbs. shortening	1 tsp. Worcestershire sauce	3 med. potatoes, peeled,
1 ½ cups strong coffee	1/2 tsp. dried oregano	1/4 cups water
	1/8 tsp. cayenne	3 Tbs. flour

Coat beef cubes with a mixture of 2 tablespoons flour and 1 teaspoon salt. In Dutch oven or heavy skillet, brown meat on all sides in hot shortening. Stir in coffee, molasses, garlic, 1 teaspoon salt, Worcestershire, oregano, and cayenne.

Cover; simmer over low heat until meat is almost tender, about 1 ½ hours. Add the 1 ½ cups water, carrot slices, onion and potato quarters. Simmer, covered, until vegetables are tender, about 30 min. Blend 1/4 cup cold water into 3 Tbs. flour; add to stew mixture. Cook; stir until mixture is thickened and bubbly. Serve in bowls. Makes 6 to 8 servings

Hot Dog and Lentil Stew

1 cup lentils	freshly ground pepper	1 sm. onion, peeled, diced
2 cups tomato juice	1 bay leaf	2 carrots, scraped, diced
1 can beef broth	4 slices bacon	1 lg. potato, peeled, diced
1 tsp. salt	1 rib celery, diced	1 lb. hot dogs

Clean the lentils, combine with **4 cups of water**, tomato juice, beef broth, salt, pepper and bay leaf. Bring to boil, reduce to simmer, cover, cook about 1 ½ hours, or until lentils are tender.

While lentils are simmering; cook the bacon until crisp, remove from pan. Add celery and onion to bacon drippings, cook over moderate heat until tender, stirring occasionally. Drain fat from celery and onions, add them to the lentils, along with the crumbled bacon, carrots and potato. Simmer another 30 minutes. Slice hot dogs and add to stew. Serve with mixed green salad.

Quick Skillet Stew

16-oz. can sm. whole potatoes	8-oz. can sliced, undrained carrots
1 can condensed cheddar cheese soup	2 Tbs. instant minced onion
1 can luncheon meat, cubed (12-oz.)	1/2 tsp. prepared mustard
	1/8 tsp. garlic powder

Drain potatoes, reserving 1/3 cup liquid; slice. In skillet, combine potatoes and reserved liquid with remaining ingredients. Heat; gently stir occasionally. Makes about 5 cups.

STEWS WITH LAMB & PORK:

"Of course you can gift wrap potatoes"

Basic Irish Stew

2 lbs. cubed shoulder lamb	1 sliced turnip	4 quartered potatoes
salt and pepper	8 small white onions	2 Tbs. flour
1 sliced onion	4 quartered carrots	2 Tbs. chopped parsley

Place meat in heavy pan, add salt, pepper, sliced onion. Pour over boiling water to cover; simmer, covered, for 1 ½ hours. Add vegetables, cook for 1/2 hour more.

Thicken gravy with flour mixed in water. Add chopped parsley. Serve with noodles or dumplings. (See pages 54,55, or 60)

Bonus: Add 1 package frozen green beans, thawed ahead of time.

Sheepherder Stew

2-3 lbs. lean lamb or	4 med. potatoes, halved	1/2 cup barley
beef, cubed	garlic salt, pepper, &	4 onions
flour	rosemary to season	6 carrots
		3 parsnips

In heavy kettle, flour, season and brown cubes of meat; drain off surplus fat. Cover with stock or water and cook slowly until nearly done. Add barley and stir often or it will stick. Simmer for 1 hour, then add other vegetables and cook very slowly for about 3 more hours keeping plenty of moisture in it.

"Heaven And Earth" Stew

2 lbs. potatoes	1/2 tsp. salt	1/2 cup grated cheese
2 lbs. sour apples	pinch of sugar	4 Tbs. butter

Peel and cube potatoes; boil 5 or 6 minutes in a pan with water covering the potatoes. Add the peeled, cubed apples, seasonings and boil 10 minutes longer. Whip everything together until a mash develops, but it should not be fully smooth. If necessary, add a little more water or broth. Blend in the butter and grated cheese. Excellent with the sausage wreath below.

Sausage Wreath:

1 sausage ring	1 lg. apple	butter for spreading
1 lg. onion	1/4 C. smoked, lean bacon	paprika for sprinkling
		1/2 cup aged Gouda cheese

Remove the skin from the sausage and cut slits in the remaining meat, but do not cut all the way through. Cut the onions into thicker half-moons, pare the apple into eights and bacon into 1 inch squares. Stuff the ingredients alternately into the slits in the sausage, daub everything with melted butter and broil for 10-15 minutes under the pre-heated broiler. Sprinkle with paprika, and cheese.

Serve with "Heaven And Earth" stew in the center of the wreath.

Lamb Stew--Just Right

2 lb. lamb neck or stew pieces minced; add garlic to taste		
cooking fat or oil	1/4 tsp. salt	8 sm. whole onions
1 ½ cups tomato juice	dash of pepper	4 carrots, pared, sliced
1 tsp. Worcestershire sauce	1/4 tsp. Italian seasoning	4 potatoes, pared, chunks

Brown lamb in skillet with fat; pour off excess fat; add meat to tomato juice, sauce, garlic, and seasonings. Cover; cook over low heat 45 minutes; add onions, carrots & potatoes. Cook 45 min. or until tender, stirring now and then.

To thicken, mix **1 tablespoon flour** with **2 tablespoons water** and blend until smooth. Slowly stir into stew. Cook, stirring, until thickened. May be served with rice or noodles. Makes 6 to 8 servings.

Variation: Cut back on the vegetables, and cut remaining vegetables into smaller pieces then add chopped mushrooms and bell peppers. Serve on rice.

Stews:

Pork And Vegetable Stew

2 lbs. boneless pork	1/2 tsp.ground sage	3 cups water
shoulder, in 1" cubes	1/4 tsp. pepper	3 med. potatoes, peeled, sliced
1/3 cup flour	3 Tbs. shortening	4 medium carrots (cut up)
2 tsp. salt	1 minced clove garlic	10-oz. pkg.frozen lima beans
	1 bay leaf	

Trim excess fat from meat. Combine flour, 1 tsp. salt, sage, and 1/4 teaspoon pepper. Coat meat with the flour mixture. Brown in hot shortening; pour off fat. Add garlic, bay leaf, and 3 cups water.

Cover tightly; simmer 40 min. Add vegetables and remaining 1 tsp. salt; continue cooking until vegetables are tender, 15-20 minutes, remove from heat, season stew with salt and pepper to taste. Make 8 servings.

Potato Stew With Smoked Sausage

1/2 cup all-purpose flour	1 lb. smoked sausage	1 Tb. minced fresh parsley
5 Tbs. butter	(Andouille or Polish)	1/2 tsp. cayenne
2 cups chopped onions	sliced 1/2" thick	1 tsp.salt; 1/2 tsp.black pepper
2 Tbs. butter	1 ½ qts. pork stock	2 qts. peeled cubed potatoes,

Heat butter in large cast iron or heavy pan over high heat until hot. With wire whisk or wooden spoon, gradually stir flour into hot butter; cook; stirring briskly, until medium brown, about 5 minutes, being careful not to scorch it.

Remove from heat; with wooden spoon immediately stir in 1 cup onions in the bowl. Continue stirring until mixture (roux) stops getting darker, about 3 minutes. Set aside.

In large skillet, heat the butter over high heat until half melted. Add the sausage pieces and cook about 3 minutes, turning and scraping pan bottom occasionally. Add the remaining 1 cup onions; turn heat to medium, and continue cooking until well browned, 6 to 8 minutes, stirring and scraping almost constantly. Remove from heat; set aside.

Bring stock to boil in 4-quart sauce pan over high heat. Add the roux by spoonfuls to boiling stock, stirring until roux is blended before adding more. Add the reserved sausage and onion mixture (including drippings), parsley, salt and the peppers. Return mixture to boil, stirring occasionally. Reduce heat; cover pan, and simmer about 10 minutes, stirring occasionally.

Now add half the potatoes; re-cover pan, bring to boil over high heat; then reduce heat and simmer until potatoes are tender, about 20 minutes, stirring occasionally. Add the remaining potatoes, return to a boil over high heat, then simmer until all potatoes are tender about 20 more minutes, stirring frequently so mixture doesn't scorch. Remove from heat; serve immediately. Makes 6 servings.

Fresh Savory Cabbage-Carrot Stew

1 lb. pork shoulder	3 large onions	1 tsp. caraway seed
3½ Tbs. butter	5 large washed carrots	3 cups broth
salt and pepper	2/3 cup baby Gouda cheese	4 large potatoes
1/4 bay leaf	1/2 medium cabbage	

Cut pork into 1" cubes and briefly fry in butter; subsequently add seasonings. Cut onion into rings; slice the carrots; layer on top of the meat. Slice cheese into strips; lay over carrots. Finally, add the cabbage cut into strips; season with a dash of salt, pepper and caraway seed. Pour the broth over the mixture; cook covered over medium heat, about 40 min. Grate the raw potatoes into the pan; cook for 5 minutes and serve. This stew tastes wonderful re-heated. You might want to double the recipe and freeze half.

STEWS WITH CHICKEN, RABBIT, AND SEAFOOD:

Mom---If I cook it do I have to eat it?

It's fun to try new recipes....Each one is such a treat.
It really is surprising though....When they're good enough to eat.

American Chicken Liver Stew

1/2 lb. chicken livers	1 sm. can tomato puree	chili powder
2 Tbs. butter	salt and pepper	8-oz. canned corn
1 onion	Worcestershire sauce	8-oz. canned peas
1 clove garlic	tabasco sauce	1 can potatoes, sliced
1 green pepper	seasoned salt	sliced tomato
1 red pepper	ground paprika	3-oz. aged cheese

Clean the livers. Wash, remove seeds and ribs of peppers, and chop finely. Chop up the onion and mince the garlic. Fry the chicken livers in butter until brown, then add the onion, garlic and peppers. Saute for 5 minutes, then stir in the tomato puree, salt and seasonings.

Drain corn and peas, add to livers with a little of the corn liquid if necessary. Stir in peeled, sliced potatoes, sliced tomatoes, grated cheese and **chopped parsley**, in that order. Heat thoroughly and serve at once.

Burgoo
(Historic Pioneer Recipe)

3 lb. broiler-fryer, cut-up	2 cups cut-up carrots	1 bay leaf
2 beef shank cross cuts	1 cup chopped onion	1 clove garlic, minced
12 cups water	1 cup chopped celery	4 ears corn
1 Tb. salt; 1/4 tsp. pepper	1 cup chopped grn. pepper	16-oz. can butter beans
6 slices bacon	2½ Tbs. dk. brown sugar	10-oz. pkg frozen cut okra
2 28-oz. cans tomatoes	red pepper	2/3 cup flour
1 C. potatoes, peeled, cubed	4 whole cloves	2 Tbs. crushed, dried, or
		1/2 C. snipped parsley

In 10 quart Dutch oven combine chicken, beef cross cuts, water, salt, and pepper. Cover; cook until meat is tender, about 1 hour. Remove chicken and beef from broth, reserving broth. Remove chicken and beef from bones; discard skin and bones. Cube beef and chicken. Set aside.

Cook bacon until crisp; drain, reserving drippings. Crumble bacon; set aside. To reserved broth in Dutch oven add cubed beef, undrained tomatoes, potatoes, carrots, onion, celery, green pepper, sugar, red pepper, cloves, bay leaf, and garlic.

Cover; simmer 1 hour, stirring often. Remove cloves and bay leaf. With knife, make cuts down center of corn kernels on each row; scrape cob. Add corn, cubed chicken, undrained beans, and okra to Dutch oven; simmer 20 minutes. Blend flour and reserved bacon drippings; stir into soup. Cook and stir until soup thickens. Salt to taste. Garnish with parsley and bacon. Serves 20 hungry people.

Rabbit Stew

1½ lb. rabbit meat, cubed	1/4 lb. fresh sauteed mushrooms
3 Tbs. vegetable oil	1/4 tsp. cayenne
1 pkg. dry onion soup mix	1/2 C. grated Cheddar cheese
1/8 tsp. ground cumin	1-2 cans Cr. Mushroom Soup
2-3 Tbs. Worcestershire	4 med. potatoes, cubed
1 soup can water	4-6 med. carrots, diced
2-3 med. onions	

Brown meat in oil. Mix all other ingredients together. Put meat in bottom of large casserole or roasting pan and pour cut-up vegetable mixture on top. Cover and bake at 350 degrees for at least 2½ hours

TIP: The method for cooking rabbit is about the same as it is for cooking chicken. The flavor is somewhat different. Some folks say it has a slightly wild taste, while others say they can't tell the difference.

Shrimp-Celery Bisque

1 cup water	1/4 cup chopped onion	2 Tbs. flour
1 cup chopped celery	1/2 tsp. salt & dash pepper	2 Tbs. butter
1 cup diced potato	4½-oz. can shrimp,	2 cup milk

In saucepan combine first five ingredients starting in left column. Simmer, covered, until vegetables are tender, about 15 minutes; stir often. Coarsely chop drained shrimp. Blend milk into flour until smooth; stir into potato mixture with shrimp and butter. Cook and stir until thickened and bubbly. Makes 4 servings.

TIP: Different spices bring out different flavors. If you want to test spices, divide the soup in 3 or 4 parts; try different spices in each part and compare the flavors.

Fisherman's Stew

2 Tbs. butter	1 egg yolk	instant mashed potatoes,
1 Tb. flour	salt, pepper & cayenne	3 servings
1 cup milk	9-oz. smoked shell-fish	3 peeled tomatoes
1/4 cup aged cheese	12-oz. can whl/kernal corn	2/3 cup aged cheese

In a saucepan, heat the butter, flour and milk until lightly simmering. Blend in the 1/4 cup grated cheese and thicken with the egg yolk. Season the sauce to taste. Grease a heat-resistant pan, pour in the drained corn.

Skin and bone the fish. Pluck off medium pieces, and lay over the corn. Pour the sauce over the fish pieces, spread the mashed potatoes evenly over the sauce, and arrange the tomato wedges over the mixture, with the 2/3 cup of cheese. Bake in pre-heated oven at 350 degrees for 25 minutes.

Owyhee Fish Stew

1/4 lb. bacon diced	1 pkg. Idahoan® Creamy	1 cup milk
2 Tbs. olive oil	Ranch Potatoes, sauce	1 lb. ling cod (or other firm
1 lg. onion, finely diced	packet reserved	flesh fish), diced
4 tomatoes, sliced	2¼ cups boiling water	pepper

In large skillet fry bacon until crisp. Discard fat and add olive oil to pan. Saute onion until tender. Add potatoes and tomatoes; saute for 2 minutes. Stir in sauce packet, water and milk; simmer over low heat for 15 minutes. Add cod and cook for another 15 minutes. Remove from heat and season with pepper. Makes 6 servings.

CORN CHOWDER:

"See mom, I told you Mikey would like it!"

Fresh Corn Chowder

1/4 lb. salt pork, diced	2 ½ cups water	1 cup fresh or frozen corn
2 Tbs. butter	1 bay leaf	snippets or cheese
2 ribs celery, sliced	salt and pepper	croutes for garnish
1 onion, sliced	2 ½ cups milk	1 Tb. chopped parsley
2 med. potatoes, diced	1 ½ Tbs. flour	

Blanch salt pork; put in **cold water**, bring to boil, drain. In kettle, melt butter, add salt pork, fry gently until it starts to brown. Add celery and onion, cook 1 minute, add the potatoes, water, bay leaf, and seasoning; bring to boil, cover, simmer 10-15 minutes or until potatoes are almost tender. Take pan from heat.

Mix a little milk into the flour making a smooth paste; stir into soup, add the remaining milk and corn; bring soup to boiling; cover; simmer 10-15 minuter or until corn is tender. Remove bay leaf; taste for seasoning; sprinkle with chopped parsley and serve with cheese croutes.

Canned-Corn Chowder

5 slices bacon	16-oz. can whole	2 cups milk
2 cups diced potatoes	kernel corn	1 tsp. salt; dash pepper
1 cup thin onion slices	1 can Cr. Mushrom. Soup	flour to thicken

Crisp-cook bacon; crumble. Reserve 2 tablespoons drippings. Cook potatoes and onion in 1 cup boiling salted water until tender. Do not drain. Stir in corn, mushroom soup, milk, salt, and pepper. Blend flour with reserved bacon drippings; add to soup mixture. Cook and stir until thick. Simmer 5 minutes. Stir often. Top with crumbled bacon. Serves 6 to 8.

Corn Chowder

Crisp crackers are the perfect accompaniment to this delicious chowder.

5 slices bacon	2 med. potatoes,	2 cups milk
1 med. onion, thinly sliced,	peeled, diced	1 can cream-style corn
& separated into rings	1/2 cup water	1 tsp. salt & dash pepper
		butter or margarine

In saucepan cook bacon until crisp. Drain bacon, reserving 3 tablespoons drippings. Crumble bacon and set aside. In same saucepan cook onion in reserved drippings until lightly browned. Add diced potatoes and water; cook over medium heat until potatoes are tender, 10 to 15 minutes.

Stir in milk, cream-style corn, salt, and pepper; cook until heated through. Pour chowder into warmed soup bowls; top each serving with crumbled bacon and a pat of butter. Makes 4 or 5 servings.

Pantry-Shelf Corn Chowder

1 Tb. butter	1/2 cup light cream	1/2 tsp. salt
2 cans whole-kernel corn	or evaporated milk	1/4 tsp. Worcestershire
1 can Potato Soup	1/2 tsp. seasoning salt	2 Tbs. cut parsley
2 soup cans milk	1/8 tsp. celery salt	nutmeg
		crisp bacon bits

Put butter in saucepan; add corn and simmer 5 minutes. Add soup, milk, cream, salts, Worcestershire. Over medium heat, bring to boil, stirring until heated through. Remove from heat; add parsley, a little nutmeg; top with bacon pieces. Serve at once. Makes 6 servings.

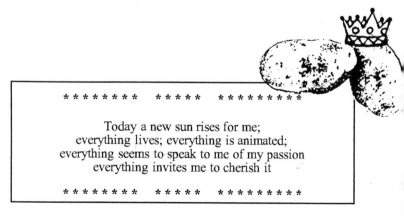

* * * * * * * *   * * * * *   * * * * * * * *

Today a new sun rises for me;
everything lives; everything is animated;
everything seems to speak to me of my passion
everything invites me to cherish it

* * * * * * * *   * * * * *   * * * * * * * *

Chowders:

Corn Chowder With Variations

Corn Chowder can be enjoyed year-round. When fresh corn isn't in season, substitute frozen or canned corn.

3 Tbs. butter	4 cups corn kernels	2 bay leaves
2 cups diced onions	4 cups milk	salt and pepper
2 cups diced potatoes		

    In a large soup pot, melt the butter and saute the onions until limp, 3-5 minutes. Add the potatoes, corn, milk, and bay leaves. Simmer for 15-20 minutes, or until the potatoes are tender.

    Cool the soup slightly. Remove the bay leaves. Puree two-thirds of the soup in a food processor or blender. Return the puree to the pot and reheat. Season to taste with salt and pepper. 6-8 servings.

Variation #1 -- Curry Corn Chowder:
Add 2-3 teaspoons curry powder to the onions when sauteing. Then proceed with the recipe.

Variation #2 -- Bacon Corn Chowder:
Brown 1/4 pound diced bacon in the soup pot and remove from the pan. Drain off all but 2 tablespoons bacon fat, and saute the onions in bacon fat instead of butter. Return the diced bacon to the soup as a garnish.

Variation #3 -- Cheese Corn Chowder:
Add 2 cups grated Swiss or Cheddar cheese to the soup after you have returned the puree to the pot.

Variation #4 -- Garden Corn Chowder:
Add 1 ½ to 2 cups cooked diced vegetables to the soup after you have returned the puree to the pot. Recommended vegetables are snap beans, lima beans, carrots, sauteed peppers, and peeled and seeded cucumbers.

Variation #5 -- Chicken Corn Chowder:
Add 1 to 1 ½ cups shredded cooked chicken to the soup after you have returned the puree to the pot.

Variation #6 -- Creamy Chicken Corn Chowder:
Use 3 cups chicken stock and 1 cup heavy cream in place of the milk. You can use evaporated milk in place of cream if you wish.

Chowders:

MEAT CHOWDERS:

*"Really!
Cheese-burger Chowder
tonight" -- Yes!"*

Quick Cheese-Burger Chowder

1/2 to 3/4 lb. ground meat	2-3 Tbs. chopped grn. pepper	2 ½ cups milk
2 C. peeled, cubed potatoes	1 Tb.instant beef bouillon	3 Tbs. all-purpose flour
1/2 cup chopped celery	1¼ cups water	4-oz. cheddar cheese
1/4 cup chopped onion	1/2 tsp. salt	

In large saucepan cook ground meat and remove most of the drippings, leaving about 2 tablespoons. Stir in potatoes, celery, onion, green pepper, bouillon granules, 1¼ cup water and salt. Cover; cook 15-20 minutes or until vegetables are tender.

Mix until smooth 1/2 cup of the milk and the flour; stir into meat mixture. Add remaining milk. Cook and stir until thickened and bubbly. Add shredded cheese and heat and stir until cheese melts. Garnish individual servings with additional shredded cheese, if desired. Makes 6 to 8 servings.

Corned Beef Chowder

1 can Cr. Potato Soup	1 pkg frozen Brussels	1 can corned beef
3 cups milk	sprouts, thawed & cut-up	pepper

In large saucepan blend soup and half the milk. Stir in Brussels sprouts and pepper. Bring to boiling, stirring occasionally. Reduce heat; simmer until sprouts are tender, 15 minutes. Add remaining milk and beef. Heat. Makes 4 or 5 servings.

---

* * * * * * * * * * * * * * * * * *
One pound of learning requires
ten pounds of common sense to apply it
* * * * * * * * * * * * * * * * * * * *

Chicken Chowder

4 lb. stewing hen, cut-up
3 tsp.salt; 3/4 tsp.pepper

3 lg. potatoes, peeled, cubed
6 med. carrots, peeled, sliced

3 med. onions, sliced
10-oz. pkg. frozen peas
1⅔ cup evap. milk

Remove pieces of excess fat from chicken. Place chicken in pieces in large kettle with 1 quart of water, 1 teaspoon salt, and 1/4 teaspoon pepper. Cover and cook slowly until chicken is tender, 2 to 3 hours. Remove chicken. Add potatoes, carrots and onions together with the remaining salt and pepper to broth in kettle. Simmer until vegetables are tender, but not mushy, about 15 minutes.

Meanwhile, remove chicken from bones and cut into small pieces. Add peas and chicken and cook 5 minutes. Stir in evaporated milk and heat to serving temperature, about 5 minutes. Makes 8 to 10 servings.

Chicken-Ham & Cauliflower Chowder

2 cups chicken broth
10 oz pkg. frozen cauliflower
1/2 med. green pepper, chopped
1 can Cream of Potato Soup
3/4 cup Creamy sauce Mix (below)

1 cup water
8 oz cooked ham, diced
1 cup sm. chicken chunks, cooked
1/2 cup grated cheese
Herb Stuffing Mix (See page 79)

In a saucepan, heat chicken broth to a boil. Cut up thawed cauliflower in bite-size pieces and add cauliflower and chopped green pepper to hot chicken broth. In a small container combine potato soup, and the Creamy Sauce Mix; blend in the water. Add to vegetable mixture in saucepan. Cook and stir until thickened and bubbly.

Stir in ham and chicken; add cheese, heat through until cheese starts to melt. Pour in serving bowls and sprinkle each with some of the Herb Stuffing Mix or seasoned croutons. Makes 4 servings.

Creamy Sauce Mix:

1⅓ cups instant nonfat dry milk powder
3/4 cups all-purpose flour

1 tsp. salt
1/2 cup butter

In mixing bowl combine milk powder, flour and 1 teaspoon salt. Cut in butter until crumbly. Place in a sealed container or a zip-lock freezer bag. Refrigerate until needed. Makes 3 cups.

Medium White Sauce: Combine 1/2 Creamy Sauce Mix with 1 cup cold water. Cook; stir until bubbly; cook; stir 2 minutes more. Makes 1 cup.

Cheese Sauce: Combine 1/2 cup Creamy Sauce Mix with 1 cup cold water. Cook and stir until bubbly. Add 1 cup shredded American cheese and stir until melted. Makes 1¼ cups.

Chicken Chowder in Crusty Bread Bowls

1/4 lb. bacon	3 cups cubed potatoes	4 Tbs. butter
2 cups chopped onions	3 cups chicken broth	1 to 2 Tbs. flour
1 cup chopped celery	salt, pepper to taste	4 cups half & half
1 cup grated carrots	2 cups chicken chunks	One bread bowl for each family member. (See below)

Brown bacon in large skillet. Remove bacon, crumble and set aside. Saute onions and celery in bacon fat until tender. In a large pan put onions, celery, carrots, potatoes, and chicken broth; simmer until tender. Salt and pepper to taste. Add chicken and bacon. Make a white sauce with melted butter, flour and half & half. Use just enough flour to thicken. If it gets too thick, add a little milk after adding the vegetable mixture until it is at the desired consistency. Pour into bread bowls.

Crusty Bread Bowls:

4 Tbs. yeast	2 Tbs. sugar	10 cups flour
4 cups warm water	4 tsp. salt	cornmeal

Dissolve yeast in water. Add sugar, salt and 6 cups of the flour. Beat 3 minutes. Gradually add remaining flour to make a stiff dough. Knead on lightly floured surface until dough is smooth and elastic.

Place in greased bowl, cover and let rise until double. Punch down and divide into 16 pieces. Form each piece into a ball and place the ball on baking sheet, sprinkled with cornmeal or roll it in the cornmeal. Cover and let rise until double in bulk,

Bake at 375 degrees for 25 minutes. Cool, cut off tops, scoop out bread to make a bowl, keep in as large a piece as possible for serving with soup. Pour hot soup into bread bowl and serve. Eat bread bowl with soup or after soup is eaten. Makes 16 large bread bowls.

TIP: For a quick white sauce make the sauce as usual. Fill ice cube trays (without the dividers) with the sauce. When frozen cut into 16 squares. Remove from trays; put into a freezer bag and freeze until needed. Drop one or two cubes into your chowder. It's fast and easy.

Sausage Wheat Chowder

1 lb. pork sausage	1/2 tsp. thyme	2½ cups tomatoes
1½ tsp. salt	1 lg. onion, chopped	1/4 tsp. pepper
4 cups water	4 cups cooked whole	1/2 green pepper, chopped
1 bay leaf	kernel wheat	1 cup diced potatoes
3/4 tsp. garlic salt		

In a large kettle, brown pork sausage. Pour off fat. Add all ingredients except potatoes and green pepper. Simmer covered 1 hour. Add potatoes and green pepper and cook, covered an additional 15 minutes until potatoes are tender. Remove bay leaf. Serve hot. Makes 8 servings.

Cauliflower-Ham Chowder

2 cups chicken broth	1 can Cream of Potato Soup
10-oz. pkg frozen cauliflower	3/4 cup Creamy Sauce Mix
1/2 small green pepper, chopped	(recipe page 77)
1 cup water	8-oz. diced, fully cooked ham
	Herb stuffing mix (see below)

In saucepan, heat canned or frozen chicken broth over medium-low heat about 15 minutes; stirring occasionally until thawed; bring to boiling. Pour over frozen cauliflower; cut up large pieces of the cauliflower. Add green pepper. In another dish, mix and blend together the water, canned potato soup and the Creamy Sauce Mix. Add this to the vegetable mixture.

Cook and stir until thickened and bubbly. Stir in ham; heat through. Serve in soup bowls. Sprinkle each serving with some of the Herb Stuffing Mix bread cubes, if desired. (Recipe below.) Makes 4 servings.

Herb Stuffing Mix:

The Herb Stuffing Mix also doubles as crispy seasoned croutons. Use them to sprinkle atop your favorite salad or to float in a hearty soup, stew or chowder.

15 slices day-old white	2 Tbs. dried parsley flakes	1/4 tsp. pepper
or whole wheat bread	1 tsp. garlic salt	3 Tbs. cooking oil
2 Tbs. minced dried onion	1/2 tsp. ground sage	

Slice bread into 1/2-inch cubes. Spread bread cubes evenly in a large shallow baking pan. Toast bread cubes in a 300 degree oven for 40-45 minutes or until golden; stirring once. Remove from oven; cool slightly. In a large mixing bowl, with a seal type lid, combine the bread cubes, onion, parsley flakes, garlic salt, sage, and pepper. Drizzle oil over all.

Put lid on container and turn the bowl several times to coat bread cubes. Store in fridge if not used at once. Makes 10 cups.

Kentucky Burgoo

1 ½ lbs. chicken wings (12)	3 ½ tsp. salt
1 med. onion, chopped (1/2 cup)	1/2 lb. ground beef
5 cups water	2 cans (1 lb.each) mixed vegetables
1 can (1 lb.) stewed tomatoes	1 sm. head cabbage, shredded
2 Tbs. bottled steak sauce	2 cups instant mashed potato flakes
1/4 tsp. cayenne	1/4 cup chopped parsley

Cut apart chicken wings at joints with a sharp knife. Combine with onion, water, tomatoes, steak sauce, cayenne and 3 teaspoons of the salt in a large heavy kettle or dutch oven. Heat to boiling; reduce heat; cover. Simmer 30 minutes.

Mix ground beef lightly with remaining 1/2 teaspoon salt; shape into 18 little meatballs. Add mixed vegetables and cabbage to chicken mixture; bring to a boil; add meatballs; reduce heat; cover. Simmer 10 minutes. Stir in potato flakes. Remove from heat.

Sprinkle with parsley. Spoon into soup bowls. Serve with hot corn bread, if you wish. Makes 6 servings.

SEAFOOD CHOWDERS:

Just one more bowl!
I promise to leave some for daddy.

Simple Clam Chowder

2 6-oz. cans clams	2 cups diced sm. potatoes	1 quart milk or half and half
1 chopped onion	3/4 cup flour	1 tsp. lemon juice
1 cup chopped celery	3/4 cup butter	1/2 tsp. sugar
		1 ½ tsp. salt & some pepper

Drain juice from clams and pour over vegetables in pan. Add water to cover and simmer until barely tender. Melt butter; add flour and blend. Cook stirring constantly. Add half and half; cook stirring with wire whip until smooth and thick. Add undrained vegetables, clams and heat. Season with lemon juice, sugar, salt, and pepper.

Curried Clam Chowder

1 cup chopped onion
1 tsp. curry powder
2 Tbs. butter
2 Tbs. flour

3 medium peeled, cubed
  potatoes
1 tsp. paprika
1/2 tsp. thyme

8-oz. can tomatoes
1 Tb. Worcestershire
2 7½-oz.can minced clams

In large saucepan or Dutch oven cook onion and curry in butter until tender. Blend in flour; add rest of ingredients except clams. Simmer, uncovered, until potatoes are tender, about 30 minutes. Add undrained clams; simmer 5 min. Makes 8 to 10 servings.

Clam Chowder With Chicken Broth

1/4 lb. bacon
1 lg. onion
1 cup chopped celery
3 cups cubed potatoes

1 cup grated carrot
3 cups chicken broth
salt & pepper to taste
4 cups half & half

1 can minced clams
4 Tbs. butter
1 Tb. flour
Crusty Bread Bowls (pg. 78)

Fry bacon until crisp; set aside. Saute onion and celery in bacon grease until tender. In dutch oven or large heavy pan put celery, onion, potato, carrot, and chicken broth.

Simmer until tender. Salt and pepper to taste. Drain clams reserving juice. Add half and half, clams and butter. Thicken juice with flour and add along with bacon. Heat through.

Clam And Pork Chowder

2 doz. shell clams or 2
  cans minced clams
1 cup water
1/4 lb. salt pork or
  bacon, minced

1/2 cup chopped onion
1½ cups clam liquor
  plus water
5 cups potatoes, diced
chopped parsley

2 cups milk
8 saltine crackers
2 cups half & half
2 Tbs. butter

Place clean clams in pot with 1 cup water, bring to boil, simmer 5 to 8 minutes or until clams open. Remove from shell and mince. Strain liquid remaining in pot. (Or if using canned clams, drain and reserve clam liquor.) Cook salt pork until browned and crisp. Remove salt pork from pan, reserving 2 tablespoons drippings. In saucepan, add onion and cook until tender. Add clam liquor and potatoes.

Bring to boil, simmer until potatoes are tender. Pour milk over saltines and let stand until soft. Stir milk mixture, half & half, reserved salt pork drippings, and butter into chowder mixture. Heat until hot enough to serve. Garnish with chopped parsley. Makes 6 servings.

New England Clam/Bacon Chowder

1/4 cup diced bacon	1/4 cup milk	1 Tb. lemon juice
1/4 cup minced onion	2 7 or 8-oz. cans minced clams	1 tsp. pepper
1 can potato soup	with liquor	

In large saucepan, cook and stir bacon and onion until bacon is crisp and onion is tender. Stir in soup and milk; heat through, stirring occasionally. Stir in clams, liquor, lemon juice and pepper. Heat.

Long Island Clam Chowder

1/2 lb. cut up bacon	6 potatoes, peeled, diced	1/4 tsp. thyme
2 onions, diced	1 quart water	1 quart shucked clams
1 green pepper, diced	1/2 tsp.salt & 1/4 tsp.pepper	1 qt. tomato juice

Brown bacon in deep pot; add onions and green pepper; cook 2-3 minutes, stirring as it cooks. Add potatoes, water, salt, pepper, thyme and cook until potatoes are tender; add chopped clams (be sure the black necks have been cut off), and tomato juice. Cook again over very low heat a few minutes until clams are tender. Serve with oysterette crackers floating on the top. Makes 8 servings.

> *TIP:* *When dicing or slicing cooked potatoes hold the paring knife over a gas flame or in boiling water. The potatoes will dice or slice easily. This is especially good when working with potatoes with a high starch content.*

Clam Chowder From Idaho

6 slices bacon, diced	2 cans chopped clams, drained,
1 medium onion, chopped	& reserved liquid
1 pkg.Idahoan® Creamy Ranch	1¼ cups heavy cream or 1 can
Potatoes, Reserve sauce packet	evaporated milk
2 cans chicken broth	4 Tbs. butter
1/4 cup chopped fresh parsley	

In a heavy saucepan fry bacon over moderate heat until golden brown. Drain all but 4 tablespoons of fat. Add onion and saute until tender. Stir in potatoes, chicken broth and reserved clam liquid. Simmer for 5 minutes, stirring occasionally.

Mix in clams, 2 tablespoons parsley and reserved sauce packet. Continue simmering and stir frequently for 10 minutes; remove from heat. Add cream or evaporated milk. Heat thoroughly. Garnish with butter and remaining parsley. Salt and pepper to taste. Excellent when served with toasted croutons or crackers.

Clam Chowder Potato Scallop
(Boy Scout Method)

7½-oz. minced clams
1 pkg. dehydrated scalloped potato mix
Liquids to make potatoes according to box directions

Drain clams, save liquid. Empty potatoes into a skillet and mix according to box directions. Add clam juice. Heat to boiling. Cover and simmer 30 to 35 minutes. Stir in clams and heat through.

Manhattan Clam Chowder

6 tsp. butter
1½ cup diced onion
1/4 tsp. pepper
1/2 cup diced grn. pepper

1 cup diced carrots
1 tsp. thyme
1 cup diced celery
9-oz. cooked beef sausage
(like beef stick from Hickory Farms)

1 cup clam juice
1½ cups diced potatoes
1/8 tsp. curry powder
12-oz. clams, drained, minced

Melt butter in large saucepan. Add onion and cook until lightly browned. Add all remaining ingredients, except clams, and enough water to cover vegetables. Bring to a boil. Cover; reduce heat and simmer 30 minutes or until vegetables are tender. Add clams; turn off heat and let stand 2 minutes or until clams are heated through. Makes 6 servings.

Low Calorie Tuna Chowder

1 can light chunk tuna
2 lg. potatoes, cubed
parsley or green onion for garnish

1 cup minced green onion
3 cans chicken broth

1 cup sliced carrot
1 cup minced celery

Drain tuna. Cook potatoes in boiling water until tender; drain. Cool; peel and cut in cubes. Meanwhile simmer vegetables in broth until tender about 15 minutes. Strain broth into blender; reserve vegetables. Add potato chunks to blender and puree until very smooth. Pour puree and vegetables into soup pot. Simmer 15 minutes, stirring occasionally. Add tuna to soup and cook 5 minutes longer. Top each serving with minced parsley or sliced green onion. Makes 8 cups.

TIP: To cleanse the hands from vegetable stains, rub them with a slice of raw potato, let stay on a little while then wash hands with soap and water...stains disappear.

Midwestern Fish Chowder

1 lb. frozen fillets
1/4 C. bacon or salt pork
1/2 cup chopped onion
1/2 cup cut-up grn. pepper

1 cup chopped celery
2 cups boiling water
1 cup diced potatoes
1 tsp. salt

dash cayenne pepper
1/4 tsp. thyme
2 cups tomato juice

Thaw frozen fillets. Skin fillets and cut into 1/2 inch pieces. Fry bacon until lightly browned; break up. Add onion, green pepper and celery. Cook until tender. Add water, potatoes, seasonings and fish. Cook about 15 minutes or until potatoes are tender. Add tomato juice; heat. Makes 6 servings.

Trout Chowder

4 cubed potatoes
1 cubed onion

2 trout, boned, cut-up
1/2 cup evaporated milk

3 tsp. whole allspice
butter and flour

Boil potatoes and onions in small amount of salted water until almost done. Put fish on top of potatoes. Dot with butter, Add milk and allspice and finish cooking about 15 minutes. Thicken with flour and water.

Idaho Trout Chowder

4 med. potatoes
2 med. carrots
2 stalks celery

4 10-12 inch trout
2 cups milk
2 Tbs. flour

1 Tb. butter
salt, pepper to taste

Dice potatoes, carrots and celery into 3/8 to 1/2 inch chunks. Cover with water and boil until completely tender. Drain off water and set aside. Clean and skin trout, boil for 5 minutes. Drain off water and allow to cool until fish can be handled. Remove all bones and flake flesh into small chunks. Add fish meat to vegetables. Add milk and flour and bring to slow boil, stirring regularly. Add butter and salt and pepper to taste. Cook until desired thickness is reached.

Serve with crackers to 6 people. This is an excellent appetizer or meal in fishing or hunting camps.

South America Shrimp Chowder

2 Tbs. lard or oil
1 onion, chopped
1 clove garlic, crushed
2 med. potatoes, peeled, diced

1 lg. tomato, peeled, chopped
2 Tb. rice, uncooked
dried red pepper
1/2 tsp. oregano

salt and pepper
1½ cups water
1 doz. medium shrimp
2½ cups milk
1/4 cup Feta cheese

In a saucepan heat the lard or oil and fry onion and garlic until brown. Add the potatoes, tomato, rice, dried red pepper, oregano, salt and pepper to taste and water. Cover with lid; simmer 15 minutes or until rice and potatoes are almost cooked. Halve shrimp lengthwise, add to chowder with the milk. Bring to a boil; simmer 2 min. Add crumbled cheese, season to taste and serve.

New England Fish Chowder With Pork

1 lb. haddock or cod	1 medium sliced onion	1 tsp. salt
1 cup boiling water	1 lg. peeled, diced potato	1/4 tsp. pepper
1/4 lb. salt pork, diced	1/2 cup chopped celery	2 cups milk
	1/2 bay leaf, crumbled	1 Tb. butter

Simmer haddock, covered, in boiling water 15 minutes. Drain, reserving broth. Remove bones from fish. Saute diced pork until crisp; remove and set aside. Saute onion slices in pork drippings until golden brown. Add fish, potato, celery, bay leaf, salt and pepper. Pour in fish broth plus enough additional boiling water to make 1½ cups liquid. Simmer covered 30 minutes. Add milk and butter; simmer 5 minutes more. Serve chowder sprinkled with diced pork, if desired. Makes 4 servings.

CROCK-POT SOUP, STEW, & CHOWDER DISHES:

"Look what we have saved because I cook with potatoes every day. Vacation--here we come!"

Potato Casserole-The Crock-Pot Way

1½ lbs. ground beef	1 lg. onion, sliced	1 can Cr. celery soup
3 med. potatoes, sliced	3 stalks celery, chopped	1 can Cr. mushroom soup
4 lg. carrots, sliced	1/2 cup pearl barley	1 or 2 soup cans water

Brown ground beef; layer meat, vegetables, and barley in crock-pot. Mix soups and water together and pour over ingredients in the crock-pot. Cover and cook on low for 6 to 8 hours.

Crock Pot Soup

1 beef round steak, cut-up	1 cup chopped celery	1 can Tomato Soup
2 cups chopped carrots	1 soup can water	2 lg. chopped onions
3 cups chopped potatoes	3 Tbs. tapioca	1 tsp. salt

Put all ingredients in crock pot. Cook on high for 3 hours. Cook on low for 2 to 3 hours or until meat and potatoes are tender, or cook on low heat for about 8 hours.

Variation: Replace steak with ground beef and add a 10-oz. can undrained peas.

Beef Stew-Crock Pot Style

2 lbs. beef chuck or stew
   meat,cut in 1" cubes
1/4 cup flour
1½ tsp. salt
1/2 tsp. pepper

3 potatoes, chopped
1/2 cup beef broth
1 stalk celery, sliced
1 tsp. paprika
1 chopped clove garlic

1 bay leaf
2 onions, chopped
4 carrots, sliced
1 tsp. Worcestershire sauce

Place meat in crock-pot. Mix flour, salt and pepper; pour over meat; stir to coat meat with flour. Add remaining ingredients; stir to mix well. Cover and cook on low 10 to 12 hours (High: 4 to 6 hours.) Stir stew thoroughly before serving.

Slow Cooked Beef And Vegetables

1 beef roast
1 pkg. dry onion soup mix

1 cup water
3 med. onions

4 med. potatoes
4 lg. carrots

Place roast in crock-pot; mix soup mix with water; pour over meat. Clean, peel vegetables. Quarter the potatoes and carrots lengthwise. Cut onions in thick slices. Place vegetables around the roast and on top if necessary. Try to get the vegetables in the soup mix. Of course as it cooks more juices will be created. Cook on low 8-10 hours. Use dripping for gravy.

Eight-Hour Crock Pot Stew

1½ lbs. beef stew meat
4 carrots, sliced
4 med. potatoes, cut-up
1 tsp salt
1 bay leaf

10½-oz. can beef broth
2 ribs celery, chopped
2 Tbs. parsley flakes
1/4 tsp. pepper
2 Tbs. quick cooking tapioca

1 med. onion, chopped
1 Tb. Worcestershire
28-oz. can whole tomatoes
   undrained

Brown meat; combine ingredients; cook in crock-pot on low 8-10 hrs.

Good Crock Pot Brown Stew

2 lb. boneless beef chuck
1 tsp. lemon juice
1 tsp. Worcestershire sauce
1 minced clove garlic
1 Tb. sugar

2 small bay leaves
2 tsp. salt
2 cups hot water
pinch allspice
8 small onions

6 carrots, halved
1 medium onion, sliced
1/2 tsp. pepper
1/2 tsp. pepper
3 quartered potatoes

Brown meat on all sides in hot fat in pressure cooker; add all ingredients, except vegetables; cook at 10 lbs. for 30 minutes. Open cooker; add vegetables; cooking 10 minutes at 10 lbs. Remove meat and vegetables, thicken liquid. Can also cook in crock pot for about 8 hours on low heat. Makes 6 servings.

Dumplings For Stew: For light, plump all-purpose dumplings, follow recipe on Bisquick package.

Quick Vegetable Soup In Crock Pot

2 lbs. stew meat
1 qt. canned tomatoes
1 Tb. Worcestershire
10-oz. pkg. frozen mixed
vegetables.

1 med. onion, diced
1-2 tsp. salt (to taste)
2 med. potatoes, diced
1 clove garlic
1 tsp. oregano

1 qt. water
2 stalks celery, chopped
1 Tb. dried basil
Schilling Salad Supreme
Parmesan cheese

Brown stew meat. Place in crock pot with all other ingredients. Shake a little Salad Supreme in for taste. Cover; cook on low for about 8 hours. Sprinkle with Parmesan. Good served with crusty French or garlic bread.

Crock-Pot Short ribs

3-4 lbs. lean beef short ribs
4 potatoes, quartered
4 carrots, quartered
1 onion, sliced

1 Tsp. sugar
1 cup beef bouillon
2 Tbs. vinegar
1 Tb. prepared mustard

2 Tbs. catsup
1 Tb. horseradish
1 Tsp. salt; 1/4 Tsp. pepper
1/4 cup flour

Brown short ribs; place vegetables in crock-pot and arrange ribs over them. Combine remaining ingredients except flour and pour over meat. Cover and cook on low 6-8 hours. Remove ribs and vegetables. Turn cooker on high. Mix flour with a little water and stir into sauce. Cook 10 to 15 minutes until thickened. Makes 6 servings.

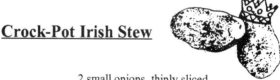

Crock-Pot Irish Stew

2 lbs. boneless lamb, cubed,
browned & drained
2 tsp. salt & 1/4 tsp. pepper
3-4 med. potatoes, peeled, quartered
(or 15-oz. can sm. potatoes)
1 small whole bay leaf
2 cups water

2 small onions, thinly sliced
2 med. carrots, peeled, cut 1/2"
slices
10-oz. pkg. frozen peas or
mixed vegetables
1/4 cup quick-cooking
tapioca to thicken stew

Season cubed lamb with salt and pepper. Place in the Crock-Pot. Add remaining ingredients except peas (omit tapioca if you don't want gravy thickened). Stir well. Cover and cook on Low 8 to 10 hours. Add peas during last 1 to 2 hours of cooking.

Crock-Pot Lamb Chop Stew

1 lamb chop per family member	other vegetables of your choice
salt, pepper & other seasonings	1/2 cup brown rice
1/2 med. potato per family member	1 can Cr. chicken/mushroom soup
1 or 2 onions, coarsely chopped	2 soup cans water
1/2 med. carrot per family member	3 Tbs. flour (to thicken stew)

Season lamb chops with salt and pepper. Place in bottom of crock-pot; add quartered, peeled potatoes, onion, carrot, & other vegetables. Add rice; mix flour with 1/2 cup of water until smooth; add soup & remaining water; mix well; pour over the meat & vegetables. Cook on low for about 8 hours.

Crock-Pot Chicken and Ham

1 chicken, cup-up	3 stalks celery, coarse-chopped
1 can Cr. Mushroom Soup	1 or 2 onions, sliced
1 can Cr. Chicken Soup	1/2 med. green pepper, sliced
1 tsp. prepared mustard	1 sm. ham slice per family member
3 med. potatoes, quartered	steamed white or brown rice
	1 sm. can drained mushrooms

Skin chicken; season with **salt, pepper** and other seasonings of your choice. Place in crock-pot; mix soups with **1 soup can of water**, and mustard; add peeled, potatoes, celery, onion, and pepper to the soup mix; pour mixture over chicken. Top with slices of ham. Cook on high for 2 hours and continue on low for 4 or 5 hours, or on low for 6 to 8 hours.

Prior to serving cover 1/4 cup white rice per family member in container of cold water, with water about 1 ½ inches above the rice. Cover and bring to boiling; boil about 2 minutes; turn off stove and let rice set until cooked. (If using brown rice, follow same directions except after bringing to a boil, turn heat to low and cook until done.) Drain and place in serving bowl.

To Serve; place rice on individual plates; add a piece of chicken and a slice of ham. Spoon on vegetable/soup mixture. Top with hot mushrooms.

Crock Pot Seafood Chowder

1 ½ lbs. cubed fresh or frozen	2-3 potatoes, peeled, cubed
fish fillets (haddock, cod, etc)	1 ½ cups water
3 slices, diced bacon	1 ½ tsp. salt
1 medium chopped onion	1/4 tsp. pepper
3/4 cup chopped green onion & tops	1 can evaporated milk

Thaw frozen fillets; cut into bite-size pieces. In small skillet, saute bacon and onion until golden; drain; put into crock pot with fish. Add remaining ingredients except evaporated milk. Cover and cook on low 6 to 9 hours or until potatoes are tender. (High 2 ½ to 3 ½ hours). Add evaporated milk during last hour.

MAIN DISHES

There are good cooks and bad cooks
There are cooks tried and true.
But I like a brave cook
Who'll try something new.
--by Carol Fielding McCabe

Information & Tips

Generally speaking, a main dish will consist of a GOOD source of protein, such as meat, eggs or cheese. A side dish may have eggs and cheeses, but have little or none of the heavier proteins such as meats.

If you are short on cream for almost any recipe, substitute undiluted evaporated milk or if only a tablespoon or two short, make up the difference by adding either butter or margarine.

When a recipe calls for onions or garlic, "fresh" is best. If substitutes are necessary use "powders" over salt. If only pastes are available follow package instructions for equivalents.

Vinegar adds a delightful sharpness to many foods. Red wine vinegar is the most intense; apple cider is the mildest. Lemon juice is a delicate substitute for either.

If you like your potatoes to retain some texture, try ricing them.

Top a casserole with frozen potato puffs, tots or logs during the last 10 to 15 minutes of baking. Bake until puffs are hot.

Use instant potato flakes to coat meats and poultry that have been dipped first in egg, beaten with a little water or milk.

An excellent quick potato trick is to crush potato chips and use instead of bread crumbs on fish and chicken.

Take care not to overcook mealy potatoes Drain them as soon as you can pierce them easily while cooking. Save the drained water to make gravies, soups or breads, since it is rich in nutrients.

Make extra mashed potatoes. They keep for several days refrigerated in an airtight container and are great for improvising or using in other recipes calling for mashed potatoes or even to fry as cakes for breakfast.

Use packaged scallop potato mix as the basis for leftover meat casseroles. The sauce comes in the package. The mix helps to make the most of leftover meat, cut in strips, to make a hearty potato-meat main dish.

There are OVER 100 varieties of potatoes available all year. Avoid if green in color, wilted, leathery, or spongy. Remember only potatoes grown in Idaho can be called Idaho potatoes! To make sure you're buying genuine Idaho potatoes, look for the "Grown in Idaho" seal on the bag.

MEATLESS DISHES:

High energy potatoes gives the strength needed to enjoy the good times in life.

Cheese 'N Potato Casserole

6 scrubbed potatoes	1 can Cr. Mushroom Soup	3 Tbs. chopped pimento
salt and pepper	3 Tbs. butter	3 hard cooked eggs, sliced
1 cup grated cheese	3/4 cup milk	

Slice unpeeled potatoes thinly. Layer in casserole; half potato slices, seasonings, grated cheese and soup. Dot with half of butter. Make second layer the same. Rinse soup can with milk and pour over casserole. Top with pimento. Cover and bake in 350 degree oven for 1 hr., or until potatoes are tender.

Remove cover and top with sliced hard cooked eggs and remaining 1/2 cup grated cheese. Return to oven until cheese is melted.

Potato Ginger Pudding (Casserole)

The ginger flavor makes this dish delightfully different. Add more if you like.

2 eggs	5 med. potatoes, cooked	1 cup raw cashew pieces
3/4 cup milk	3/4 cup sesame seed meal	2 Tb. thin sliced ginger root
1 cup cottage cheese	1 medium onion	1 tsp. salt

Put the egg and milk into a blender and buzz; add the cottage cheese and buzz again until smooth. Drop in the onion quarters and buzz again until the whole mixture is smooth. When you mash the potatoes, leave the skins on for the vitamins and fibre plus their color and texture will make the casserole more interesting. Stir the blender mixture into the mashed potatoes along with the remaining ingredients. Turn the mixture into an oiled 2-quart casserole.

Bake at 350 degrees for 1 hour, until the top is lightly browned and a toothpick comes out clean. This is a dish high in nutritional value.

Creamy Hard-Boiled Egg

2 lb. red potatoes, peeled,
"Egg Mayonnaise" (page 16)
2 Tbs. warm water
1⅓ Tb. prepared mustard

1/2 tsp.salt; 1/8 tsp.pepper
1/4 chopped onion
1/4 cup finely chopped
green bell peppers

4 hard-boiled eggs, halved,
separated yolks and whites.
(use yolks in the egg
mayonnaise recipe)

Boil potatoes until tender; cut into small pieces. Meanwhile, make Egg Mayonnaise and add, water, mustard, salt, and pepper, mixing well; set aside. Finely chop egg whites and set aside. Drain hot cooked potatoes and place in a large bowl; add onions, bell peppers, egg whites, and mayonnaise mixture; mix well, breaking up some of the potatoes (creamy textured with some lumps in it). Serve immediately or chill. Good either way. Makes 8 to 10 servings.

Potato & Egg Casserole

4 medium potatoes
1 tsp. salt
1/4 tsp. pepper

1/4 tsp. nutmeg
3 Tbs. bacon fat
4 eggs

1/2 cup grated process
American cheese
3/4 cup evaporated milk

Peel potatoes; slice thinly; sprinkle with salt, pepper and nutmeg. Heat bacon fat in a skillet; add potatoes; cook till browned and tender, stirring often.

Spread potatoes in a greased 1 qt. casserole; sprinkle with cheese. Break eggs carefully over cheese; cover with evap. milk. Bake in preheated 350 degree oven 15 to 20 minutes, or until eggs are set. Serve at once. Makes 4 servings.

Potato Nests

2 lb. potatoes
2 eggs

3 ½ Tb. flour
salt, nutmeg

3-oz. butter

For spreading: 1 egg yolk. **For sprinkling:** 1-oz. grated cheese.

Cook the potatoes in salt water, drain and pass through the strainer. Mix in mixing bowl with eggs, flour, and seasonings. Add the melted butter.

Fill a piping bag with the mixture and pipe small round forms around the outer part of a greased pie pan. Continue adding round forms on top of each other until they reach the top of the pie pan. Paint the rings with yolk of egg; sprinkle with cheese and bake in moderate oven until golden yellow. Fill the center of the pan with cooked, seasoned meat, such as ground beef, ham, or fish. Add mushrooms and vegetables for variety.

Best Potatoes Au Gratin

In **buttered** 3-quart baking dish, arrange alternate layers of **6 cups cooked diced potatoes** & **1½ cup grated sharp cheddar cheese**; sprinkling each layer with **1 tablespoon onion** and dot with **butter**. Mix **3 eggs, 1½ cups milk, salt and pepper to taste** and pour over potato mixture. Sprinkle with **1½ cups additional grated cheeses**. Bake at 325 degrees for 45 minutes or until set. Serves 12.

Egg And Beet Salad
(main course salad)

4 lg. cooked beets, or 1 can sliced beets	10-12 new potatoes 6 scallions chopped	6 hard-cooked eggs 1/2 cup mayonnaise

Horseradish Cream:

1 Tb. sugar	2 Tb. prepared horseradish	1/2 tsp. salt
1 ½ tsp. dried mustard	1/2 cup heavy cream or	black pepper, freshly ground
2 Tb. wine vinegar	condensed milk	

Skin; slice; cook; drain beets. Cook peeled potatoes in boiling salted water for 15-20 minutes or until tender. Drain.

To make horseradish cream, mix sugar and mustard with vinegar; stir in horseradish and cream and mix together; season to taste with salt & pepper.

Quarter or slice potatoes; mix while still warm with the horseradish cream and chopped scallions or green onions. Mix in the beets, pile in the center of a serving dish. Halve the eggs, arrange around the edge and coat each egg with a spoonful of mayonnaise. Makes 6 servings.

PREPARED MEAT DISHES:

"Hot Dog!
Just the way I like it.
Bring on the fries!"

Full O' Baloney

1 ½ C. cubed raw potatoes	1 can Cream Celery Soup	2 lg. slices cheese, quartered
1 ½ cups cubed bologna	2 Tbs. minced green pepper	

Heat oven to 350 degrees. Mix all ingredients except cheese in 1 ½ quart baking dish. Bake covered 1 hour & 15 minutes. Remove cover; top with cheese. Broil until bubbly and browned. Makes 4 servings.

Leftovers: Cover and reheat in oven or microwave. Add 1 to 2 tablespoons milk, if needed.

Wiener Boats

4 wieners	1 Tb. green onions
4 cups mashed potatoes	1/2 cup grated Am. cheese

Slit wieners lengthwise, but do not cut in two; place in shallow baking dish. Combine mashed potatoes, and chopped green onions; pile down the middle of each wiener. Sprinkle cheese over potatoes. Bake 20 to 25 minutes in moderate oven 400 degrees. Sprinkle with paprika; serve. Makes 4 servings.

Hot Dog-Potato Bake

1 can Cream Celery Soup	1 Tb. prepared mustard	2 cups whole potatoes,
1/2 cup milk	1 lb. frankfurters, cut	drained, sliced
1-2 Tbs.dried parsley flakes	in 1" pieced	

In 2-qt. casserole, combine soup, milk, parsley, and mustard; stir in potatoes and franks. Bake 400 degrees for 30 minutes or until hot; stir. Makes about 6 cups.

Broiled Stuffed Wieners
with tater tots & beans

4 wieners	2 dill pickles, sliced	4 strips bacon
1 Tb. prepared mustard	2 2x4" slices of cheese	1 or 2 cans baked beans
		2 cups Tater Tots

Slit wieners lengthwise, but do not cut in two; spread with mustard. Insert one slice pickle, one slice cheese into each wiener. Wrap one strip bacon around each wiener; fasten with toothpicks. Broil until brown on all sides.

In separate containers heat beans and Tater Tots in fry pan or microwave. Add juices in bottom of broiler pan to beans.

On a serving dish pile beans in center; arrange the wienes & Tater-Tots around the beans. Garnish with fresh parsley and olives. Serves 4.

Frank-Potato Pie

4 or 5 frankfurters, (cut 1")	1 can Tomato Soup drained	1 egg, beaten
1/2 cup chopped onion	4 ser. pkg. instant mashed	1/2 cup shredded sharp
2 Tbs. butter, melted	potatoes	Am. cheese
16-oz. can green beans		

Cook frankfurters and onion in butter until franks are browned and onion is tender. Stir in drained green beans and tomato soup. Turn into a 1½ quart casserole. Set aside. Prepare mashed potatoes according to package directions, except reserve the milk. Add beaten egg. Slowly add enough of the reserved milk to make potatoes hold shape. Mound potatoes on top of frankfurter mixture. Bake, uncovered, at 350 degrees for 25 minutes; top with cheese. Bake until cheese is melted, about 5 minutes. Makes 6 servings.

Eggs Flamenco
(Baked Eggs)

6 Tbs. butter
3 potatoes, peeled,
  blanched, diced
3 franks or cooked
  smoked sausage

Salt and pepper
3 Tbs. cooked peas
2 red bell peppers
  cut in strips
1 Tb. chopped parsley

4 tomatoes, peeled, seeded,
  chopped
8 eggs
3 Tbs. light cream
1/4 tsp. cayenne pepper

Melt butter in a frying pan; add potatoes and cup-up franks or sausages and cook over medium heat until potatoes start to brown; shaking pan occasionally to avoid sticking. Season; add peas and peppers and cook 5 minutes or until peppers are soft. Add tomatoes and parsley; cook until very hot; spread mixture in bottom of a buttered shallow oven-proof dish. Break the eggs on top, sprinkle with salt and pepper and pour the cream over top.

Bake in moderate oven (350) for 8-10 min. or until eggs are just set. Sprinkle with a very little cayenne pepper just before serving. Makes 4 to 6 servings.

TIP: Frankfurter Fun! Make weenie people and place on top of your casseroles. Olive slices can be used for the eyes, raisins for the nose, etc. For extra fun make each one different.

Or make dancing weenie people. Use part of a weenie for the head. A full weenie for the body, and for each leg and each arm section use 1/2 of a weenie.

Have fun making their various positions.

Frankfurter Scallop

4 med. potatoes, peeled, sliced
1 med onion, peeled, thinly sliced
8 frankfurters, cut in 1-inch chunks
1 ½ cups skim milk

4 tsp. flour
1 tsp. salt
dash paprika
1 Tb. prepared mustard

In a 9-inch baking pan, layer half the potatoes, all the onion, then frankfurters and remaining potatoes. In small bowl, combine milk, flour, salt, paprika and mustard. Pour over casserole. Bake at 375 degrees for 1 hour or until hot and bubbly. Makes 6 servings.

Tip: To "de-fat" franks, drop in pan of boiling water; remove from heat and let stand 10 minutes; drain. Some of the fat in the franks will melt into the water and be discarded.

BEEF DISHES:

> "Hooray!
> You passed the test.
> You chose potatoes over
> Stove Top Stuffing."

Tater-Tot Casserole

1 lb. ground beef	1 can Cream Mushroom Soup	1 pkg. frozen tater tots

Spread browned meat in 9x9" baking dish. Pour a can of Cream of Mushroom Soup over meat. Cover with tater tots. Bake 1 hr. at 350 degrees.

Variation: Replace mushroom soup with chicken soup or use the chicken/mushroom combination soup.

Cucumber, Potato & Meat Boat

3/4 lb. ground beef	1 cup sour cream	3 med. potatoes, mashed
1 med. onion, chopped	3 cucumbers (6" long)	1/2 to 3/4 C. grated cheese
1 small pkg. taco mix (dry)	1/4 cup water	

Cook together the beef and onion in a fry pan until meat is browned. Do not over cook. Add package of dry taco mix, salt & pepper if needed, and 1/4 cup water. Mix well; simmer, stirring occasionally, until water has evaporated. Add 1/4 cup sour cream and mix thoroughly. Cover to keep warm until needed.

Peel cucumbers; cut in half lengthwise; scoop out seeds. Using new or left over creamy potatoes fill the cucumber boat mounding the potatoes an inch or so above the boat. Separate the mashed potatoes making a trough down the middle. Spoon ground beef mixture into the potato trough, mounding above the potatoes. Be generous with the sprinkling of cheese on top of the meat.

Place in oven or microwave heating just long enough to melt the cheese. Serve at once with slices of tomatoes or a fresh green salad. Makes 6 servings.

Variation: Younger children love to substitute and place a cooked wiener in the trough of the mashed potatoes. And of course, sprinkle with cheese.

Bacon And Beef Stuffed Potatoes

| 4 large potatoes | 2 Tbs. butter | 4 slices bacon |
| salt and pepper | 1/2 lb. ground beef | watercress or parsley |

Scrub and bake potatoes in 400 degree oven 1 hour or until almost done. Cut in half, lengthwise. Cut top off potato, scoop out enough hot potato to make room for the beef and bacon to fit inside. With a fork fluff the remainder of the potato; sprinkle with a little salt and pepper and add a little butter to each. Salt and pepper uncooked beef and make 4 long rolls (they should be a tight fit into the potato opening); cut bacon strips in half and place 2 halves on top of beef rolls; replace the potato tops.

Return potatoes and meat to oven for 20-25 minutes, or until meats are cooked. After about 15 minutes in the oven, remove potato lids to allow bacon to crisp. Replace lids and place each potato on a serving tray and garnish with watercress or fresh parsley. Serve hot. Makes 4 servings.

Stuffed Peppers

4 large green peppers	1¼ cup potato chips	1/4 cup catsup
salt	3/4 cup buttermilk	paprika & poultry
2 cup meat mix, (below)	2 eggs, beaten	seasoning

Slice the top off the green peppers; remove seeds; rinse peppers. Place peppers in deep container; cover with boiling water. Cover; let peppers sit for 10 minutes. Drain; sprinkle cavities with salt. In mixing bowl, combine the thawed "Ground Meat Mix", 1 cup crushed potato chips, buttermilk, eggs, catsup, and 1/4 tsp. poultry seasoning. Fill peppers with the meat mixture. Place filled peppers in 8x8x2-inch baking dish. Sprinkle with remaining potato chips and paprika. Bake in 375 degree oven for 30 minutes or until heated through. Makes 4 servings.

Ground Meat Mix: 3 eggs, 2 cups bread crumbs, 1 cup chopped celery, 3 lbs. ground beef, 1 cup shredded carrot, 1 cup chopped onion.

In a mixing bowl, beat eggs slightly. Stir in soft bread crumbs, celery, onion, carrot, and 1 teaspoon salt. Add meat; mix well. Cook half the mixture at a time until meat is browned. Drain fat; cool. Divide into 2 cup portions. Place in freezer bags; label and place in freezer, or use in the above recipe.

New Potato Meat Ring

Mix together:

1 lb. ground beef	1/4 lb. ground pork	1/4 lb. ground ham
2 cups grated raw potatoes	2 eggs, slightly beaten	1/2 cup chopped onion
1 tsp. salt	1/2 tsp. thyme	1/2 tsp. rosemary
		1/2 tsp. sage

Bake in greased 8-inch ring mold at 350 degrees 1 hour. Unmold on serving platter. Fill center of ring with creamed new potatoes. Makes 6 servings.

Stuffed Baked Potatoes

4 very lg.Idaho potatoes	1 cup chopped or 4-oz.	1 Tb. chopped chili pepper
1 Tb. oil	canned mushrooms	salt and pepper
2 onions, chopped	2 Tbs. chopped parsley	1/4 cup Swiss or
1 lb. ground beef	1 Tb. chopped thyme	Cheddar cheese

Wash potatoes; rub with salt, prick with fork; bake in 350 degree oven for 1 hour or until very soft. Cut in half lengthwise; scoop out pulp and mash it. In a skillet heat oil, add onions and fry until brown. Stir in ground beef and cook over moderate heat until brown. Stir in the mushrooms, parsley, thyme, chili pepper, and salt and pepper to taste, then cook 1 minute longer.

Take from the heat; mix in the potato pulp and spoon the mixture back into the potato shells. Scatter the tops with grated cheese and bake in a 350 degree oven for 20 minutes or until heated through and browned.

The potatoes may be prepared earlier in the day and heated just before serving. Makes 4 to 6 servings.

Potatoes And Beef Gravy Dinner

Peel; cut-up and boil **4 medium potatoes**. Add **salt** and cook until tender. Mash the potatoes, adding **milk** and a little **butter** if desired. While potatoes are cooking, cook in a fry pan **1/4 pound ground beef**; season with **salt & pepper** and your favorite seasonings. Try cayenne!

When meat is done, add **1 cup evaporated milk** and **2 cups whole milk** (leave fat in unless it is excessive). Make a thickening out of **flour** and **cold milk**; add this to the mixture, stirring constantly until thickened. The gravy should be semi-thick.

Spoon gravy over potatoes on individual dinner plates. This is excellent with green salad; cold french-style beans, which you have drained well and added a tablespoon of Miracle Whip and lightly tossed together.

Potato Meat Roll

Mix together and set aside: 1 ¼ lb. ground beef, egg, slightly beaten, 1 ½ tsp. salt, 1/2 lb. ground ham, 1/4 cup chopped onion, 1/2 cup bread crumbs.

Mix together: 1 egg, slightly beaten, 1/2 can condensed mushroom soup, 1/8 tsp. pepper, 1 tsp. salt, and 2 cups unseasoned mashed potatoes.

Shape meat mixture into 10x14-inch rectangle on waxed paper. Place potato mixture lengthwise across meat rectangle.

Roll like a jelly roll and bake seam side down at 350 degrees for 1 ¼ hours. Remove the wax paper as you roll. Makes 8 servings.

Stuffed Pita Bread

Bread:

3 ½ to 3 ½ cups flour	1 ½ cups warm water	1 ½ tsp. salt
1 pkg. yeast	1/4 cup shortening	

In large bowl, mix 2/3 cup flour, yeast mixed with warm water, shortening and salt. Beat with mixer 2 min. until gluteny. Gradually add rest of flour. Use enough flour to make a soft, workable dough. Cover; let rest in warm place 15 min. Divide in 12 equal portions. Roll each between floured hands into very smooth ball. Cover and let rest 10 minutes.

Using fingers, gently flatten balls without creasing dough. Cover; let rest 10 minutes. On a well-floured surface, lightly roll one piece of dough at a time into a 7" round, turning dough over once. Do not stretch, puncture or crease dough. Work with enough flour so dough does not stick.

Place on a baking sheet. Bake two at a time at 450 degrees about 3 minutes or until dough is puffed and softly set. Turn over with a spatula; bake about 2 minutes more or until dough begins to lightly brown. Repeat with remaining dough, baking one batch before rolling and baking the next.

Filling:

1 Tb. butter	10-oz. can beef broth	1 Tb. water
1 lg. onion, chopped(1 cup)	(condensed)	1 Tb. cornstarch
1 lb. ground beef	2 Tbs. Worcestershire sauce	1/2 cup sour cream
2 Id. Potatoes, baked, diced	1 tsp. dried dill weed	

In large skillet melt butter; saute onion until tender. Mix the onions with ground beef, and potatoes; brown; cook to your liking over medium heat, stirring to keep meat mixture from sticking and to help break it into small chunks. Add condensed broth, Worcestershire sauce and dill weed. Blend cornstarch with water; add to skillet. Bring to boiling, cook 1 minute.

Reduce heat to low, stir in sour cream. **DO NOT BOIL.** With sharp knife, cut a crease across center of pita bread, being careful not to cut through the bread. Spoon meat mixture onto pita bread. Fold bread in half. Serve immediately. Makes 12 hand-held pita bread treats.

Potato Burgers

1/2 lb. ground beef	1 tsp. salt	1 Tb. snipped parsley
1 cup grated raw potatoes	3 Tbs. fat or oil	2 Tbs. minced onion
1/8 tsp. pepper	1/2 tsp. dry mustard	

Mix meat, potatoes, onion, pepper, salt. Shape into 8 patties. In hot fat in skillet, saute patties until crisp and brown; then remove from skillet; keep warm. Add mustard and parsley to dripping in skillet; heat; pour over patties. Makes 4 servings

Potato Coated Meat Loaf

1 lb. ground beef	salt, pepper	1 lb. potatoes
1/2 cup bread crumbs	1/4 tsp. cayenne pepper	2 Tbs. butter
1/2 cup cold milk	1 onion finely chopped	hot milk to mix
1 egg, beaten	1/4 tsp. dry mustard	2 Tbs. chopped parsley

Put ground beef in a mixing bowl with bread crumbs, cold milk, egg, 1 tsp. salt, cayenne pepper, mustard, and onion. Mix all together very thoroughly. Put in a greased 1 lb. loaf pan and bake in a 350 degree oven for 45 minutes.

Meanwhile, peel potatoes and cook in boiling salted water until tender (about 15-20 minutes). Mash well with butter and enough hot milk to make creamy mashed potatoes. Beat in salt, pepper, and 1 tablespoon parsley.

Turn cooked meat loaf out of tin; put it on a baking tray. Coat loaf in mashed potatoes and return to oven for about 15 minutes or until beginning to brown. Serve garnished with chopped parsley. Serves 4.

Dairy Meat Loaf

Mix together:

1 lb. ground beef	1 cup bread crumbs	1 cup grated carrots
1/2 cup raw potatoes	1/2 cup cottage cheese	1/2 cup sour cream
1/2 cup chopped onions	1/2 tsp. salt	1/4 tsp. marjoram
1 tsp. Worcestershire sauce	2 Tbs. horseradish (opt)	

Shape into loaf; bake 1 hr. at 350 degrees; serve hot or cold. Freezes well.

Variation: Using day old or new mashed potatoes, add some butter and cream or evaporated milk, salt and pepper, and whip together until fluffy. Spoon this on top of the meat loaf in a semi-smooth spread. Brush a thin layer of butter over the top and bake for about 5 minutes longer or until potatoes are slightly brown (You could broil for faster results).

Garnish with herbs such as dried chives, or parsley. Fresh parsley looks great, as does sprinkles of paprika.

Easy Meat Loaf

Mix together:

1 lb. ground beef	2 eggs, slightly beaten	1 tsp. salt
1/2 cup grated raw potatoes	1 cup grated raw carrots	1/4 tsp. pepper
1/2 tsp. onion salt		

Form into loaf; bake at 375 degrees for 1 hr. Serve hot or cold. Serves 4.

Variation: Mix together 1/4 cup tomato paste, 3 tablespoons catsup, 1/2 teaspoon prepared mustard, and 2 or 3 tablespoons brown sugar. Ten minutes before the meat loaf is done, spread this mixture across the top. Add a few sprinkles of dried chives or parsley on top of the tomato paste mixture for color. Return to the oven and cook 10 minutes longer.

Dutch Oven Meat Balls

Mix together:

1 lb. ground beef	1 egg, slightly beaten	1 tsp. salt
1/2 cup bread crumbs	1/4 cup tomato sauce	1/8 tsp. pepper
1 tsp. onion juice	1/8 tsp. allspice	

Shape into 12 meat balls. Brown in 2 tablespoons oil in a Dutch oven then add.

3 cups water	3/4 cups tomato sauce	3 med. cubed potatoes
1½-oz. pkg. dry onion soup	1½ cups sliced carrots	10-oz. pkg. frozen peas
1 cup cubed green pepper		

Add meat balls to above mixture; bring to a boil and cook over low heat for 30 minutes until vegetables are done. Makes 4 servings.

Mushroom Meatballs

1 lb. lean ground beef	1 cup carrots, grated	1/2 can (2/3 cup)
1 egg	1 cup potatoes, grated	evaporated milk
1/2 tsp. onion salt	1/2 cup bread crumbs	1 can Cr. Mushroom Soup

In a small bowl, combine beef and egg. Add all other ingredients except soup and milk. Mix together and form into 1-inch meatballs. Brown in an oven-proof skillet using only enough oil to prevent sticking. Combine soup and milk; pour over meat; cover; bake for 25-30 minutes at 375 degrees.

Poor Boy's Supper

1½ lbs. ground beef	1/2 cup dry bread crumbs	1 Tb. shortening
1 sm. potato, peeled, grated	1 egg	1 can Cr. Mushroom Soup
1 sm. onion, peeled, grated	1½ tsp. salt	1 soup can milk
1/2 carrot, grated	1/8 tsp. pepper	1 C. cooked long grain rice

Combine meat, grated vegetables & bread crumbs. Add egg, salt & pepper. Mix until blended. Shape into meat balls. Brown in shortening over low heat. Combine soup, milk & rice in a casserole. Add meat balls; cover & bake at 350 degrees for 30 minutes. Serve with stewed tomatoes. Makes 6 to 8 servings.

Meat Balls

1 lb. ground beef	1 egg	1 small onion, chopped
2 med. carrots, grated	2 small potatoes grated	salt and pepper
1/4 cup bread crumbs		

Mix ingredients well and make small meat balls. Brown. Make a white sauce with 2 Tbs. butter, 2 cups milk, 2 Tbs. flour and 1 can Cream Mushroom Soup. Pour over meat balls. Bake at 350 degrees for 30 minutes.

Koenigsberg Meat Balls

Mix together:

1/2 lb. ground beef	1 cup boiled, riced potatoes	1/2 lb. ground veal
2 eggs	1 Tb. anchovy paste	1 Tb. butter
1/4 cup herring, chopped	1 Tb. flour	2 Tbs. chopped onion (very
1/4 tsp. pepper & 1 tsp. salt		fine)

Form into 12 dumpling meat balls; roll in **flour** and set aside. To make gravy, place **1 cup chopped onion, 1 Tb. butter, 2 Tbs. flour, and 1/4 tsp. salt** in a cooking pan and saute until onion is brown and flour is cooked. Add **2/3 tablespoon vinegar** and **3 cups water**. Bring to a boil; place dumpling meat balls in gravy, and simmer for 20 minutes. Makes 4 servings.

Variation: To the gravy, add 1 tablespoon capers and 3 chopped anchovies or 2 tablespoons chopped herring. One egg yolk may also be added.

Chili Beef Hash

1 lb. ground beef	1/2 tsp.salt,& dash pepper	3 cups diced raw potatoes
1/2 cup water	1 cup sliced celery	1/4 cup chili sauce
2 Tbs. shortening	1 can Golden Mushrm. Soup	

In a skillet brown beef, cook potatoes and celery in shortening. Pour off fat; add remaining ingredients. Cover; cook over low heat about 10 minutes. Stir occasionally. Makes about 4½ cups.

Beefburger Stack-Ups

2 beaten eggs	Pkg. inst. mashed potatoes	1/2 cup chopped green onion
1/4 cup milk	(4 servings)	2 Tb. canned pimento
1 tsp. salt & dash pepper	1 cup boiling water	1/4 tsp. salt
1 tsp. Worcestershire	1/2 cup sour cream	3 slices sharp Am cheese
1½ lb. ground beef	1/4 C. chop'd grn. pepper	catchup, heated

Combine eggs, milk, tsp. salt, Worcestershire sauce, and pepper. Add beef & mix. Make 12 patties; place one in 6 individual casserole dishes. Stir mashed potatoes into boiling water. Add sour cream; green onion, pimento, & 1/4 teaspoon salt; spoon over meat patties. Cover with remaining patties. Bake at 375 degrees for 45 minutes. Top with cheese sliced in halves. Bake until cheese melts, about 2 minutes more. Serve with warm catsup. Makes 6 servings.

---

* * * * * * * * * * * * * *

When the hour of need arises, the hour of preparation has passed.

* *

Shipwreck

4 med.potatoes,peeled,diced	1/2 cup uncooked rice	1 soup can water
1 small onion, diced	1 lb. lean ground beef	salt and pepper to taste
2 cups celery, diced	1 can tomato soup	

Put vegetables in buttered casserole dish. Add rice. Crumble uncooked ground beef over the top. Mix soup and water together and pour over everything. Season to taste. Bake 350 degrees 60 to 90 minutes until vegetables are tender. Serve while hot. Makes 4 to 6 servings.

Cheeseburger Casserole

1 lb. lean ground beef	1 can whole kernel	1 Tb. Worcestershire sauce
1 med. onion, chopped	corn, drained	2 egg yolks, beaten
2 Tbs. melted shortening	1 cup Am. cheese grated	1½ cups potatoes,
1 tsp. salt & 1 tsp. pepper	3/4 cup catsup	seasoned, mashed

Brown ground beef and onion in melted shortening in large heavy fry pan. Drain off meat drippings. Mix in seasonings, canned corn, cheese & catsup, and Worcestershire sauce.

Spoon mixture into well greased 1½ quart casserole. Blend egg yolks in mashed potatoes. Spread over meat mixture. Bake at 350 degrees for about 30 minutes. For a crispy topping, place under broiler several minutes before serving. Makes 6 servings.

Potato, Sour Cream & Egg Casserole

4 medium potatoes	1 lb. ground beef	1/2 C. grated Am. cheese
1 tsp. salt & 1/4 tsp. pepper	1/2 tsp. seasoning salt	1/2 cup Mozzarella cheese
3 Tbs. bacon fat	1 cup Cr. Mushroom Soup	4 eggs
1 small chopped onion	1 Tb.Worcestershire sauce	1/2 cup sour cream
		1/2 cup evaporated milk

Peel potatoes; slice thinly. Sprinkle potatoes with salt & pepper. Heat bacon fat in heavy skillet; add potatoes and cook until about tender (still chewy), stirring frequently. In another skillet spray lightly with "Pam", add onions, ground beef and seasoning salt; cook until done, stirring frequently.

Add 1/2 can of Cream of Mushroom Soup and Worcestershire sauce to meat mixture; mix well; set aside. Spread potatoes evenly in a lightly greased casserole; spread the beef mixture evenly over the potatoes; sprinkle with the cheeses.

Break the yolks of the eggs and stir lightly (do not over stir); pour over the cheese. Mix the sour cream and evaporated milk together until smooth; pour over the egg; do not stir. Bake in preheated 350 degree oven until eggs and creams are set, about 20 to 30 minutes. Makes 6 servings.

Cauliflower Casserole

1½ lb. ground beef	1/2 cup bread crumbs	1/2 cup Cheddar cheese,·
salt and pepper	1 egg yolk	grated
pinch each: ginger,	3 Tbs. milk	1 parboiled cauliflower
allspice & sugar	3 Tbs. flour	1/2 cup milk
2/3 cup mashed potatoes	2 Tbs. butter	

Mix ground beef, salt, pepper, spices, potatoes, bread crumbs, egg yolk, and milk; shape into small balls. Dredge in flour; brown slowly in butter in casserole. Push meatballs to edges; put cauliflower in center; cover with 1/2 cup milk. Bake, covered, in 350 degree oven for 20 minutes. Sprinkle cheese on cauliflower; bake, uncovered, for 15 minutes more, or until cauliflower is brown. Add liquid if necessary.

Something Special Potato Casserole

1½ lbs. ground beef	1/3 cup water	1 tsp. sugar
1½ cup onion, chopped	1/2 tsp salt,	5 med. potatoes, thinly
32-oz. spaghetti sauce	1/4 tsp. pepper,	sliced into circles
		8-oz. Mozzarella cheese

Brown beef and onions; drain fat. Add spaghetti sauce, water, salt, sugar, pepper; simmer 2 minutes to blend flavors. In 9x13" pan, spoon in 1/3 of meat mixture; top with 1/2 potatoes; layer of meat; layer of potatoes. End with layer of meat. Cover dish with foil and bake at 375 degrees for 1 hour. Remove foil and sprinkle with cheese. Bake 10 minutes more. Makes 8 servings.

Variation: Add 1 cup plain yogurt.

Ground Beef And Rice Ball Casserole

Mix together:

1/2 lb. ground beef	1/4 cup evaporated milk	1½ tsp. salt
1/4 lb. ground fresh pork	1/2 cup chopped onions	1/4 tsp. pepper
1 egg, slightly beaten	1/2 cup cooked rice	1/4 tsp. poultry seasoning
1/2 cup cold mashed potatoes		

Form into 8 equal balls and place in large covered baking dish. Mix 2½ cups tomatoes with 3/4 cup water and pour over patties. Cover and bake at 350 degrees for 1 hour. Remove cover and bake 30 minutes longer, basting with sauce occasionally. Makes 4 servings.

Country Bean Casserole

3 Tbs. butter
1 onion, diced
1½ cup ground beef
   and pork

4 peeled tomatoes
1 can cut green beans
salt and pepper to taste
2 Tbs. catsup

instant mashed potatoes
2/3 cup aged cheese
parsley
1 tsp. paprika

Heat butter; saute the onion until glazed. Add ground beef and pork; braise. Slice peeled tomatoes into eights; drain the beans, add to the meat. Season to taste with salt, pepper and the catsup. Prepare mashed potatoes as directed on package.

Grease a pan; add a layer of mashed potatoes; add the meat-vegetables mixture. Top with more mashed potatoes and sprinkle with grated mature cheese and parsley. Brown in a preheated oven at 400 degrees for 15-20 minutes. Makes 2 to 3 servings.

Note: Most recipes calling for instant mashed potatoes can be substituted with potatoes you cook and mash yourself.

Potato Beefed-Up Pie

2 lbs. ground beef
1 cup evaporated milk
2 cups soft bread crumbs
3 eggs

2 tsp.salt; 1/2 tsp.pepper
1 tsp. dry mustard
1/2 tsp. thyme
1/2 cup minced onion

4-oz. American cheese, cubed
2 C. prepared instant
   mashed potatoes
1 Tb. butter

Combine beef with evaporated milk, bread crumbs, eggs, salt, dry mustard, pepper, thyme, onion and cheese cubes. Turn mixture into a greased 10-inch pie plate. Bake in preheated 350 degree oven 50 minutes.

Remove from oven; increase heat to 450 degrees. Prepare potatoes according to package directions. Pipe potatoes through a pastry tube in a lattice design on top of meat; dot with butter. (Or, you can spread potatoes lightly all over top of pie and decorate with a fork, making criss-cross lines. Return to oven; bake 10 minutes longer. Makes 8 servings.

Meat-Shell Potato Pie

1 can Cr. mushroom soup
1 lb. ground beef
1/4 cup chopped onion
1 egg slightly beaten

1/4 C. dry bread crumbs
2 Tbs. chopped parsley
1 tsp. salt; dash pepper

2 cup mashed potatoes
1/4 cup shredded cheese
bacon, cooked, crumbled

Mix thoroughly 1/2 can soup, beef, onion, egg, fine bread crumbs, parsley, and seasonings. Press firmly into 9" pie plate. Bake at 350 degrees for 25 minutes; spoon off fat. Frost with potatoes; top with remaining soup, cheese and bacon. Bake 10 minutes more or until done. Makes one 9" pie.

Meat 'N Tater Pie

2 cups Rice Krispies	1/3 cup milk	1/2 c. shredded Cheddar cheese
1 tsp. salt; 1/8 tsp. pepper	1 lb. ground beef	paprika
1/2 tsp. ground sage	2 eggs, beaten	1/4 cup chopped onion
1 Tb. catsup	2 cup mashed potatoes	2 Tbs. melted butter

In large mixing bowl, combine 1 cup cereal, salt, pepper, sage, catsup, and milk. Add beef. Mix until combined. Press evenly in 9" pie pan to form meat shell. Set aside.

In small mixing bowl, beat eggs a little. Add seasoned potatoes and onion. Mix well. Spread evenly over meat shell and bake in 350 degree oven 35 minutes.

While meat is cooking, crush rest of cereal until it measures 1/4 cup. Combine with butter or margarine.

Remove pie from oven and sprinkle cheese over top evenly. Top with cereal and bake 10 minutes longer or until cheese melts. Sprinkle with paprika.

Tango Pie

1 cup dry bread crumbs	1 Tb. sugar	1/2 tsp. red pepper flakes
3 ½ cups water	1 tsp. white pepper	1 cup raisins
2 tsp. salt; 1 Tb. paprika	2 tsp. ground nutmeg	1 C. stuffed green &/or black
1/2 cup butter	1 med. onion, sliced thin	olives
1 cup milk & 1 cup heavy	2 Tbs. oil	salt & pepper to taste
cream or evaporated milk	1 lb. lean ground beef	4 hard-boiled eggs,
5 C. (dry flakes) potatoes	3 med. tomatoes, chopped or	chopped
3 eggs	tomatoes chop'd, drained	1 beaten egg with 1 Tb. milk

Preheat oven to 375 degrees. Grease the bottom and sides of a 9-inch pan or a 3-quart casserole; coat well with bread crumbs. Bring water, salt and butter to a boil. Remove from heat; add milk and cream. Gently stir in potato flakes. Let sit for one minute then stir in 3 eggs one at a time. Add sugar, white pepper and nutmeg. Cover and set aside. Saute the onion in oil until tender. Add ground beef; cook for 5 minutes, stirring frequently. Mix in tomatoes, red pepper flakes, raisins, olives, paprika, salt and pepper. Heat thoroughly; remove from heat.

Spread a little more than half the potatoes over the bottom and sides of pan. Spoon in beef mixture; spread evenly. Arrange hard-cooked eggs on top; cover with remaining potatoes. Brush top with beaten egg and milk mixture. With a fork make a criss-cross pattern. Bake for 30 minutes. Cool 10 minutes before serving. Makes 8 to 10 servings.

Australian Shepherd Pie

Cook **2 pounds potatoes**, in boiling salted water until tender. Meanwhile saute in **butter** 3 minutes, **2 chopped onions, 1 crushed clove garlic, 1/2 cup green pepper**, and **1/2 cup thinly sliced celery**, then add **1 lb. ground beef**. Cook until brown. Sprinkle in **3 Tbs. flour**. Blend in **1½ cups water, 2-ounces tomato paste and salt and pepper to taste**. Simmer 5-10 minutes. Place in greased oven dish. Mash potatoes, with **butter, salt, pinch nutmeg, and 3/4 cup milk**. Reheat. Cover meat mixture with potatoes. Make light designs with fork on top of potatoes. Bake in moderate oven 350 degrees for 30 minutes. Makes 4 servings.

Spoon Bread Meat Pie

1 cups meat broth	1 ½ cups cooked, cubed	1 Tb. chopped pimento
1 Tb.cornstarch & 2 Tbs.	potatoes	1/4 tsp. salt
cold water	1 C. cooked,sliced carrots	Spoon Bread Topper
2/3 cups mayonnaise	1/2 cup chopped onion	(recipe below)
1 ½ cups chunked,stew meat,	1 cup shredded Am. cheese	
cooked		

In saucepan, add 1 cup broth. Combine cornstarch and water. Stir into broth. Cook and stir until thickened and bubbly. Blend in mayonnaise. Add cooked stew meat, potatoes, carrots, onion, cheese, pimento, and salt. Heat through. Turn into a greased 2-quart casserole. Add Spoon bread Topper. Bake in 400 degree oven for 40 minutes or until golden. Makes 4 to 6 servings.

Spoon Bread Topper:

1 cup yellow cornmeal	1 cup meat broth	2 eggs
2 Tbs. baking powder	1/2 cup milk	1 Tb. melted butter
1/2 tsp. salt		

In mixing bowl, combine cornmeal, baking powder, and salt. Heat the broth to boiling and add to the cornmeal mixture in bowl; mix well. Add milk, eggs, and melted butter thoroughly, using rotary beater. Pour the cornmeal batter over hot meat pie mixture. Bake as directed in recipe.

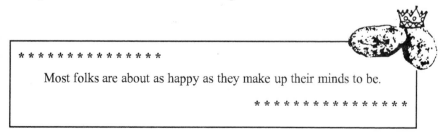

* * * * * * * * * * * * * *

Most folks are about as happy as they make up their minds to be.

* * * * * * * * * * * * * * * *

Beef Steak Pie

1 ½ lbs.beef round	2 Tbs. shortening	1/8 tsp. pepper
steak (1"cubes)	2 cups water	2 C. diced, raw potatoes
1/4 cup all-purpose flour	1 tsp. salt	milk
1 large chopped onion	1/4 tsp. crushed thyme	Easy Egg Pastry single crust
		(see below)

Place beef cubes and flour in mixing bowl with a sealing lid. Shake well to coat meat. In large skillet, cook beef and onion in shortening until beef is browned and onion is tender. Add water, salt, thyme, and pepper. Cover; simmer 1 ½ hours. Add diced raw potato; cover; simmer 20 minutes. Turn meat mixture into a casserole; season to taste with salt and pepper.

Roll out pastry (recipe below), on floured board; roll a circle larger than the casserole. Place pastry over hot mixture; seal to edge of casserole. Cut slits in pastry for escape of steam. Brush pastry with milk. Bake in 450 degree oven until golden, about 15 minutes. Makes 6 servings.

Easy Egg Pastry:

3 cups flour	1 cup shortening	1/3 cup water
1/2 tsp. salt	1 egg	1 tsp. vinegar

Put flour and 1/2 tsp. salt in mixing bowl; mix; add shortening and cut into small pieces with pastry blender. Combine egg, water and vinegar until blended. Make a well in dry ingredients; pour in egg mixture. Mix until it forms a ball. Refrigerate until ready to use. This will make one double crust pie or two single crust pies.

TIP: For good pie crust watch the amount of water you use. Using too much water will turn the crust tough. You want the crust soft and pliable. Add water slowly and carefully.

Special Ground Beef Pie

1 lb. ground beef	1 lb. can beans or	5 med. potatoes, cooked
1 med. onion, chopped	corn, drained	1/2 cup warm milk
salt and pepper to taste	1 can tomato soup	1 egg, beaten
		1 cup Cheddar cheese

Brown meat and onion. Add seasonings, beans or corn (or a half can of each), and soup. Pour into casserole. Mash hot potatoes; add milk and egg. Season and drop in mounds over meat. Bake at 350 degrees for 25-30 minutes. Add grated cheese to top of pie and cook until slightly melted. Makes 6 servings.

Variation: Replace ground beef with 1 ½ to 2 cups diced cooked beef (roast).

106

Garnished Beef Pastries

Easy Egg Pastry (pg. 106)	2/3 cup chopped turnip	1 tsp. salt; 1/4 tsp. pepper
1 med. chopped potato	or carrot	milk
1/2 cups chopped onion	1 lb. beef round steak, cut	1 Tb. sesame seed
	in 1" cubes	catsup

Place potato, turnip, carrot (or rutabaga), and onion in mixing bowl with beef cubes. Add salt and pepper; mix well. Set aside.

Divide dough into 5 portions. Using rolling pin, roll out each portion to a 7" circle. Place about 2/3 cup of the beef-vegetable filling in the center of each circle; bring sides of pastry over filling. Pinch edges to seal, leaving openings for steam to escape. Brush pastry lightly with milk and sprinkle with sesame or poppy seeds. Carefully transfer pastries to an ungreased baking sheet. Bake in 375 degrees oven for 35 to 40 minutes or until golden brown. Serve with catsup, if desired. Makes 5 servings.

Ground Beef Roll

Biscuit dough	1/2 cup milk	1 onion, chopped
1 ½ cups ground beef	2 cups flour	1 carrot, grated
4 Tbs. shortening	1 potato, grated	2 tsp. baking powder

Brown meat in shortening; drain. Using your favorite biscuit dough; roll out to 1/4 inch thick. Mix browned meat with other ingredients. Spread on top of dough. Roll up like a cinnamon roll. Bake at 450 degrees for 20-25 minutes. Serve with brown gravy or mushroom soup.

Beef Pot Pie From Leftovers

1/2 cup minced onion	3 Tbs. flour	2 cups cubed leftover roast beef
1/2 cup diced celery	1 C. sliced cooked carrots	1 Tb. Worcestershire
3/4 cup sliced mushrooms	1/2 tsp. salt; 1/8 tsp. pepper	1 cup left over gravy
2 Tbs. fat	2 C. diced leftover potatoes	2 Tbs. chopped parsley
		Easy Egg Pastry (page 106)

Cook onion, celery, mushrooms in fat over low heat about 10 minutes or until tender; stir in flour. Add remaining ingredients except the pastry; blend; cover; simmer 10 minutes. Pour into greased casserole or 8"x8"x2" cake pan.

Roll pastry 1/8 inch thick. Place on top of meat-vegetable mixture; brush with slightly beaten egg white or ice water. Make several gashes in center. Bake 20 minutes in hot oven 450 degrees. Makes 6 servings.

Smothered Beef Casserole

3 lb. round roast or rolled
   rump of beef, with fat
1/4 lb. salt pork or bacon,
   with some fat
Salt and pepper

pinch of cinnamon
pinch of allspice
3-4 carrots, quartered
2 onions, quartered
1 clove of garlic, crushed

2 cups red wine
about 2 cups water
3-4 med. potatoes, peeled,
   quartered

In a large flameproof casserole, place sliced pork or bacon and set beef on top. Add the spices with salt and pepper to taste and put vegetables around the meat. Add garlic and wine and enough water to almost cover the meat.

Cover tightly with the lid and cook just below simmering over very low heat on top of the stove or in a low oven (300 degrees) for 3-4 hours, or until the meat is very tender and the gravy is reduced by half. Add the potatoes 20 minutes before the end of the cooking time. This dish reheats well. If planning to reheat, do not cook potatoes completely during first cooking. Makes 6 servings, with leftovers.

Note: Wine alcohol is destroyed with cooking, the wine flavor does remain.

Ragout Of Beef

2 lbs. lean, well trimmed
   round steak, cubed
3/4 cup chopped onion
2 beef bouillon cubes
salt & dash pepper

1/2 cup red wine
16-oz. can tomatoes
1 tsp. Worcestershire sauce
2 Tbs. flour
1 tsp. paprika

dash garlic powder
2 tsp. salad oil
4 med. potatoes, peeled,
1 cup celery, chopped
   cubed

In large, heavy Dutch oven or skillet; brown meat and onions in oil. Drain off any accumulated fat. To meat and onions, add 2 cups water and remaining ingredients except potatoes and celery.

Cover and simmer 1 hour or until meat is almost tender. Add potatoes and celery. Cook 30 min. more or until meat and veggies are tender. Serves 8.

Note: Wine alcohol is destroyed with cooking, the wine flavor does remain.

Hash-Stuffed Peppers

6 medium green peppers
1 cup water
1/2 tsp. salt
2 Tbs. butter or margarine

1/2 cup minced onion
2 cups diced, cooked,
   corned beef
1 cup diced, cooked potatoes

1/2 cup bread crumbs
8-oz. can tomato sauce
1 Tb. Worcestershire sauce

Cut a thin slice from the stem end of each green pepper; scoop out seeds. Bring water and salt to a boil in a large saucepan; add peppers. Simmer covered for 5 minutes; remove peppers; drain. Melt butter in a medium-size saucepan; add onion and saute 2 minutes. Stir in remaining ingredients. Spoon mixture into pepper shells. Place in a greased 6x10x1½ inch baking pan; bake, uncovered, in preheated 350 degree oven until hot, about 30 minutes. Makes 6 servings.

New England Boiled Dinner

3 lbs. boneless corned beef brisket	1 Tb. mixed whl. pickle spice	4 med. potatoes, halved
2 cloves garlic, halved	9 small onions 6 med. carrots, halved 1 sm. cabbage, wedged	2 turnips, pared, cubed 1 lb. butternut squash

Put enough cold water in kettle to just cover beef. Tie garlic and spice in cheesecloth bag; add to kettle. Quarter and add 1 onion to kettle. Bring to boil; reduce heat. Cover; simmer about 1 ½ hours. Add remaining whole onions, carrots, potatoes, turnips and squash.

Bring to boil. Cover; simmer 30 minutes. Add cabbage; bring to boil; simmer, uncovered, 15 minutes. Remove from kettle and place on serving platter. Makes 8 to 10 servings.

Note: To carve meat, place fat-side up on cutting board. Carve across grain in thin slices starting at pointed end; place on platter with vegetables.

Low-Cal Corned Beef And Cabbage

4 lbs. corned beef round*	3 bay leaves	1 large head cabbage,
2-3 cloves garlic, minced	4 med. potatoes, peeled,	cut in wedges

In large kettle place corned beef, garlic and bay leaves; add water to cover. Heat water to boiling; skim surface. Cover and simmer over low heat about 4 hours or until meat is almost tender.

Remove cover and skim off all surface fat. Add quartered potatoes; cover and cook 15-20 minutes. Add cabbage and simmer until meat and vegetables are tender, about 10 minutes more. Makes 8 servings, about 310 calories each. (One serving equals 1/4 lb. corned beef, 1/2 potato and 1/2 cup cabbage.)

* Ask for corned beef <u>round</u> instead of brisket; it has far less fat!

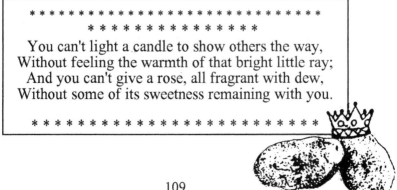

```
* * * * * * * * * * * * * * * * * * * * * * * * * * * * *
      * * * * * * * * * * * * * *
```
You can't light a candle to show others the way,
Without feeling the warmth of that bright little ray;
And you can't give a rose, all fragrant with dew,
Without some of its sweetness remaining with you.
```
      * * * * * * * * * * * * * * * * * * * * * * * * * *
```

Corned Beef Brisket Dinner

3 ½ lb. corn beef brisket	6 med. potatoes, peeled	prepared mustard
1/2 cup chopped onion	3 small carrots, peeled	1 ¼ cup brown sugar
2 cloves garlic, minced	6 cabbage wedges	dash ground cloves
whole bay leaves	2 turnips, cut in eights (opt.)	

Place corned beef in Dutch oven or heavy saucepan and barely cover with hot water. Add onion, garlic and bay leaves. Cover; simmer 3 to 4 hours or until tender. Remove meat from liquid; keep warm. Add potatoes, carrots and turnips to liquid in Dutch oven; cover and bring to boiling. Cook 10 minutes. Add cabbage and cook 20 minutes longer.

Meanwhile, glaze meat. Spread fat side of meat lightly with mustard. Combine brown sugar and cloves; sprinkle over mustard. Bake in shallow pan at 350 degrees for 15-20 minutes. Arrange corned beef and vegetables on warm platter for serving. Makes 6 servings.

Yankee Pot Roast

4 lb. beef pot roast	1 bay leaf	1 turnip, peeled, diced
3 Tbs. shortening	1/2 tsp. celery seed	4 carrots, quartered
2 cloves garlic, crushed	1 cup tomato juice	1 lb. can sm. white potatoes 1
tsp. thyme	8 small white onions	drained
salt, pepper & flour		

Dredge meat in seasoned flour, brown slowly on all sides in hot shortening for about 20 minutes. Add garlic, seasonings, tomato juice. Simmer; covered, for about 2¾ hours. Add vegetables; cook 30 minutes more, adding potatoes for last 15 minutes of cooking.

> *TIP: Experienced cooks do a roast with the fat side up. The juice soaks down into the meat and keeps it basted and moist.*

Everyday Pot Roast

3 to 4 lb. beef chuck	6 to 8 stalks celery	6 to 8 carrots
1/3 cup horseradish	6 to 8 small onions	3 potatoes, cut in half
Salt and pepper		

Roll meat in flour; brown on all sides in hot fat. Spread with horseradish. Season with salt and pepper. Add a little water; cover and cook slowly 2 to 2 1/2 hours at 300 degrees. Add vegetables and continue cooking 1 hour. Serves 6.

Stuffed Roast Beef

3 lbs. boned rump of beef	1/2 tsp. salt & pepper	oil (for brushing)
2 Tbs. softened butter	4-5 med. potatoes, cubed	watercress (for garnish)
2 tsp. Dijon-style mustard	4-5 med. tomatoes, halved	

For Stuffing:

1 onion, finely chopped	2 C. white bread crumbs	salt and pepper
2 Tbs. butter	1 tsp. thyme	1 egg, beaten
1/2 lb. ham, ground	1 Tb. chopped parsley	1 ½ Tbs. milk

Stuffing For Roast Beef: Fry onion in butter until soft. Stir in ham, bread crumbs, thyme, parsley, pepper and salt. Stir in beaten egg to bind the mixture: adding a little milk if stuffing is dry. Fill the stuffing into the cavity left by the bone: enlarging it with a knife if necessary to form a pocket. Reserve any extra stuffing.

Beat the softened butter with mustard, salt and pepper until smooth; spread on top of beef. Set beef in roasting pan; cook at 375 degrees, basting often, for 1 hour or until meat is cooked. Mix the remaining stuffing with the potatoes in a baking dish. 40 minutes before the end of cooking, sprinkle 2 tablespoons pan juices over the potatoes and bake them in the oven with the beef until tender and browned.

Brush tomatoes with the oil; sprinkle with salt and pepper and bake them in the oven with the meat for 10-15 minutes or until tender, or broil them. Set the beef on a platter: arrange tomatoes around it and pile the potatoes at each end. Garnish with watercress. Makes 4 or more servings.

TIP: Has your potatoes gotten a little old? If so, you can improve the flavor by adding a little sugar to the water in which they are boiled.

Irish Chuck Roast

3 ½ lbs. boneless chuck roast (2" thick)	2 cans Golden Mushrm. Soup	1/2 tsp. celery seed
	1/2 cup canned tomatoes	6 small potatoes, halved
2 Tbs. shortening	1 Tb. prepared horseradish	1 med. head cabbage, cut-up

In lg. heavy pan brown meat in shortening; pour off fat. Add soup, chopped tomatoes, horseradish, and celery seed. Cover; cook over low heat 2 hours. Add potatoes; place cabbage (6" wedges) on top.

Cook 1 hour more or until done. Stir occasionally. Spoon off fat; thicken sauce if desired. Makes 6 servings

Favorite Pot Roast

4-5 lb. bottom round/beef	2 Tbs. parsley	1 cup wine vinegar
1/4 cup flour	1/2 tsp.salt;1/4 tsp.pepper	6 peeled potatoes, quartered
3 Tbs. cooking oil	2 bay leaves	6 scraped carrots, cut in
1 onion, sliced thin	2 cups water	1" pieces

Pat the beef with flour all over, until it's kind of powdered-looking, then heat the oil in a Dutch oven-or any other large pot with a cover. Brown the meat (with cover off) on all sides in hot oil. Add onion, salt, pepper, parsley and bay leaves; pour the water and vinegar around the meat and let it boil. Cover and turn heat lower and cook on top of range for about 2-3 hours.

About 30 minutes before done, put in the quartered potatoes and carrot chunks. Cover and continue cooking until done. To thicken the gravy stir 2 tablespoons flour with a little cold water until mixed; then mix with the hot gravy stirring well until it boils and gets thick. Slice the meat and serve it with the gravy. Makes 6 to 8 servings.

Roast Beef & Browned Potatoes

For best flavor and least shrinkage a beef roast should weigh at least 4 pounds. Choose Standing Rib, or Rolled Rib for this recipe. Allow about 1/2 lb. raw boneless meat per serving.

Heat oven to 325 degrees. Season **roast** with salt and pepper. Place fat-side-up on rack in open pan. Standing rib roast needs no rack. If you have a meat thermometer, insert through outside fat into thickest part of meat. Do not baste, cover, or add water. When meat is roasted to liking serve immediately on hot platter with **Browned Potatoes** (below) and **parsley** garnish. Serve brown meat juices in a separate bowl. You may thicken juice a little if you like.

Browned Potatoes:

Pare 2 or 3 medium potatoes. Cook in 2" boiling salted water about 20 minutes, until almost done; drain. Add to roast last 30 minutes; turn potatoes to brown evenly. Makes 2 servings of potatoes.

Oven Beef Hash

2 cups chopped, cooked potatoes	1¼ cups finely crushed crackers (about. 32)	1 Tb. Worcestershire sauce
13-oz. can evap. milk	1/3 C. finely chopped onion	1/8 tsp.dried, crushed oregano
1½ cups chopped cooked beef	1/2 cup shredded carrot	1/8 tsp. pepper & 3/4 tsp. salt
	1/3 cup parsley	1 Tb. melted butter

Lightly stir together potato, evaporated milk, beef, 1 cup of the crushed crackers, carrot, onion, parsley, Worcestershire sauce, and seasonings. Turn into 1½ quart casserole. Combine remaining crumbs and melted butter or margarine; sprinkle atop casserole. Bake, covered, at 350 degrees until heated through, 35 to 40 minutes. Makes 4 to 6 servings.

Beef Miroton
(leftover beef)

2 Tbs. butter	1 cup beef consomme	5 med. potatoes, boiled
1/2 lb. onions, chopped	1/4 tsp. pepper: 1/2 tsp. salt	1 lb. leftover beef
1 Tb. flour	1 Tb. vinegar	2 Tbs. fresh bread crumbs

In a skillet, heat 1 tablespoon butter. Add onions and cook until slightly browned; sprinkle with flour and cook until browned, stirring constantly. Stir in consomme, salt, pepper, and vinegar. Bring to boil, cover and cook over low heat for 25 minutes.

Meanwhile, cut potatoes into slices about 1/2 inch thick. Butter an oven-proof casserole and arrange potatoes in crown, each slice overlapping another.

Cut meat into thin slices; place in center of potato crown; pour onion mixture over meat. Sprinkle with bread crumbs and dot with remaining butter. Bake at 450 degrees for 10 minutes. Makes 4 servings.

Skillet Steak Casino

1 lb. boneless round steak (1/2")	3/4 cup water
2 Tbs. shortening	1/4 cup chili sauce
1 can Cream of Onion Soup	3 med. potatoes, quartered
	9-oz. pkg. frozen cut green beans

Pound steak; cut into serving-size pieces. In skillet, brown steak in shortening; pour off fat. Add soup, water, and chili sauce. Cover; cook over low heat 30 minutes. Add potatoes; cook 45 min. longer. Add beans. Cook 20 minutes longer or until done; stir occasionally. Makes 4 servings.

Spanish Veal Chops

3 Tbs. flour	2 C. sliced, peeled onion	1 bay leaf
1 tsp. salt & 1/4 tsp. pepper	1 cup canned tomatoes	3 cups mashed potatoes
6 loin or rib veal chops	1/2 cup water	1 tsp. salt for potatoes
5 Tbs. fat drippings	1 Tbs. chopped parsley	2 Tbs. cornstarch & water

Combine flour, salt, pepper; coat chops. Melt fat in fry pan; add chops; brown on both sides; remove to warm platter. Saute onions in fat 5 minutes; place chops on top of onions. Add tomatoes, water, parsley, bay leaf, salt, pepper. Cover; simmer one hour.

Place hot mashed potatoes on platter, making a level bed. Remove chops from fry pan and place on top of potatoes.

Mix cornstarch, water to a paste; add a little liquid from pan; add paste to remaining liquid; cook until thickened; pour over chops. Serves 4.

Veal Chops Entree

1/2 lb. piece of bacon	1/2 Tb. flour	salt and pepper to taste
16 small onions peeled	1 ½ cups stock	3 medium potatoes, peeled
1 cup (1/4 lb.) mushrooms	4 Tbs. butter	1 Tb. chopped parsley
		4 large veal chops

Cover bacon in pan of water; simmer 45 minutes. Let cool in liquid, then drain. Cut bacon into strips 1-4 inch thick and 1 ½ inches long. Blanch onions and drain. Quarter mushrooms. In a skillet heat butter; brown veal chops on both sides. Transfer chops to a plate. Add mushrooms, onions and bacon to the cooking pan. Saute until onions are golden brown; stir in flour until smooth; add stock; bring to boil while stirring. Season to taste with salt and pepper, return chops to skillet and cover. Simmer on top of stove for 20 minutes.

Quarter potatoes lengthwise; blanch; add to the chops. Continue cooking 20 minutes longer or until both potatoes and chops are tender. Taste for seasoning and sprinkle with parsley. Makes 4 servings.

Veal Fricassee

2 lbs. cubed veal, rump	1/2 cup hot water	2 Tbs. fat
1/4 cup flour	1/2 cup diced celery	1 cup cubed raw potatoes
1 cup sliced raw carrots	1 ½ tsp. salt; 1 tsp. pepper	1/2 cup diced onion

Roll veal in flour; brown in fat in heavy fry pan; add remaining ingredients. Cover; cook over low heat 30-35 minutes. If necessary, add more water during cooking; thicken gravy if desired. Makes 4 servings.

Idaho Beef Stroganoff

4 Tbs. chicken broth	3 ¼ cups water	4 cups (dry flakes)
1 tsp. minced garlic	12 Tbs. butter	mashed potatoes
Salt & pepper	4 Tbs. oil	1 ½ lbs. flank or round
1 Tb. dry mustard	3 med. onions, sliced thin	steak sliced thin
3 Tbs. sugar	1 lb. mushrms. sliced thin	2 cups sour cream
1/2 tsp. dry dill weed	1 cup milk	

Preheat oven to 300 degrees. In a glass or ceramic bowl combine broth, garlic, salt and pepper. Toss meat with broth mixture and let marinate for 15 minutes. In a small bowl make a paste with mustard, sugar, dill, salt, pepper and 4 tablespoons water; set aside. Over medium heat, melt 2 Tbs. butter with 2 Tbs. oil. Add onions and mushrooms. Cover and simmer for 10 minutes.

While vegetables cook, bring 3 cups water, 1 teaspoon salt and 8 tablespoons butter to a boil. Remove from heat; add milk. Gently stir in potato flakes. Keep warm in oven. Remove vegetables; discard liquid. Add remaining 2 tablespoons butter and oil to same skillet. Cook over high heat until butter begins to brown. Stir-fry well drained meat in 4 batches. Return meat and vegetables to pan. Reduce heat; stir in mustard paste and sour cream until meat is well-coated. Cover; simmer for 5 minutes. Make a hole in each serving of potatoes and fill with stroganoff.

Main Dishes

PORK DISHES:

"Should Grandma help you mash your potatoes, Dear?"

Pork Chop Oven Dinner

6 pork chops, 3/4" thick	1/2 cup water	8 tsp. ground cloves
3 Tbs. all-purpose flour	1/4 cup dry sherry	6 sm.carrots,halved lengthwise
1/4 tsp. pepper; 3/4 tsp. salt	1/2 Tb. snipped parsley	6 sm.potatoes,peeled,halved
1/4 tsp. garlic salt	1 bay leaf	1 med, onion, thinly sliced

Trim fat from chops. Heat fat in skillet. When 2 tablespoons melted fat accumulate, remove trimmings. Combine flour, salt, dash pepper, and garlic salt; dip chops in mixture. Brown chops in hot fat; about 15 minutes per side.

In a 3-quart casserole, combine water, sherry, parsley, cloves, pepper and bay leaf. Sprinkle carrots and potatoes generously with salt; place in the liquid. Arrange the pork chops on top; add onion slices. Cover. Bake at 350 degrees for 1¼ hours or until vegetables and meat are tender; basting once or twice. Skim off excess fat; remove bay leaf. Trim with parsley, if desired. Makes 6 servings.

Smoked Pork Chops On A Potato Apple Bed

Most supermarkets carry smoked pork chops. You can substitute regular chops, but the flavor will change.

6 C. peeled, sliced potatoes	1 Tb. diced onion	6 smoked pork chops
1 cup peeled sliced apples	1 cup grated Swiss cheese	1½ cup hot horseradish cream sauce (recipe below)

Preheat oven to 350 degrees. Boil the potatoes until just tender, about 10 minutes. Grease a 9"x13" baking dish. Combine the potatoes, apples, and onion, and spoon into the baking dish. Sprinkle the cheese on top.

Sear the pork chops by rubbing the fatty ends of the chops around a hot frying pan, then laying the chops in the frying pan, and browning quickly on both sides over high heat. Place the pork chops on the potatoes. Cover the dish loosely with foil and bake for 30 minutes more. Pour horseradish sauce over. Makes 6 servings.

Hot Horseradish Cream Sauce: In a saucepan, melt **2 tablespoons butter**, and stir in **2 tablespoons all-purpose flour** to make a sauce. Add **1 cup milk**, a little at a time; stirring well after each addition to prevent lumps. Add more milk if the sauce is too thick; if too thin continue cooking until it thickens. **Add 4 teaspoons prepared horseradish, 1 teaspoon Dijon-style mustard**, and **salt and pepper to taste**. Pour the hot sauce over the hot dish prepared above.

Pork Loin-To-Perfection

3-4 lbs. pork loin rib-roast	1/2 cup water	1 medium bay leaf ·
2 Tbs. shortening	1/2 cup chopped onions	1 Tb. paprika
1 can Golden mushrm. soup	1/2 tsp.salt-dash pepper	6 med. carrots, cut-up
		4 med. potatoes, halved

In large heavy pan, brown meat in shortening; pour off fat. Add soup, water, onion and seasonings.

Cover; cook over low heat 1¼ hours. Stir occasionally. Add carrots and potatoes. Cook 1 hour longer or until done. Remove bay leaf. Thicken if desired. Makes 4 to 6 servings.

Danish Pork Chops

6 center cut pork chops, trimmed	2 chicken bouillon cubes	1 C. apple, chopped
	1 tsp. salt; dash pepper	1 Tb. lemon juice
4 med. potatoes, peeled, quartered	1 tsp. curry powder	sugar (optional)
	2 cups water	

In large, heavy skillet, brown pork chops on both sides. Drain off any accumulated fat. Add potatoes, bouillon cubes, salt, curry powder, pepper and 2 cups water. Cover and simmer 45 minutes or until pork chops are almost tender. Add apples and lemon juice; simmer 15 minutes more. Just before serving stir in little sugar to taste, if desired. Makes 6 servings

California Bake

4 loin pork chops, 2" thick	3 Tbs. California walnuts, chopped	salt, pepper, flour
2 Tbs. butter		1 cup milk
1/4 onion, chopped	1/2 cup bread crumbs	1 lb. can sm. potatoes, drained
3 Tbs. parsley, chopped	3 Tbs. orange juice	4 orange slices

Have butcher cut pocket in each chop. Brown onion in butter; mix in parsley, walnuts, crumbs, orange juice, salt, pepper, and stuff chops with mixture. Secure openings with skewers and string. Dredge in flour; slowly brown chops on both sides in same pan used for onion.

Transfer chops to baking dish; cover with milk and bake; uncovered, in 350 degree oven for 1 hour. Add potatoes; lay orange slice on each chop; bake for 20 minutes more, or until tender. Makes 4 servings.

Country Dinner

2 ½ lb. smoked pork shoulder roll
16-oz. can sauerkraut, drained
2 cups apple juice

1 large bay leaf
6 medium potatoes, peeled
6 small onions
6 small carrots, quartered

Place the pork shoulder roll in a 5-quart Dutch oven; add drained sauerkraut, apple juice, and bay leaf. Cover; simmer 1 hour. Add the potatoes, onions, and carrots. Simmer, covered, until tender, about 1 hour longer. Remove meat and vegetables to warm serving platter. Make 6 servings.

Potatoes In Hot Sauce

4 or 5 med. potatoes
1/4 cup oil
2 cloves garlic, crushed
1 med. onion, chopped

1 fresh green chili pepper,
    seeded, chopped
1 cup milk
1/4 cup crumbled Feta

chopped parsley (optional)
salt, pepper & cayenne
1 egg, hard-boiled, sliced
hot or cold pork roast

Boil the potatoes in their skins in salted water for 15-20 minutes or until tender. Drain and peel them; cut in slices. In a large skillet, heat the oil and fry crushed garlic, onion and fresh chili pepper until brown. Add milk, then put in the potatoes and heat thoroughly. Sprinkle the mixture with the cheese, chopped parsley (opt.), salt, pepper and cayenne to taste and spoon into a serving dish. Decorate with slices of hard cooked egg and slices of pork. Makes 6 servings.

Red Flannel Pork Hash

2 C. diced cooked pork roast
1/3 cup salad oil
1/2 cup chopped onions

16-oz. pkg. hash browns
1/2 tsp.salt; Dash of pepper
1 can Cream Chicken Soup

16-oz. jar, pickled beets,
1/4 cup chopped parsley
Egg, sliced, hard cooked

In skillet brown pork and cook onion in 2 tablespoons oil until tender. Add remaining oil, potatoes, salt, and pepper. Cook 10 minutes. Stir in soup, chopped drained beets, and parsley. Heat; stir occasionally. Garnish with egg and additional parsley. Makes about 5 cups.

Fancy Ham Scallop

4 Tbs. flour
4 Tbs. butter
1 cup bouillon
1 lg. can evaporated milk

1 tsp.Worcestershire sauce
Salt and pepper
dash cayenne
2 cups diced ham

2 lg. potatoes thinly sliced
2 green peppers, cut in rings
1 sm. onion, thinly sliced
1/2 cup ripe olives, chopped
2 Tbs. parsley, chopped

Stir flour into melted butter; add bouillon, evaporated milk, seasonings, and cook, stirring, until sauce thickens. Arrange all remaining ingredients except parsley in greased casserole in layers.

Pour the sauce over the meat mixture and bake, uncovered, in 375 degree oven for 30 minutes. Sprinkle with parsley and serve.

Ham Potato Bake

2 (16-oz.) cans sliced,   1 Cream Mushroom Soup   1/8 tsp. pepper
  drained potatoes   1 cup Am. cheese, sharp   1 cup soft bread crumbs
1 cup shredded carrots   1/4 cup milk   1 Tb. butter, melted
1 ½ C. cubed cooked ham   1 Tb. minced onion, fresh or instant

Set oven 350 degrees. Place 1/2 the potatoes and carrots in 2-quart casserole. Combine ham, soup, 1/2 cup shredded cheese, milk, onion, and pepper.

Pour half of the soup mixture over the potatoes. Repeat layers. Combine crumbs, remaining shredded cheese, and butter; sprinkle over the casserole. Bake until heated through, about 45 minutes. Makes 4 to 6 servings.

Ham And Potatoes Au Gratin

12-oz. can chopped ham   3-oz. can chopped mushrooms, drained
1 pkg. Au Gratin Potato mix   1 tsp. Worcestershire sauce

Cut meat in 8 slices and place in baking dish. Top with potato slices from mix. Sprinkle mushrooms over potatoes along with cheese-sauce mix from potato mix.

Continue as directed on package, but add Worcestershire sauce to the butter and boiling water called for. Cover and bake at 400 degrees for 40 minutes. Makes 4 servings.

Baked Potatoes & Ham Casserole

1/4 cup butter   1/4 tsp.Tabasco peppersauce   10-oz.pkg frozen chopped
1/2 cup chopped onion   2 cups milk   spinach, thawed & drained
3 Tbs. flour   1 tsp. lemon juice   4 Idaho potatoes, baked
1 tsp. salt   1/8 tsp. nutmeg   1 ½ cup ham, chopped

Melt butter in a saucepan; add onion and cook until tender. Blend in flour, 1/2 teaspoon salt and Tabasco sauce. Stir in milk, stirring constantly, until mixture thickens and comes to a boil. Remove from heat; stir in lemon juice, nutmeg and spinach.

Peel cooked potatoes; chill and cut into 1/8 inch slices. Place a layer of potatoes in a greased 2-quart casserole; sprinkle with **1/4 teaspoon salt**. Sprinkle with half the cooked ham and half the spinach sauce. Repeat with remaining potatoes, remaining 1/4 teaspoon salt, ham and sauce.

Cover and bake in preheated 375 degree oven 45 minutes, or until heated through. Makes 6 servings.

Eggs Suzette

4 Idaho potatoes	1/4 cup stock	4 eggs
1 cup sliced mushrooms	1 cup ham, cut in strips	3/4 Tbs. hot milk
1/4 cup butter	salt and pepper	1/4 cup grated Swiss or
2 tsp. flour	1 cup Mornay Sauce (below)	Cheddar cheese

Scrub potatoes; rub with salt; bake in oven 350 degrees for 1 1/4 hrs. or until tender. Saute mushrooms in 2 tablespoons butter in a small pan. Stir in the flour, then the stock; bring to a boil and cook 1 minute. Add the ham; heat thoroughly; season to taste and set aside. Make mornay sauce. Soft cook or poach the eggs and keep in warm water. Cut tops off potatoes (lengthwise); scoop out pulp. Put into warm bowl, mash and beat in 2 tablespoons butter and the hot milk to make a puree.

Put a quarter of the mushroom and ham mixture into the bottom of each potato; place a well drained egg on top and coat with mornay sauce. Top with potato puree, or fill a pastry bag fitted with a star tube and pipe potato to cover eggs completely. Sprinkle with grated cheese and brown under the broiler or in a hot oven (400 degrees) for about 10 minutes.

Mornay Sauce:

Melt 1½ tablespoons butter in a sauce pan; remove from heat and stir in **1½ tablespoons flour.** Pour in **1/2 cup milk**; blend until smooth with whisk or wooden spoon. Add another **1/2 cup milk**; season lightly with **salt** and **pepper**, and bring to a boil, stirring continuously. Simmer 2 minutes; remove from heat and gradually stir in **1/4 cup grated cheese**, and a little **dry mustard**. Makes 4 servings.

Golden Potatoes And Ham

1/4 cup chopped onion	1 tsp. Worcestershire sauce	4 cups potatoes, sliced thin
2 Tbs. butter	1 tsp. dry mustard	10-oz. pkg. frozen cut beans
2 Tbs. flour	1/8 tsp. pepper	2 cups cooked ham
1½ cups evaporated milk	8-oz. Cheddar cheese	

In saucepan, cook onion in butter until tender; stir in flour until smooth. Add milk, Worcestershire, mustard and pepper; cook and stir until thickened. Add cheese; stir until melted. Add potatoes, beans and ham. Turn into greased 2-quart baking dish. Cover; bake at 350 degrees for 50 minutes. Uncover; bake 25 minutes or until potatoes are tender. Garnish as desired. Makes 5 to 6 servings.

Ham And Cheese Potatoes

2 cups boiling water	3/4 cup milk
2 Tbs. butter	1 can Bean & bacon soup, undiluted
1 pkg. Au Gratin Potatoes mix	1½ to 2 cups cubed ham

In a casserole dish combine the above ingredients. Bake uncovered in a 400 degree oven for 40 minutes, or until potatoes are tender.

Candela Potatoes

6 servings mashed potatoes   1 cup diced ham   1/2 cup whipping cream
1 C. shredded Cheddar cheese

Heat oven to 450 degrees. Spread mashed potatoes in a 2 qt casserole. Cover with ham. Whip cream until stiff; fold in cheese. Spread mixture over ham. Bake for 10 to 15 minutes or until golden brown. Makes 8 servings.

Potatoes, Ham And Sauerkraut Pie

1 ½ cup mashed potatoes   4 slices pineapple   4 slices aged cheese
4 slices ham   1/2 cup grapes   (Gouda or other)
3 onions   1 cup sauerkraut, drained

Spread potatoes on bottom of baking pan; lay ham slices on top of potatoes. Cut the onion into small cubes and pineapple into strips, and combine them together with the halved grapes and the sauerkraut. Pile the mixture on the potatoes and ham; topping it off with slices of aged cheese. Brown under the broiler until the cheese begins to melt.

Eggs Savoyarde
(baked eggs)

Thick slice(1/4 lb)uncooked   1 onion, sliced   1 egg
ham cut in strips   1 sm. root celery, peeled,   6 Tbs. heavy cream
3 Tbs. butter   sliced (celeriac)*   1/4 cup grated Gruyere
3 potatoes, sliced   salt and pepper   cheese

In a shallow saucepan melt butter and cook the ham for 1-2 minutes. Add the sliced vegetables; season; cover the pan with a tight-fitting lid and cook over low heat for 20 minutes or until the vegetables are tender but not browned.

Spread the ham mixture in a buttered oven-proof dish. Break the eggs on top; spoon the cream on top and sprinkle with grated cheese. Bake in a moderate oven (350 degrees) for 8-10 minutes or until the eggs are just set.

* **Root celery or celeriac** looks like a large turnip or rutabaga. It tastes like regular celery and is good whether prepared on its own or added to beef and lamb stews. If possible choose small young roots as large ones can be quite tough. Peel celeriac before using.

Potato Crust--Ham And Cheese Pie

2 cup creamy mashed   2 Tbs. prepared mustard   1/2 cup cottage cheese
potatoes   1 lb. ham, cooked, cubed   2 slices cheddar cheese

Mix mashed potatoes and mustard. Spread in bottom of baking pan. Add ham cubes in layer on potatoes. In electric blender, blend cottage and crumbled cheddar cheese until fairly smooth. Spread over ham. Bake at 350 degrees for 30 minutes or until casserole is heated through. Makes 4 servings.

Cheesy Shepherd's Pie

4-6 strips cut up bacon	2 Tbs. butter	8-oz. cooked lean meat
celery salt	2 large onions, chopped	3-oz. grated cheese
salt, pepper,	5-oz. mushrooms, sliced	1 ½ lbs. potatoes
nutmeg		milk to cream potatoes

Fry the bacon slowly until crisp. Crumble the meat in the pan; stir until it is light brown and add the salt and other seasonings. Melt butter in a pan; saute the chopped onions; add the sliced mushrooms and saute for 5 minutes more.

Fill a buttered oven-proof dish with layers of bacon, meat, onion, mushrooms and cheese. Reserve a little cheese for the top. Top with a layer of creamy mashed potatoes. Sprinkle with the remaining cheese. In a pre-heated oven cook at 400 degrees for about 20 minutes or until crust is golden brown.

Crispy Potatoes

4 strips bacon	32-oz. frozen shredded	1/4 cup fresh parsley, chopped
2 onions, diced	potatoes	2 C. longhorn shredded cheese
few scallions or grn. onions	2 cans Cream chicken soup	1 Tb. garlic salt
3 Tbs. butter	1 pint sour cream	2 C. Wheaties or Corn Flakes

Cook bacon until crisp; break into pieces. Saute onions and/or scallions, in 1 tablespoon bacon fat until golden (not brown). Add thawed, shredded potatoes, soup (without water added), and sour cream. Mix together, add parsley, cheese and garlic salt.

Put in 9x13 shallow baking dish. Mix together Wheaties or Corn Flakes with melted butter; pour over mixture in baking dish. Bake in 350 degree oven 45 to 50 minutes, until golden brown and crispy; cover. If you wish to prepare this in advance, cover and keep in fridge a few days before you bake it.

Cheese, Bacon & Potato Galette

1/4 lb. processed cheese	8 medium potatoes	1 ½ to 2 cups chicken stock
1/4 lb. sliced bacon	2 Tbs. butter	salt and pepper

Set oven at 400 degrees. Cut each slice of cheese into 4 pieces; cut each slice of bacon in half. Peel potatoes; cut them into very thin slices.
Rub half the butter around an oven-proof dish; arrange the potatoes in it; seasoning lightly between the layers. Pour in enough stock to almost cover the potatoes; spread with bacon and cheese on top; dot with remaining butter.

Bake in heated oven until potatoes are tender and the cheese and bacon are browned and crisp, adding more stock if the dish seems dry.

Potato-Cabbage Casserole

3 lg. unpeeled Idaho potatoes	2 Tbs. flour	1/2 cup milk
1/2 lb. bacon, cut/2" strips	1/2 tsp. dried thyme	6 cups finely shredded cabbage
1 cup sliced onion	1/2 tsp. salt	1 cup Swiss cheese
	1½ cups beer	

Steam potatoes in 1 inch boiling water 30 to 40 minutes, or until tender. Slice potatoes; unpeeled, into 1/2-inch slices; set aside. Cook bacon in a large skillet until crisp; set aside. Pour off all but 2 Tbs. bacon fat; saute onion in same skillet until golden. Stir in flour, thyme and salt. Gradually add beer and milk; stir, over low heat, until mixture boils and thickens into a sauce.

In 3-quart casserole; layer half the cabbage, potatoes, bacon, cheese and sauce; repeat with remaining ingredients. Cover and bake in preheated 375 degree oven 30 minutes. Uncover and bake 15 minutes longer, or until cabbage is tender. Makes 4 servings.

Scalloped Sausage and Potatoes

1 lb. bulk pork sausage	1/4 cup flour	1 cup sharp Am. cheese
4 cups sliced potatoes	salt to taste	1½ cups milk

In skillet crumble sausage; brown it lightly; drain. Place half of the sliced potatoes in a 2 quart casserole. Combine flour and salt. Sprinkle half the seasoned flour mixture over the potatoes.

Top with half the browned sausage and shredded cheese. Repeat layers with remaining potatoes, flour mixture, sausage, and cheese. Pour milk over all. Cover and bake at 350 degrees until potatoes are tender, 50-60 minutes. Uncover and bake 10 minutes longer. Makes 4 to 6 servings.

Potato & Sausage With Tomato Sauce

4 Tbs. butter	1 tsp. salt	6 C. cooked diced potatoes
5 Tbs. all-purpose flour	1/4 tsp. Worcestershire	8 sausages, cooked
2½ cups tomato juice	1/4 C. green pepper	parsley for garnish
	1/4 C. chopped onion	

Heat oven 350 degrees. Blend melted fat, and flour into paste, add tomato juice; cook until thick. Cook slowly; stir for about 15 minutes. Stir in salt, Worcestershire sauce, shredded green pepper, and onion. Simmer in sauce for about 3 minutes.

Place diced potatoes in glass dish; pour sauce over potatoes. Arrange the sausage on top of potatoes. Bake for 35 minutes. Garnish with parsley.

Quick Idaho Skillet Dinner

1 lb. Italian sweet sausage cut in 1/2 "slices or 1 lb. bulk sausage	3 C. frozen Idaho hash brown potatoes 10-oz. pkg. frozen	1 tsp. lemon juice 1/8 tsp. pepper 1/2 tsp. salt
1/2 cup onions, chopped	Italian green beans 2 tomatoes, peeled, cut-up	2 Tbs. water

In large skillet brown sausage over medium heat. Add onion and cook until tender. Add frozen hash browns and cook uncovered 10 minutes; stirring occasionally. Add remaining ingredients and simmer; covered, 10 minutes, or until green beans are tender. Makes 4 servings.

Saucy Links

8-oz. Brown'n Serve sausage links	1 can Cream Mushroom or Celery Soup	2 Tbs. chopped parsley 2 C. sliced, cooked potatoes
1/2 cup milk	1/4 tsp. prepared mustard	1 cup sliced cooked carrots

Brown sausage; pour off fat. Stir in soup, milk, mustard, and parsley. Add potatoes and carrots. Heat; stir occasionally. Makes about 4 cups.

Country-Style Sauerkraut & Sausages

8 Brown n Serve Sausages, in 1"pieces	16-oz. can Bavarian-style sauerkraut, drained	1 egg, beaten 2 Tbs. grated onion
1 Tbs. butter	2 Tbs. brown sugar	2½ cups mashed potatoes

In skillet brown sausages in butter on medium heat 5-6 minutes, turning frequently. Stir in sauerkraut and brown sugar; warm through. Pour mixture into a greased 2-quart casserole; set aside.

Add egg and onion to mashed potatoes; stir well. Spread potato mixture over sauerkraut; bake in preheated 350 degree oven, uncovered, 25 minutes. Makes 4 to 6 servings.

TIP: When a recipe calls for an egg added to mashed potatoes, you may elect to use two egg whites instead. Well beaten egg whites will add to the looks of the dish. If the mashed potatoes do not call for an egg, try adding a well beaten white to greatly enhance the taste of the potatoes as well as the looks.

LAMB AND VENISON DISHES:

"Honey, just wanted you to know---you're the cook again tonight."

Braised Venison

3-4 lb. roast of venison	marinade for game (below)	kneaded butter (see page 125)
thinly peeled rind of 1	1 Tb. red currant jelly	mashed potatoes for servings
orange & lemon	2-3 Tbs. heavy cream (opt)	

For braising:

2 Tbs. oil or meat drippings	2 onions, diced	2 stalks of celery, diced
2 diced carrots	bouquet garni	1½ cups jellied stock
		salt & pepper

Venison is the meat of deer. It has no natural outer layer of fat, so it lacks succulence & tenderness. It is usually marinated before cooking. Put the meat in a deep bowl; pour over the marinade, leaving the vegetables on top. Add the orange and lemon rinds; cover and refrigerate 2-3 days, turning the meat occasionally. Take the meat from the marinade and pat dry with paper towels.

In a deep skillet; heat the oil or drippings and brown the meat on all sides. Take meat out, then add onions, carrots and celery in the skillet, cover and cook gently for 5-7 minutes. Replace the venison and add bouquet garni with the stock, strained marinade and seasoning. Bring the mixture to a boil; cover pot with foil, then with the lid and braise in a moderately low oven (325 degree) for 2-3 hours or until venison is very tender. Remove the venison and keep warm.

Strain the gravy; skim off fat; bring to a boil and whisk in kneaded butter a little at a time until the gravy is the consistency of heavy cream. Add the red currant jelly, stir until melted and taste for seasoning. Arrange the venison on a platter and spoon over the sauce. Pipe a border of mashed potatoes around the platter just before serving. If you like, add 2-3 tablespoons cream to the sauce just before serving. Makes 6 servings with leftovers.

Marinade For Game:

2 cloves garlic, minced	2 med. onions, sliced	2 med.carrot, sliced
1½ cups Burgundy or	2 stalks celery, sliced	10-12 peppercorns
any robust red wine	3 Tbs. red wine vinegar	3 strips lemon rind
3 Tbs. olive oil	8 allspice or juniper berries, crushed	

Combine all vegetables (thinly sliced, minced or chopped) and the other ingredients in a saucepan; bring to a boil and simmer 10 minutes.

Main Dishes

Kneaded Butter:

Mix **1 tablespoon flour** and **2 tablespoons butter** together as a paste on a plate with a fork. When using paste, add small pieces at a time to thicken a mixture or liquid (usually at the end of the cooking process).

Note: Wine alcohol is destroyed with cooking, the wine flavor does remain.

Pot Roast Leg of Lamb
with Spring Vegetables

4-5 lb. leg of lamb	1/2 cup white wine	1 pkg. frozen peas
1/4 cup butter	10 new potatoes, peeled	1 pkg. frozen lima beans
1/2 clove garlic, crushed	1 bu. baby carrots or 1 pkg.	salt and pepper
1 Tb. chopped parsley	frozen	1 tsp. sugar

For sauce: fat from cooking liquid, 6 Tbs. light cream and, 1 Tbs. flour.

For stock: shank bone of lamb, 8 peppercorns, 1 onion, salt, 1 stalk celery and 1 carrot.

For stock; place shank bone of lamb in a saucepan with remaining stock ingredients and add water to cover. Put lid on pan and simmer 2 hours or until stock is very concentrated. Strain.

Trim any skin and fat from leg of lamb. Cream the butter in a bowl with a wooden spoon and work in garlic and parsley; spread over the lamb and leave 15 minutes. Place in large container; cover; cook 30 minutes, (until meat has changed from pink to grey color but not browned). While cooking shake the container occasionally to prevent lamb from sticking. Add wine and simmer gently; uncovered, until it has been reduced by one-third.

Add 1/2 cup stock from shank bone and season. Cover and roast in 375 degree oven for 1 to 1 ½ hours or until meat is very tender. (Check meat after 30 minutes of roasting time. If cooking too fast you may need to lower your oven heat as the meat should cook gently.)

If vegetables are fresh add potatoes and carrots to the pan after 30 minutes of roasting, and peas 30 minutes before the end of the cooking time. Strain and reserve gravy, leaving meat and vegetables; if canned or cooked frozen vegetables are used, add vegetables; turn oven to low; add sugar; cover and keep hot in oven.

For sauce, skim fat from cooking liquid; mix with flour and stir back into liquid. Heat in a small pan; stirring until boiling; simmer 2-3 minutes. Add cream and reheat. Taste for seasoning. Arrange meat on a platter, surrounded by vegetables and spoon a little sauce on top. Makes 6 or more servings.

Note: Wine alcohol is destroyed with cooking, the wine flavor does remain.

Lamb Ring With Potato Puffs

2 lbs. lean ground lamb	2 Tbs. onion, minced	dash pepper
3 eggs	1 Tb. parsley, chopped	3 cups mashed potatoes,
1/2 C. grn. pepper, chopped	1 tsp. salt	creamy

In large bowl, combine lamb, 2 eggs, green pepper, onion, parsley, salt and pepper. Press into 8-inch ring mold. Bake at 350 degrees for 1 hour. Spoon off any accumulated fat. Un-mold onto large, shallow baking pan. Beat remaining egg into mashed potatoes. Spoon into individual mounds around lamb ring. Bake at 425 degrees for 10 minutes or until potatoes are lightly browned. Serves 6 to 8.

Venison Roast

1 med. cut venison shoulder roast	1/2 cup flour	dash celery salt
	2 Tbs. fat	dash garlic salt
4 Tbs. baking soda	6 med. potatoes	1 Tb. parsley flakes
1 C. vinegar & 2 cups water	6 medium-sized carrots	2 Tbs. vegetable flakes
1 tsp. each: salt & pepper	4 med. onions	dash paprika

Trim all fat from shoulder roast. Rub thoroughly with baking soda. Wash thoroughly with mixture of vinegar and 1 cup water. Rinse with cool, clear water. Salt and pepper on both sides. Rub both sides with flour. Brown in melted fat on top of stove. When browned on both sides, add **1 cup water**.

Cut potatoes, carrots and onions and place on top and around roast. Add seasonings. Cover tightly. Cook about 3 hours at 275 degrees. If desired, venison roast can be marinated overnight in vinegar, salt and water prior to roasting. This helps eliminate wild flavor of meat.

CHICKEN DISHES:

"I speak the whole drumstick."

Chicken 'N Potato Casserole

1 pkg. Idahoan Scalloped potatoes	1 can Cream mushroom soup	1 cup cooked peas
	1 cup diced cooked chicken	1/4 cup chopped pimento

Heat oven to 400 degrees. Prepare potatoes according to pkg. directions. Stir in undiluted soup; gently mix in chicken, peas and pimentos. Bake in 2-quart casserole uncovered for 45 minutes or until potatoes are tender. Makes 5 servings.

Chicken-Potato Casserole

This casserole fits into the fast pace of today's busy families. It is as quick and easy as it is tasty. Also ideal for microwave oven.

1 pkg. Au Gratin Potatoes
1 can evaporated milk
2 ½ cups boiling water
2 Tbs. chopped onion
1 can Cr. of Mushrm. Soup

2 C. cut-up cooked chicken
  or beef, or 2 6½-oz.
  cans tuna, drained
1 can sliced, drained
  mushrooms

2 Tbs. butter or margarine
1 cup Cheddar cheese
1/2 cup crushed Corn Flakes
  or cracker crumbs

Heat oven to 400 degrees. Mix all ingredients except cheese and corn flakes in ungreased 2-quart casserole; sprinkle with shredded cheese.

Bake uncovered until potatoes are tender, about 35 minutes; sprinkle with corn flakes. Bake 5 minutes longer. Let stand 5 minutes before serving. Makes 6 servings.

Casserole-Roasted Chicken

3 lb. broiler-fryer
1 ½ tsp. salt
1/4 tsp. pepper
16 small white onions,

12 small new red potatoes
3 Tbs. butter
3 Tbs. vegetable oil
1/2 cup boiling water

1 envelope instant chicken
  broth or 1 tsp. bouillon
1 tsp. leaf basil, crumbled
1 Tbs. parsley

Sprinkle chicken cavity with 1/2 tsp. of the salt and pepper. Peel onions. Scrape potatoes. Melt butter with the vegetable oil in a large heavy flameproof casserole or Dutch oven. Add chicken; brown on all sides.

Combine boiling water and chicken broth in a 1-cup measure, stirring until dissolved; add to casserole with chicken. Place onions and potatoes around chicken; sprinkle with basil and remaining 1 teaspoon salt; cover.

Bake in slow oven (325 degrees,) basting once or twice with juices, 1¼ hrs, or until chicken and vegetables are tender. Sprinkle with parsley. 4 servings.

Chicken In The Garden

1 broiler-fryer, quartered
1 ½ tsp. salt
1 tsp. dried leaf tarragon

2 Tbs. butter or margarine
1 lb.sm. new potatoes,pared
2 Tbs. snipped fresh chives

2 Tb. chopped fresh parsley
1 Tbs. fresh lemon juice
2 C. diagonally cut celery
1 lb. asparagus

Sprinkle chicken on both sides with 1/2 teaspoon salt and 1/2 teaspoon tarragon. Heat butter or margarine in large skillet; add chicken, skin side down, and brown slowly; turn, and brown other side. Transfer the chicken to a shallow 3 or 4-quart casserole. Add potatoes (whole, halved or quartered) to the butter in skillet; cook slowly over low heat for about 5 minutes and add to casserole. Sprinkle chicken and potatoes with chives, parsley, lemon juice, and drippings from skillet. Cover tightly with lid or aluminum foil.

Bake in 375 degree oven 30 min. Remove from oven and remove cover. Add celery pieces and asparagus. Sprinkle vegetables with remaining 1 teaspoon salt and 1/2 teaspoon tarragon; spoon juices in casserole over asparagus. Cover and return to oven for 20 to 30 minutes or until asparagus is tender.

Saucy Chicken Casserole

3 whole chicken breasts,
  cooked, cubed
1 cup cooked rice
2 Tb. instant minced onion

1 can Cr. of Mushrm. Soup
1/2 cup dairy sour cream
4-oz. can mushroom stems
  and pieces, drained

1/2 cup water chestnuts, sliced
1 can (17-oz.) peas, drained
1 cup crushed potato chips

Blend together chicken, rice, onion and soup in a large bowl. Gently fold in sour cream, mushrooms, sliced water chestnuts and peas. Spread mixture in a greased 8-inch-square casserole; cover and bake in preheated 350 degree oven 30 minutes. Sprinkle potato chips over top; bake, uncovered 10 minutes longer. Makes 8 servings.

Chicken Chip Bake

2 cups cubed cooked
  chicken
1/2 tsp. salt   ,
2 Tbs. lemon juice

2 cups sliced celery
1/3 cup toasted slivered
  almonds
2 tsp. grated onion

3/4 cup mayonnaise
1/2 cup process Am.
  cheese, shredded
1 cup potato chips, crushed

Combine all ingredients except cheese and potato chips. Pile lightly in 1-1/2 quart casserole. Sprinkle with cheese, then potato chips. Bake at 425 degrees until heated through, about 20 minutes. Makes 5 or 6 servings.

Chicken Casserole Delight

3 ½ lb. roasting chicken
2 Tbs. butter
12 baby onions

1/4 lb. bacon
1 cup mushroom chunks
1 Tb. flour

2 or 2 ½ cups stock
3 med. potatoes, quartered
salt and pepper
2 Tbs. chopped parsley

In a large casserole dish heat the butter; when foaming put in chicken, breast down. Brown the bird all over on low heat about 15 minutes.

Blanch onions (or scallions) and bacon separately in cold water; bringing to a boil and draining.

Remove chicken from cooking container; add onions. bacon and mushrooms to container and cook until brown; stirring occasionally. Stir flour into container; pour in stock; bring to boil. Replace the chicken; cover and bake at 350 degrees for about 1 hour.

Peel medium-sized potatoes, quarter, add to container 30 minutes before the end of cooking. When potatoes and chicken are tender, remove chicken, cut into serving pieces and return to container. Taste sauce for seasoning and sprinkle with parsley before serving. Makes 4 or more servings.

Deep-Dish Chicken Pie

6 med. potatoes, peeled, quartered
6 med. carrots, scraped, quartered
1 small onion, chopped (1/4 cup)
1/4 cup chopped green pepper

2 Tbs. butter
1 can Cr. Chicken Soup
3 cups chunks of cooked chicken,
   boiled, roasted, or broiled
Biscuit Wedge Topping (See below)

Cook potatoes and carrots in boiling salted water in large saucepan 15-20 minutes, or until tender; drain, saving 1 cup of liquid for next step.

While vegetables cook, saute onion and green pepper in butter, until soft in saucepan; stir in chicken soup and 1 cup saved liquid. Spoon vegetables and chicken into 8-cup casserole; pour sauce over.

Bake in hot oven 425 degrees, 15 minutes while making Biscuit Wedge Topping, (see below); arrange biscuits on top of hot mixture; bake 15 minutes longer, or until biscuits are golden.

Biscuit Wedge Topping: Sift **1½ cups sifted flour, 2 tsp. baking powder** and **1/2 tsp. salt** into medium sized bowl; cut in **1/4 cup (half stick) butter or margarine**; add **1/2 cup milk** all at once; stir just until blended. Turn dough out onto lightly floured pastry cloth or board; knead lightly 1/2 minute; roll out to a 7-inch round; cut into 6 wedges; brush tops lightly with milk; sprinkle with **1/4 teaspoon poppy seeds**.

Chicken The Fast Idaho Way

5½-oz. pkg Id. Au Gratin Potatoes
1 chicken bouillon cube
1/4 cup grated Parmesan cheese
3/4 cups sliced celery

1½ cup chicken, cooked, diced
1 pkg. (10-oz.) frozen spinach,
   thawed, drained
1/4 cup chopped onions

Empty potato slices into large bowl; sprinkle with cheese sauce mix. Dissolve bouillon cube in boiling water called for in package directions; add with milk called for on package to potatoes and mix well (omit butter). Add remaining ingredients and mix well. Turn into 2-quart casserole. Bake as directed, 30-35 minutes in 400 degree oven. Makes 4 servings.

Chicken And Potato Curry

2 C. thinly sliced potatoes
2 hard-cooked eggs, sliced

2 C. chicken, cooked, cubed
1/2 cup water

1 can Cr. of Potato Soup
1 Tb. curry powder

In 9-inch baking pan, arrange in layers as follows; 1 cup potatoes, eggs, chicken, remaining 1 cup potatoes. In small bowl, blend soup, curry powder and 1/2 cup water; pour over casserole. Bake, uncovered, at 375 degrees for 1 hour or until potatoes are tender. Makes 4 or 5 servings.

All-In-One Supper Casserole

1 can Cr. of Chicken Soup	1 cup diced chicken	1 pkg. frozen peas, thawed
1/2 cup milk	1 C. sliced ham cut in strips	1 pkg. tater tots

Combine soup, milk, chicken, thinly-sliced ham strips and peas in casserole dish; top with tater tots. Bake at 425 degrees for 40 minutes. Makes 4 servings.

Chicken Pie

1 4-lb. chicken	3 C. cooked, diced potatoes	1 Tb. salt; 1/8 tsp. pepper
1 tsp. salt	1 C. cooked or canned peas	1 cup milk or cream
2 stalks celery	1 C. cooked chopped carrot	2 cups chicken broth
1 med. sliced onion	4 Tbs. butter or margarine	dash nutmeg
1 bay leaf	4 Tbs. flour	1/2 tsp. Worcestershire
		pinch tarragon

Put cleaned chicken in large Dutch oven or saucepan; add boiling water to cover chicken half-way. Add 1 tablespoon salt, celery, onion and bay leaf. Cover; simmer until tender; allow 1 to 1½ hours for roaster; 3-4 hours for older fowl; additional water may be added if necessary.

Remove chicken; allow to cool. Strain broth; add water if necessary to make 2 cups; skim off fat as it cools. Remove skin from chicken; cut meat into 1" cubes. Arrange chicken, potatoes, peas carrots, in casserole or shallow baking pan. Melt fat in sauce pan; remove from heat. Stir in flour, salt, pepper. Add milk, chicken broth, nutmeg, Worcestershire sauce, and tarragon.

Cook over low heat, stirring constantly until thickened. Pour over chicken-vegetable mixture. Top with baking powder biscuits or flaky pie crust. Brush with milk. Bake 20-25 minutes in hot oven 425 degrees. Makes 6 servings.

Variation #1: Part chicken, part ham may be used. Leftover chicken and/or ham may be used.

Variation #2: Heap fluffy mashed white or sweet potatoes on top instead of biscuits or pie crust.

Variation #3: A bed of rice or noodles may line the bottom of the baking pan before adding the chicken-vegetable mixture. Instead of topping with biscuits or mashed potatoes you may wish to top with crumbled potato chips, or buttered Corn Flakes, or even crushed pretzels.

Variation #4: If you need a filling dish that will serve more people try lining the bottom of the pan with mashed potatoes as well as topping with fluffy mashed potatoes.

Potato-Flake Chicken

Mashed potato flakes make the coating for oven-crisp chicken.

2/3 cup evaporated milk
1 tsp. salt; 1/8 tsp. pepper
1 tsp. mixed Italian herbs

1 envelope (1½ cups instant
mashed potato flakes)
2 2-lb. broiler-fryers, cut up

Quick Cream Gravy
(See recipe below)

Pour evaporated milk into a pie plate; stir in salt, pepper and Italian herbs . Empty mashed potato flakes into a second pie plate. Dip chicken pieces into evaporated milk mixture, then into potato flakes to coat well. Place in single layer on ungreased cookie sheet, skin-side up.

Bake in a 350 degree oven for 1½ hours, or until tender and golden brown. Serve with Quick Cream Gravy. Makes 6 servings.

Quick Cream Gravy: Blend 1/4 cup evaporated milk into 1 can (10 ounces) chicken gravy in small saucepan. Heat slowly, until bubbly-hot and smooth.

Neapolitan Chicken

Families that love spaghetti and potatoes will welcome this chicken-and-potatoes with spaghetti-sauce flavor.

2 fryers (2 lbs. ea.) cut-up
1/4 cup flour
1 tsp. salt; 1/8 tsp. pepper
2 Tbs. salad oil
1/2 cup onion, chopped

1 clove garlic, minced
1 cup water
1 envelope spaghetti-sauce
mix
3 med. tomatoes, chopped

1/4 cup, cut-up parsley
6 med. potatoes, pared, cut
1" cubes
1 lg. green pepper, cut into
wide strips

Shake chicken with flour, salt and pepper in a paper bag to coat well. With oil in fry pan brown, a few pieces at a time; place in a 8-cup baking dish. Saute onion and garlic until softened in same frying pan; stir in water, then spaghetti-sauce mix; heat to boiling. Stir in tomatoes and parsley. Simmer; uncovered; 15 minutes. Pour over chicken in baking dish; top with potato cubes and pepper strips; cover.

Bake in moderate oven (350 degrees) 1½ hours, or until chicken is tender. Serves 6.

Chicken, Turkey or Goose Stuffing

1⅛ cups butter
3/4 cups minced onions
1/2 cup snipped parsley
2¼ tsp. salt

1/4 cup dried celery
1½ tsp. poultry seasons
1/4 tsp.pepper

9 cups day-old bread,
crumbs or 1/2" squares
9 cups mashed potatoes or
tater tots

In hot butter in deep kettle, saute onions until tender. Combine rest of ingredients; add to onions; heat well without browning; stirring frequently. Loosely stuff neck and body cavity of a 10-pound bird.

Creamed Chicken On Potato Patties

3/4 cup Creamy Sauce Mix (pg. 77)
1⅛ cup water
1½ cups cooked chicken chunks

1 cup fresh or frozen peas
1-oz. can chopped mushrooms, drained
potato patties from mashed potatoes

In a saucepan, combine the Creamy Sauce Mix and water. Cook and stir until thickened and bubbly; cook and stir 1 to 2 minutes more. Stir in cooked chicken, peas, and drained mushrooms; heat through. For each serving, place a hot Potato Patty on serving plate; ladle some of the chicken mixture over top. Or you can line pie pan with the potato mixture. Makes 6 servings.

Italian Chicken Potatoes

3 lb. broiler-fryer,cut up
1 cup tomato juice

2 med. potatoes, diced
1 tsp.salt; dash pepper; garlic

1 small onion, sliced
1/2 tsp. oregano

Bake chicken pieces; skin-side up, at 350 degrees for 30 minutes, or until golden brown; basting occasionally with pan juices. Drain off fat.
Add remaining ingredients; cover; bake 30 min. more or until chicken and vegetables are tender; basting frequently during cooking. Serves 4-6.

Chicken Loaf

1 boiling chicken
1 cup chicken broth
1 can Cr. Celery Soup

1 can Cr. Mushroom Soup
little poultry seasoning
and/or sage

1 cup mashed potatoes
1 large pkg. Ritz crackers,
crushed

Boil chicken until tender; set aside 1 cup broth. Cut chicken in small pieces. Mix broth with Cream of Mushroom, Cream of Celery Soups, potatoes, chicken and seasonings.
Line pan with cracker crumbs; 2/3 on bottom; add chicken mixture and sprinkle remainder of crumbs on top. Heat until hot or bake for 10-15 minutes in medium hot oven. Serve in squares.

Palouse Potato Delight

pkg.Idahoan Western Style
  Potatoes (save sauce pkt)
1 sm. onion, finely chopped
2 cups boiling water

1¼ cups milk
1/2 cup mayonnaise
1 tsp. curry powder
1/2 tsp ground coriander

1/2 tsp ground cardamon
1/4 tsp. ground turmeric
1 cup cooked lentils
2 C. chicken, cooked, diced

Preheat oven to 400 degrees. In a greased 3-quart casserole mix together potatoes, onion and boiling water. Bake uncovered for 20 minutes.
For curry sauce combine sauce packet, milk, mayonnaise, curry, coriander, cardamon, and turmeric in a saucepan. Cook on low heat until thickened. Cover; set aside. Mix lentils and chicken into potato mixture. Carefully fold in curry sauce. Return to oven and bake for 15 minutes.

132

Tater-Dipped Chicken

2 eggs, slightly beaten
1/4 cup water

1/2 tsp. salt; 1/8 tsp. pepper
12 chicken pieces

2 C. instant-mashed potatoes
1 cube butter

Heat oven to 400 degrees. Combine eggs, water, salt, & pepper. Dip chicken pieces in egg mixture; roll in potato flakes.

Meanwhile, melt butter in baking pan. Place layer of coated chicken pieces; skin side up, in pan of melted butter. Bake, uncovered 30 minutes. Turn and bake 30 min. longer. Makes 12 servings.

Louis Salad
(main course salad)

1 ½ cups diced cooked
  chicken or turkey breast
1 ½ cups diced cooked beets

1 ½ cups Gruyere cheese
2 med. potatoes, boiled,
  drained, diced

2 sm. grn. peppers, core, diced
6 Tbs. vinaigrette dressing
  (see page 19)
sm. head of romaine lettuce

For Garnish: Mild sliced onion, 2 sliced boiled eggs, 1 Tb. chopped chives

Mix chicken, beets, diced cheese, potatoes and peppers with the vinaigrette dressing; cover and let stand 1-2 hours. Divide the lettuce into leaves and place around a salad bowl. Pile the chicken mixture in the center; decorate with onion and egg slices and sprinkle the top with chives. Makes 4 servings.

Chips And Chicken

5 boneless, skinless whole
  chicken breasts
1 ½ cups pineapple juice
1/3 cup sour cream

1/3 cup milk
2/3 cup Cr. Celery Soup
2 3-oz cans deviled ham

1/4 C. grn. pepper, finely cut
2 ½ cups crushed potato chips
1/3 cup melted butter

Marinate boneless chicken breasts in pineapple juice 1 hour at room temperature, or overnight in fridge. Reserve 1/2 cup juice for basting. Heat oven to 375 degrees.

Mix sour cream, milk, undiluted celery soup and 1 can deviled ham. Stir in green pepper and potato chips. Pat inside of chicken breasts dry; spread with rest of deviled ham. Divide potato chip filling into 5 parts; spoon on each piece of chicken. Roll-up, fasten with skewers. Combine butter with 1/2 cup pineapple juice and warm over low heat. Place chicken upright in baking dish and baste.

Bake at 375 degrees for 50 minutes; basting at 15 minute intervals. Serve on a platter garnished with slices of fresh green pepper and tomato. Makes 5 servings.

133

Tarragon Chicken With Asparagus

3 Tbs. vegetable oil	salt to taste	1 lb. fresh asparagus
1 ½ lbs. skinned, boned	3 C. cooked, cubed, potatoes	1 Tb. lemon juice
chicken thighs; 1" pieces	1/2 cup water	1 tsp. dried tarragon

Heat 1 tablespoon oil in a Dutch oven. Add 1" chicken chunks; sprinkle with salt and cook over high heat; stirring often until browned. Reduce heat to medium and, stirring often, continue cooking until chicken is no longer pink in center.

Meanwhile heat remaining 2 tablespoons oil in a large skillet over medium heat. Add cooked, peeled, cubed potatoes and spread into an even layer. Cover and cook 3 minutes. Turn over; cover and cook 3 minutes longer until lightly browned and tender.

While potatoes cook, bring water to boiling in another skillet (large enough for the asparagus). Cut tough ends off; wash and add to the water. Cook 5 to 7 minutes until crisp-tender. Stir lemon juice and tarragon into chicken. Serve with the potatoes and asparagus. Makes 4 servings.

Chickenettes

4 chicken breasts	8 strips (1x3" Swiss cheese)	Accent (optional)
4 strips (1x3") boiled ham	Lawry's seasoned salt	instant potato flakes
		2 eggs, slightly beaten

Cut chicken breasts in two and remove all bones; make a slit in breast, the long way of meaty part. Place one slice of ham between 2 slices of cheese and stuff into slit in chicken breast. Roll meat and bring skin together and fasten with toothpicks making sure all the stuffing is well covered. Season with Accent and Lawry's salt.

Dip in potato flakes, then egg and again in potato flakes. Place in oiled baking dish; seam side down and bake in 350 degree oven for 45 minutes; then turn carefully with spatula, so as not to disturb coating and bake 45 minutes more until golden brown. Makes 4 to 6 servings.

Cheesy Patty Cakes

1/2 C. finely chopped celery	1 egg, beaten	dash pepper
2 Tbs. butter	1/4 cup sharp Am. cheese	1 cup chopped cooked turkey
1 ⅓ cups water	1 tsp. instant, minced onion	1/3 cup dry bread crumbs
4 servings instant potatoes	1 tsp. dried parsley flakes	cheese sauce (see pg. 77)

In skillet cook celery and butter until tender. Stir in water. Bring to boil; stir in mashed potatoes, egg, shredded cheese, onion, parsley, and pepper. Mix in turkey. Shape 12 patties; coat with crumbs. Cook on hot greased griddle over med. heat about 2 minutes on each side. Serve with Cheese Sauce.

Turkey-Tomato Bake

1/2 cup chopped onion	1 ½ cups chopped,cold turkey	1/4 cup shredded Am. cheese
1/2 cup chopped celery	1 can tomato soup	9-oz. pkg. frozen French-fried
1 Tb. butter	1/3 cup catsup	crinkle-cut potatoes
17-oz. can w/kernel corn, drained		

In skillet cook onion and celery in butter until vegetables are tender but not brown. Add corn, turkey, soup, catsup, and cheese. Turn into an 8x8x2" baking dish. Place potatoes on top. Bake, uncovered, at 425 for 25 min.

Turkey And Potato Bake
(or diced ham or chicken)

2 med. potatoes, peeled, sliced	2 cups turkey, cooked	1 can Cream Celery Soup
	1 med. onion, sliced	1/2 cup skim milk

In non-stick 8-inch baking pan, arrange in layers as follows: potatoes, turkey, onion slices. In small bowl, blend soup and milk; pour over potato/turkey mixture. Cover and bake at 375 degrees for 45 minutes. Uncover and bake 15 minutes longer or until potatoes are tender. Makes 4 servings.

Turkey Or Chicken Casserole

1/2 cup celery, diced	2 cups rice, cooked	3 C. cooked turkey or chicken
1/4 cup green pepper	2 cans Cream Chicken Soup	1 cup mayonnaise
1/4 cup onion, chopped	1 tsp. salt	4 boiled eggs, diced
2 Tbs. butter	2 tsp. lemon juice	1 cup crushed potato chips

Saute celery; chopped green peppers and onion in butter. Mix all ingredients except potato chips. Put into greased casserole. Top with potato chips and cook until heated through.

Turkey Hash Oven-Style

1 ½ cups coarse ground cooked turkey	1 cup cubed, cooked potato
1 can evaporated milk (2/3 cup)	1/4 cup snipped parsley
1/4 cup chopped onion	1 Tb. melted butter
1 tsp. Worcestershire sauce	1/4 cup crushed saltine crackers
1/4 tsp. ground sage	(about 7 crackers)

Stir together all ingredients except crackers and butter. Add **1/2 teaspoon salt; dash of pepper**. Turn into greased 1-quart casserole. Toss together crumbs and butter; sprinkle atop hash. Bake, uncovered, at 350 degrees until heated through, about 30 minutes. Makes 4 servings.

Roast Stuffed Goose

1 young goose, about 8 lbs.	1/4 tsp. ground ginger	1/4 cup port
2 Tbs. butter	1 ½ cups stock from	1 tsp. cornstarch mixed to
1/2 tsp. salt; 1/4 tsp. pepper	goose giblets	paste with 1 Tb. water

For Potato Stuffing:

3 med. onions, chopped	4 large potatoes,peeled,cut	1/2 tsp. sage
1/2 cup butter or cream	in 8 pieces	salt and pepper

For Garnish:

1/4 cup butter	1/2 cup red currant jelly	2 Tbs. red wine vinegar
10 sm. tart apples, peeled, cored		

Stuffing For Fowl: Cover onions with cold water; bring to boil; simmer 5 minutes, or until tender. Drain. Boil potatoes in salted water 15-20 minutes until soft; drain; return to pan. Dry over very low heat, shaking occasionally. Mash with potato masher or fork; add butter or cream, beating until potatoes are light. Take from heat, stir in onions, sage and season well.

Set oven at 375. Fill goose body with stuffing; sew or close each end. Cream 2 Tbs. butter with seasoning and ginger; spread over breast of bird. Set in roasting pan, roast for about 2 ½ hours; basting and turning bird occasionally to brown evenly. After 2 hours cooking, pour off fat; spoon the port over goose and continue cooking until skin is crisp.

For a garnish melt butter in baking dish. Put in apples; baste them with butter; bake in the same oven as the goose for 40 minutes, or until golden-brown. Put red currant jelly in pan with vinegar; melt over gentle heat.

Remove goose from oven; remove stitching and set on a hot platter. Arrange apples around and spoon melted jelly over them. Skim any fat from juices in roasting pan; add stock and boil well to dissolve juices.

Adjust seasoning and thicken, if desired, with the cornstarch mixture. Place in a gravy boat. Serve while hot. Makes 6 or more servings.

Cornish Game Hen Dinner

4 cornish game hens	black pepper, fresh-ground	lemon juice
	6 Tbs. butter, melted	

For Garnish: Watercress, lemon quarters and straw potatoes (see page 137)

With scissors, cut through backs of birds. Cut away the backbone; lay hens flat on a chopping block; skin side up; press down sharply with the palm of the hand so breastbone cracks and the bird lies flat. Run a skewer through legs to keep the birds flat. Sprinkle with pepper & lemon juice & brush with melted butter, keeping some for basting. Let set for 30 min.

Heat broiler. Place hens on broiler rack; skin side up; cook slowly until browned; brushing with butter from time to time. When brown, turn over; continue to broil other side, allowing about 7 minutes on each side.

Arrange cooked hens on a platter; pour over any juices from the broiler pan and garnish with watercress, lemon quarters and straw potatoes.

Straw Potatoes: Peel **1 lb. potatoes**, square the sides, as for French fries. Cut into slices 1/8 inch thick, then cut 1/8 inch wide. Soak in cold water for 30 minutes and dry thoroughly on paper towels. Heat pan of fat to 350 degrees.

Place the potatoes in a frying basket and fry 3-4 minutes or until soft. Lift out, heat fat to very hot, 375 degrees, put potatoes back in fat and cook 1 minute longer or until "straws" are golden-brown and crisp. Drain well. Sprinkle with **salt** and serve at once.

SEAFOOD DISHES:

"We'll siiiiiing for foooood."

Perfect Tuna Casserole

1 can Cr. Celery or Mushroom Soup	1 can (7-oz.) tuna fish, drained, flaked	1 cup cooked peas
1/4 cup milk	2 hard-cooked eggs, sliced	1/2 cup crumbled potato chips

Combine soup and milk in a buttered 1-quart casserole; stir in tuna, eggs and peas. Bake in preheated oven at 350 degrees for 25 minutes; stir. Top with crumbled chips; bake 5 minutes longer, or until hot. Makes 4 servings.

Tuna Casserole

1/3 cup butter	1 small onion, chopped	10-oz. pkg. frozen peas, thawed
3 Tbs. cornstarch	2 7-oz. cans tuna, drained	1 cup Cheddar cheese
1/2 tsp. salt; 1/4 tsp. pepper	8-oz. pkg elbow macaroni, cooked, drained	Crushed potato chips
3 cups milk		

Melt butter in a small pot over medium heat. Blend in corn starch, salt and pepper. Remove from heat and gradually stir in the milk until real smooth. Cook and stir all the time until the mixture comes to a boil and bubbles for 1 minute. Stir in the onion. Place the tuna, cooked macaroni, peas and shredded cheese in a greased 2-quart casserole. Stir in the sauce until it's well mixed. Sprinkle on a thick topping of crushed potato chips. Bake this in a 350 degree oven for over 20 minutes and serve hot. Makes 6 servings

Tuna-Broccoli Casserole

10-oz. pkg. frozen broccoli   1 can Cr. of Mushroom Soup   1/2 cup crushed potato chips
7-oz.can tuna,drained,flaked   1/2 soup can of milk

Heat oven to 450 degrees. Cook broccoli about 3 minutes; drain; Place in 1 ½ quart baking dish. Cover with tuna. Mix soup and milk; pour over tuna. Sprinkle potato chips on top. Bake 15 minutes. Makes 4 servings.

Tuna Potato Bake

1 can Cream of Celery Soup   2 Tbs. chopped parsley   4 cups cooked potatoes, cubed
1/3 cup water   1 tsp. lemon juice   2 7-oz. cans tuna, drained,
1/4 cup mayonnaise   1/8 tsp dry mustard   3 slices processed cheese cut
        in half diagonally

In a casserole dish blend soup, water, mayonnaise, parsley, lemon juice, and mustard. Stir in potatoes and flaked tuna. Bake at 400 degrees for 30 minutes or until hot; stir. Top with cheese. Bake 5 minutes longer or until cheese melts.

Tuna-Potato Scallop

3 cups potatoes, peeled, sliced   3/4 cup grated, processed, Am. cheese
7-oz. can tuna, drained, in pieces   2 Tbs. finely cut pimento

Set oven at 375 degrees. Grease 6x10 baking dish; put half the potatoes into the bottom of dish. Put half the tuna over potatoes. Top with half the cheese and pimento. Repeat, using the rest of the potatoes, tuna, cheese and pimento. Mix thoroughly and pour over mixture in baking dish: **1 can Cream Mushroom Soup** and **1 cup evaporated milk**. Bake for 50 minutes, or until potatoes are tender. Take from the oven and top with:

1/2 cup grated, processed Am. cheese   4-oz. can mushroom stems and pieces,
2 Tbs. finely cut pimento   drained

Bake 10 minutes more, or until cheese melts and mushrooms are hot. Serve hot. Makes 4 to 6 servings.

Baked Tuna Or Salmon Pie

2 pie crust pastry (pg. 106)   1/2 cup milk   1/2 lb. Am. cheese, sliced
2 C. diced cooked potatoes   1 tsp. salt & 1/8 tsp. pepper   1 can Cr. Tomato or Mushrm.
1/4 cup chopped grn. onion   6½-oz. can tuna or 7-oz. can   Soup
2 Tbs. chopped grn. pepper   salmon, drained, flaked

Heat oven; 425 degrees. Mix potato, onion, green pepper, milk, salt and pepper; spread in pastry-lined 9" pie pan. Place tuna, then cheese over mixture. Cover with top crust; make slits; bake 35-40 minutes. Cut in wedges and serve with light thinned Cream of Tomato or Mushroom Soup. Makes 6 servings

Tuna Hash

1 Tb. butter	2 C. potatoes, cooked, diced	1/2 cup onion, chopped
2 7-oz. cans drained tuna	1 can (7¾-oz.) chicken	3 Tbs. pimento, chopped
1 tsp. celery salt	gravy or make your own	dash pepper

In medium skillet, heat butter. Meanwhile, in medium bowl, combine remaining ingredients. Spread tuna mixture in skillet and cook 15 minutes until browned on one side. Turn over and cook 15 minutes more until heated through and browned on other side. Makes 2 servings.

MISCELLANEOUS FISH DISHES:

"Looking good. I think I'll let you do this every night."

Fish And Spud Bake

1 lb. fresh or frozen	3 med. potatoes, peeled,	salt and pepper
perch or other fish	quartered	1/4 cup milk
10-oz. pkg. frozen spinach	1 beaten egg	3/4 cup Herb Stuffing (pg. 79)
milk for potatoes	1/2 cup dairy sour cream	2 Tbs. melted butter
		Lemon slices (optional)

Skin fish fillets; set aside. In medium saucepan, cook chopped spinach according to package directions. Drain; pressing out excess liquid. Cook potatoes in boiling water just until tender; drain; mash; blend in beaten egg and sour cream. If necessary, add enough milk to make potatoes fluffy, yet stiff enough to hold their shape. Season with salt and pepper, if desired. Stir in well-drained spinach.

Turn into 6x10x2-inch baking dish. Dip fish fillets in the 1/4 cup milk, then in crushed Herb Stuffing Mix. Place atop potato mixture; drizzle with the melted butter or margarine.

Bake, uncovered, in 350 degree oven for 30-40 minutes or until fish flakes easily when tested with a fork. Serve with lemon slices, if desired. Makes 4 or 5 servings.

Fish Casserole

2/3 cup smoked bacon	2 med. cucumbers	1/2 bay leaf
2 med. onions	1 ½ lbs. codfish fillet or	juice from 1/2 lemon
1 cup broth	other fish	3/4 cup baby Gouda
4 med. potatoes	4-5 sm. peeled tomatoes	

Cube the bacon; cut onion into rings; saute together until glazed. Add the broth. Add the following ingredients in layers: peeled potatoes and cucumbers, cut into small cubes or slices. If desired, spoon out the pulp and cut cucumber into 1-inch sticks.

Cut the salted fish fillets into 2 inch cubes, and lay the whole tomatoes on top. Add the seasonings; boil, and simmer for 20 minutes. Sprinkle lemon juice on top of casserole, (or put in dish and serve with the casserole.) Then blend in the cubed Gouda (cheese); let melt and serve. Makes 2 servings.

Favorite Potato Cheese Halibut

6 halibut filets or white	1 ½ tsp. horseradish	dash hot pepper sauce
fish, cut 3/4" thick	1/2 cup Swiss cheese, grated	1/2 tsp. garlic salt
1/2 cup mayonnaise	1/3 cup Parmesan cheese	white pepper to taste
1/4 cup lemon juice	2 Tbs. onion, minced	2/3 cup Idahoan Mashed
		Potatoes (dry flakes)

Preheat oven to 450 degrees. Cover broiler pan with aluminum foil and grease well. In medium bowl mix mayonnaise, lemon juice, horseradish, Swiss cheese, grated Parmesan cheese, onion, hot pepper sauce and garlic salt. Add white pepper to taste. Fold in potato flakes and mix well.

Spread mixture evenly over fillets. Place filets on broiler pan. Reduce oven temperature to 400; bake for 10-15 minutes. Turn oven to broil and cook until tops are golden brown. Fish flakes when done. Makes 6 servings.

Salmon Shepherd's Pie

15 ½-oz. can salmon	1/4 cup each, butter & flour	1 cup Cheddar cheese
10-oz. pkg. frozen peas	1/2 tsp. salt; 1/4 tsp. pepper	2 tsp. instant minced onion
4-oz. can mushrooms,	2 cups milk	3 cups mashed potatoes
		Parmesan cheese

Drain and flake salmon; remove bone. Cook and drain frozen peas. Combine salmon, mushrooms, and peas.

In a saucepan, melt butter; stir in flour, salt and pepper. Gradually add milk; blending for a smooth sauce. Add shredded cheese and stir until melted. Add onion and stir in. Combine sauce with salmon, mushrooms and peas.

Spoon this into a greased 2 quart casserole dish. Spoon mashed potatoes on top of salmon mixture. Sprinkle with parmesan cheese. Bake at 350 degrees for 20-25 minutes or until potatoes are lightly browned, and bubbly hot. Makes about 4 servings.

A Slimming Salmon Loaf

2 sm. cans salmon, drained
1 Tb. onion, minced
1/2 tsp. salt; dash pepper

2 eggs
1 Tb. parsley, chopped

1 cup mashed potatoes, using
skim milk

In medium bowl, with fork, combine all ingredients until well blended. Spread in baking dish, or individual baking molds. Bake at 375 degrees for 40 minutes in loaf pan or baking dish; 20 minutes in individual molds. Makes 5 servings, about 180 calories each.

Salmon Potato Strata

16-oz. can salmon, drained
1 med. onion, chopped
1/2 cup chopped celery

4 eggs
2 cups low fat milk
1 ½ tsp. salt, divided

1/4 tsp. dried dill
1/8 tsp pepper
4 med. Idaho potatoes (6
cups) unpared, sliced

In large bowl combine salmon, onion, celery, eggs, milk, 1/2 teaspoon salt, dill and pepper; mix well. Cut potatoes into thin slices. Place half of potatoes in greased 1 ½ quart baking dish. Sprinkle with 1/2 teaspoon salt and spread half of salmon mixture over potatoes. Repeat with remaining potatoes, salt and salmon.

Bake uncovered in a 350 degree oven 1 ¼ hours, or until potatoes are tender when pierced with a fork. Remove from oven and let stand 5 minutes before serving. Makes 8 servings.

Salmon Potato Pie

4 cups grated raw potatoes
1 ¼ cup minced onion
4 eggs
1/4 cup all-purpose flour

1/2 tsp. salt; 1/8 tsp. pepper
1/4 cup vegetable oil
1 C. cream or evap. milk
3 Tbs. minced, fresh dill

2 cups cooked salmon
1 ½ cups Cheddar cheese
paprika

Mix potatoes, 1/2 cup of the onion, 1 egg, the flour, salt, and pepper. Grease a 10" pie pan and press the potato mixture into the pan to make a crust. Brush the crust with oil and bake at 400 degrees for 20 minutes.

In a fry pan, heat 1 tablespoon of the vegetable oil and saute the remaining 3/4 cup onion until translucent; 3 to 5 minutes. Remove the skin and bones from the salmon and break it up. Beat together the remaining 3 eggs, cream, and dill.

When the crust is done, remove from the oven and reduce the heat to 350 degrees. Sprinkle the sauteed onion over the bottom of the pie. Arrange the salmon over the onion. Cover with grated cheese and sprinkle with paprika. Brush the edge of the crust with oil, and bake the pie for 30-40 minutes or until it is set. Allow the pie to sit for 10 minutes before serving. Makes 8 servings.

Dilled Salmon Pie

1 beaten egg	1 Tb. melted butter	4 serving pkg. instant mashed
1/2 cup milk	1/2 tsp. salt	potatoes
2 cups soft bread crumbs	16-oz. can salmon	dill sauce (see below)
1 Tb. chopped onion	1 egg	

Mix together egg, milk, crumbs, onion, butter, and salt until crumbs are moistened. Add drained flaked salmon with bones and skin removed; mix well. Turn into greased 8-inch pie plate.

Prepare instant potatoes according to package directions; omitting milk. Beat in the remaining egg. Spoon around edge of pie. Bake at 350 degrees for 30 to 35 minutes. Pass Dill Sauce. Makes 4 to 6 servings.

Dill Sauce:

Melt **1 tablespoon butter or margarine**. Blend in **1 tablespoon all-purpose flour**. Stir in **1¼ cups milk, 1 teaspoon sugar, 3/4 teaspoon dried dill-weed, and 1/2 teaspoon salt**. Cook and stir until thickened and bubbly. Combine **1/2 cup dairy sour cream and 1 tablespoon lemon juice**. Gradually stir into hot mixture. Heat through but do not boil.

Alaska Salmon Moroccan-Style

1 sm. onion, sliced	4 tsp. honey	1½ tsp. lemon juice
2 clove garlic, minced	1 tsp. grated lemon peel	6 (4-6-oz. ea.) thawed Alaska
1 Tb. olive oil	3/4 tsp. ground cumin	salmon fillets
1 can (28-oz. whole peeled	salt,black pepper & cayenne	1 pkg. fried hash browns
tomatoes, chopped	pepper to taste	2 Tbs. toasted almonds
		2 Tbs. chopped cilantro

Saute onions and garlic in olive oil in a medium skillet over medium high heat until golden. Stir in tomatoes, tomato liquid, honey, lemon peel and cumin. Simmer 10-15 minutes. Stir in lemon juice and season with salt, pepper and cayenne, to taste. Season salmon fillets with salt and pepper.

Broil 4-6 inches from heat, allowing 10 minutes per inch of thickness, measured at thickest part. Fry 1 package of hash browns;, place some on each plate. Place each steak on top of hash browns. Top with tomato sauce; sprinkled with chopped almonds and cilantro.

Quickie Salmon Potato Casserole

16-oz. can red salmon	1/4 tsp. celery salt	1½ biscuits of shredded
1 can potato soup	1/8 tsp. black pepper	wheat, broken into shreds
1/2 cup evaporated milk		1 Tb. butter

Drain salmon; remove dark skin and bones. Break salmon into 1-inch pieces. Heat potato soup with milk, celery, salt and pepper; add salmon. Pour mixture into a well-greased casserole. Cover with shredded wheat; dot with butter. Place under broiler a few minutes to brown. Makes 4 servings.

New Potato-Stuffed Rainbow Trout

New potatoes, black olives and capers (optional) make a savory stuffing for rainbow trout. A green salad completes the menu.

1 ½ lbs. red new potatoes, cooked
1/2 cup fresh parsley, chopped
1/4 cup capers (optional)
1/4 cup green or black olives, sliced
1 tsp. olive oil
3/4 tsp salt
1/2 tsp.freshly ground black pepper

1 tsp. fresh lemon juice
salt & freshly ground black pepper
4 whole boned Idaho Rainbow Trout,
  (8-oz. each) or other fish
1/2 cup chicken or vegetable broth
olive oil
2 lemons, thinly sliced

Cut potatoes into large cubes. Put into mixing bowl with parsley, capers, olives, 1 tsp. olive oil, 3/4 tsp. salt and 1/2 tsp. freshly ground black pepper. Mix well and set aside.

Sprinkle inside of each trout with lemon juice, salt and pepper. Stuff each trout with one-fourth of potato mixture. Pour broth into baking pan. Place stuffed trout in pan. Brush trout with olive oil and top with lemon slices. Cover pan with foil and bake at 400 degrees for about 15 minutes, until trout flakes easily with a fork. Makes 4 servings.

Shrimp Stuffed Potatoes

6 med. potatoes
1 ½ Tbs. butter

1 3/4 tsp salt;1/4 tsp.pepper
1/2 cup milk

6-oz. can shrimp
1 tsp. fresh lemon juice

Scrub and bake potatoes in a hot oven, 375 degrees, about 1 hour or until tender when tested with a fork. Cut a horizonal slice off the top. Scoop out potato. Add butter or margarine and mash with the potato. Beat in salt, ground black pepper, and milk. Save 6 shrimp for garnish and add remaining shrimp (broken into pieces) to potatoes along with lemon juice and mix well.

Spoon mixture back into potato shells and garnish each with a whole shrimp. Makes 6 servings.

Shrimp Broccoli Dish

1 lb. fresh or frozen
  broccoli

2 Tbs. onion, minced
dab of butter

2 cans Cream of Shrimp Soup
8-oz. cream cheese
crushed potato chips

Cook broccoli as directed until tender. Put in greased 9x13-inch pan. Saute onion in butter, until slightly browned. Heat soup (no water added) and add cream cheese and onion. Mix well. Pour over broccoli. Top with crushed potato chips. Makes 4 servings.

Scallops with Red Wine/Mushrooms

1 lb. scallops	1 clove garlic, crushed	2 tomatoes, peeled, cut in
1/4 cup water	2 Tbs. flour	8 pieces
juice of 1 sm. lemon	3/4 C. fish or veg.stock	1/4 cup browned bread crumbs
3 Tbs. butter	2 tsp. tomato paste	1/4 cup melted butter
1 onion chopped	salt & black pepper	mashed potatoes for piping
1 cup mushrooms	3/4 cup red wine	1 Tb. chopped parsley

In a shallow pan, combine scallops, water and lemon juice. Cover and poach 3-4 minutes. Drain scallops, reserving the liquid. Melt 3 tablespoons butter in saucepan, add finely-chopped onion; cover; cook gently 2 minutes. Add quartered mushrooms; increase heat, cook briskly until tender. Remove from heat; stir in garlic, flour, stock or cooking liquid, tomato paste and seasoning. Bring to a boil, stirring, and simmer 2-3 minutes.

Boil wine in small pan until reduced by one-third. Add to the sauce and simmer another 5 minutes. Add tomatoes to sauce with the scallops and spoon into baking dishes. Sprinkle with bread crumbs tossed in melted butter. Spoon or pipe mashed potatoes around the outside. Bake at 400 degrees for 5-7 minutes or until brown. Scatter with chopped parsley just before serving. Makes 4 servings.

Chip And Cheese Scallops

1 lb. frozen scallops	1/2 cup milk	2 Tbs. canned pimento
1 Tb. chopped onion	3-oz. can chopped,	1 Tbs. snipped parsley
3 Tbs. butter	mushrooms, drained	1/2 cup shredded cheese
3 Tbs.all-purpose flour	2 Tbs. Parmesan cheese	1 ½ cups potato chips,
1/8 tsp. pepper		crushed

Thaw frozen scallops; rinse. Cover with cold water; bring to boil; reduce heat; simmer 2 minutes. Drain, reserving 1 cup liquid. Slice scallops about 1/4" thick. Cook onion in butter until tender. Blend in flour and pepper. Add reserved cooking liquid and milk. Cook and stir until thickened. Remove from heat. Stir in mushrooms, grated Parmesan cheese, chopped pimento, parsley and scallops. Turn into 1 ½ quart casserole; sprinkle with shredded cheese and top with potato chips. Bake at 350 degrees for 20-25 minutes. Makes 6 servings.

AN AWARD WINNING RECIPE:

This recipe is taken from a magazine called "COUNTRY", (a wonderful magazine). The section taken from is entitled...**The Best Cook in the Country!** This recipe was submitted by Norbert Manko of Iron Mountain, Michigan. The article, in part, says: "...looked forward to retirement. Like most men, he wanted to devote time to new hobbies. But unlike most men, Norbert's favorite hobby became cooking!" His recipe freezes well. Try it---you will love it---I did!!!

Swedish Potato Sausage

15 pounds potatoes, peeled	5 to 7 tablespoons salt
3 pounds onions, peeled	4 tablespoons pepper
3 pounds boneless pork butt	3 tablespoons ground allspice
3 pounds ground beef	1 ½ teaspoons ground nutmeg
1/3 cup all-purpose flour	1/2 to 3/4 cup milk

In a food grinder using the coarse disk, alternately process the potatoes, onions and pork. Combine with the ground beef. Mix until well distributed. Combine all dry ingredients and sprinkle over potato/meat mixture. Add milk and mix well. Sausage may be made into patties or stuffed into hog casings. Use immediately or freeze in serving-size portions. Makes about 20 pounds of potato sausage.

SIDE DISHES

Creamed potatoes are truly delicious
A side dish that wins every time
If you want to be a great hostess
They'll make your meals sublime.
--by Carol Fielding McCabe

Information & Tips

Idaho potato cooks **DO NOT** wrap potatoes in foil and call them a **"BAKED POTATO"**. A potato wrapped in foil is a steamed potato. The taste is totally different.

New potatoes with delicate skins should be scrubbed; unpeeled, except removing of a narrow belt around the potatoes which helps to keep them from bursting during cooking.

Mashed potatoes prepared by steaming them unpeeled and passing them through a hot ricer or food mill have far more flavor than those which have been peeled before boiling.

Mashed potatoes are great by themselves but try them seasoned with chives, tarragon, chili powder, curry, or any favorite herb or spice. The bland flavor of potatoes is delicious with high-speaking seasonings.

Dehydrated potato flakes and granules can't always be used interchangeable in a recipe, because they are not equal by volume measure. Substitutions may be made based on weight measure or on the amount of dehydrated potatoes needed to make equal amounts of mashed potatoes.

When not immediately using uncooked peeled potatoes, soak in cold water to prevent darkening. Do not keep in water too long as nutrients will be lost.

Never throw away beef or chicken broth. Freeze in containers to use later with potato dishes not calling for meat, but wanting the meat flavor.

A party tip to cut down the high cost of entertaining: use frozen french fries for appetizers. Cook them crisp, serve with a ketchup or sour cream dip, cheese, or sprinkle with curry or chili powder. They'll be the life of the party--and so economical.

Potatoes are a rich source of vitamin C. They are richer in nutrients than in calories. A medium-sized potato provides as much vitamin C as an orange; it furnishes several B vitamins, important trace minerals and vegetable protein. The potato's potassium level is as great as banana's, but it contains fewer calories.

CREAMED STYLE
SIDE DISHES:

"The potatoes aren't the only "appealing" thing in the kitchen."

Dorene's Scalloped Potatoes

1 can Cr. Mushroom or
  Cr. Chicken Soup
1 cup evaporated milk
milk to cover

salt & pepper to taste
6 heaping cups sliced,
  pared potato
1 ½ cups grated carrots

2 large onions, chopped
1/2 cube butter
1/2 cup grated cheese

In a large electric frying pan set at medium heat, stir together until smooth the creamed soup, evaporated milk, milk, salt and pepper. Mix together the potatoes, carrots, and onions. Add to the mixture in the frying pan, stirring until well mixed. The semi-thick liquid should cover the potatoes. If not, add milk and mix in. Place the butter in small pats on top of the potato mixture.

Cover and let cook until potatoes are tender but not over cooked. They are best when slightly chewy. Stir occasionally with a pancake turner being careful not to break up the potato slices. (You may have some sticking on the bottom of the pan in the area of the heating element. If the heat is low enough this will not be a problem as it will mix together when stirred. If it sticks too much do not try to mix it in.) Place in a serving dish and sprinkle with the grated cheese. Cover and let set until cheese is melted. Serve hot or cold. Makes 8 or so servings.

Note: This dish can be cooked in the electric fry pan, the oven or the dutch oven. It is a wonderful basic scallop potato recipe. I call this my "clean out the fridge" dinner. Left over cooked or canned (drained) vegetables or meats can be added just before it's done. After adding the left overs, top with grated cheese, then cook until vegetables are heated through and cheese is melted, about 10 minutes.

Variation #1: Replace the Cream of Mushroom soup with Cream of Celery soup, add 3 diced ribs of celery, replace the cheese with shredded sharp cheese and garnish with thin slices of tomatoes and sprigs of parsley.

Variation #2: Use the Creamy Chicken Mushroom Soup, add any combination of vegetable, such as chopped onions, chopped celery, chopped green pepper, grated carrots, chopped cabbage, or cauliflower, or broccoli, and etc. Add a tablespoon or two of salsa. Top with both mozzarella and cheddar cheese.

Variation #3: Turn this side dish into a main dish by browning ground beef and adding to the potato mixture.

"My" Easy Scalloped Potatoes

1 lb.frozen hash browns   1/2 pt. sour cream   1 cup grated sharp cheese
  (not Southern style)   1/4 cup diced onion   1/2 can Cr. Chicken Soup
salt and pepper   1/4 cup melted butter

Place ingredients in a greased casserole. Mix together 1 cup crushed corn flakes, 1/4 cup melted butter and place on top of the ingredients in the casserole. Bake, uncovered, for 45 minutes at 350 degrees.

Cheesy Scalloped Potatoes

1 can Cheddar Cheese Soup 1 to 2 Tbs. salsa.   1/2 cup chopped celery
1/2 soup can evaporated milk 5 to 6 cups sliced potatoes 1/2 cup grated Mozzarella
cheese
1/2 soup can milk   1 or 2 chopped onions   1/2 cup grated Cheddar cheese
seasoning salt   3/4 cup grated carrots

In a baking dish stir together until smooth the Cheddar Cheese Soup, evaporated milk, milk, seasoning salt and salsa. Mix together the potatoes, onions, carrots and celery; add to the soup mixture, adding more milk if a thinner mixture is desired. Liquid mixture should coat the vegetables well.

Cover with lid or foil and let cook until potatoes are slightly chewy. Ten minutes before done sprinkle the grated cheese evenly over the potatoes. Finish cooking, uncovered until cheese melts, about 10 minutes.

Fast Potato-Vegetable Scallop
with packaged potatoes

5½-oz. pkg. dry   1/2 cup sliced onion   2 Tbs. butter
  scalloped potato mix   1/4 tsp. celery seed   1/2 cup shredded sharp process
10-oz. pkg.frozen   2½ cup boiling water   American cheese
  mixed vegetables

Preheat oven to 400 degrees. Place dried potatoes from mix in 1½ quart casserole. Sprinkle with the envelope of sauce mix from package. Top with frozen mixed vegetables, sliced onion, and celery seed. Pour boiling water over all; stir until well combined. Dot with butter. Cover; bake until potatoes are tender, about 35 minutes. Uncover; sprinkle with shredded cheese. Return to oven until cheese melts, 2-3 minutes more. Makes 6 servings.

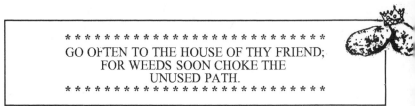

* *
GO OFTEN TO THE HOUSE OF THY FRIEND;
FOR WEEDS SOON CHOKE THE
UNUSED PATH.
* *

Side Dishes

Heavenly Potatoes

2 lbs. frozen cubed potatoes
  or 8 med. cooked, sliced
3/4 cube butter, melted
1 pint sour cream

2 cans undiluted Cr. of
  Chicken Soup
1 med. onion, chopped
1/2 tsp. salt

2 cups grated cheese
2½ cups crushed corn flakes
6 Tbs. butter, melted

Combine all ingredients except the last two. Put in a 9x13 inch baking dish. Mix 6 tablespoons melted butter and corn flakes together and sprinkle over top. Bake in a 350 degree oven for 45 minutes. (So good! One of my favorite recipes)

Creamy Au Gratin Potatoes

1/2 cup chopped onion
1 can Cr. Mushroom Soup

3-oz. pkg. cream cheese,
  cut in cubes

3-4 C.frozen hash-browns
1/3 cup shredded cheese

Cook onion until tender. Stir in undiluted soup and cream cheese cubes; cook stirring constantly until smooth and hot. In casserole, alternate layers of frozen potatoes and hot cream sauce ending with a sauce layer. Cover and bake 45 minutes or until sauce is bubbly and potatoes are tender. Remove from oven and sprinkle with shredded cheese.

Potato And Tomato Au Gratin

4 med. potatoes, peeled
1 pat butter
1 cup cheese sauce

1 egg, beaten
2 med. tomatoes, sliced
1 onion, finely chopped

salt and pepper
1½-oz. aged cheese
parsley

Thinly slice the potatoes; put a layer in the bottom of buttered casserole dish. Cover with half the cheese sauce. Pour the egg on top then add the slices of tomato, the onion, salt, pepper and the rest of the potatoes. Pour remaining cheese sauce over the top.

Sprinkle with grated cheese; bake in pre-heated oven 325 degrees for 30 minutes until golden brown and cooked through. Sprinkle with finely-chopped parsley. Makes 4 servings.

Potatoes And Peas Au Gratin

2 lb. small new potatoes
1 bu. green onions, sliced

2 cups frozen peas
2 cups thin cream sauce

1/4 cup grated cheese

Cook potatoes with jackets until tender; peel. Cook onions and peas together in **bacon grease** until tender. Make a cream sauce with **2 tablespoons butter, 2 tablespoons flour, 1 teaspoon salt and 2 cups milk**. Arrange vegetables in buttered baking dish. Add cream sauce; sprinkle with grated cheese. Brown at 350 degrees for 20 minutes. Makes 6 servings.

Variation: Replace the cream sauce with 1/2 can Cream Chicken or Cream Mushroom soup, 1/3 cup evaporated milk and 1 cup sour cream.

147

Potatoes Au Gratin

4 med. potatoes	1/2 cup Am. cheese, grated	1 cup crumbs
1/2 green pepper or pimento	3 Tbs. butter	3 slices bacon
2 cups med. thick white sauce		

Boil, peel and slice the potatoes in half-inch slices. Cut the pimento or green pepper in thin shreds. Prepare a medium white sauce (below). Grate the cheese and add to the white sauce; stir until blended. Melt butter; pour over the crumbs.

Set oven at 350 degrees, and lightly grease the casserole. Assemble the casserole in this manner; place alternate layers of sliced potatoes, white sauce, and a sprinkling of the pimento or green pepper, top this mixture with crumbs. Lay the strips of bacon on top. Bake covered for 20 minutes. Take the top off for browning, and cook another 10 minutes.

Creamy White Sauce Mix: **1⅓ cups nonfat dry milk, 3/4 cup all-purpose flour, 1 teaspoon salt, 1/2 cup butter**: In mixing bowl, combine milk powder, flour, and salt. Cut in butter until crumbly. Place in a sealed container and refrigerate until needed. Makes 3 cups.

Medium White Sauce: In a saucepan combine **1/2 cup "Creamy Sauce Mix"** and **1 cup cold water**. Cook and stir until bubbly. Cook and stir 2 minutes more. Makes 1 cup.

New Potato Gratin With Garden Vegetables

3 lbs. new, peeled, sliced potatoes	salt and pepper to taste
3 cups sliced, or chunked fresh	2 cup heavy cream
garden vegetables, such as green	1 ½ cup chicken broth
onions, turnips, spinach or chard,	1/2 cup grated Swiss cheese
peas, beans, cabbage, etc.	

Heat oven to 350 degrees. Peel and thinly slice potatoes. Peel if needed, slice or cube garden vegetables. Toss together lightly. Place potatoes and vegetables in greased baking dish and sprinkle with salt and pepper. Mix cream and chicken broth. Pour at edge of dish to barely cover mixture.

Bake covered 1/2 hour, then uncovered for additional 1/2 hour or until done. Sprinkle cheese on top and return to oven until cheese is melted. Excellent served with sliced fresh tomatoes and chives or parsley.

Creamy Potato Bake

4-6 servings mashed potatoes	2 Tb. parsley
4-oz. whipped cream cheese	1/4 cup diced onion
1 beaten egg	

Combine cheese and potatoes; beat well. Stir in egg, onion, parsley. Turn into greased 1-quart casserole and bake at 400 degrees for 30 minutes. Serves 4-6.

Cauliflower With Potato Au Gratin

1 cauliflower, divided into sprigs
4 medium potatoes, sliced
Mornay Sauce (see below)

2 Tbs. butter
1/2 cup grated Gruyere or Parmesan
   cheese for sprinkling

Parboil potato slices in boiling salted water for 8-10 minutes, or until almost tender; drain. Cook cauliflower in boiling salted water for 8-10 minutes or until just tender; drain. (A bay leaf added to the water will remove any odor of cauliflower.) Arrange the potatoes overlapping in a shallow buttered baking dish, and put the cauliflower sprigs around the edge. Spoon the mornay sauce into the center to coat the potatoes. Dot the cauliflower with butter; sprinkle the whole dish with grated cheese and bake in a moderately hot oven (375 degrees) for 10-15 minutes or until browned.

Mornay Sauce: Add together 1½ tablespoons butter, 1½ tablespoons flour, 1 cup milk, 1/4 cup grated Gruyere or dry Cheddar cheese, 1/2 teaspoons prepared mustard, salt and pepper. Mix well.

Hot Curried Potatoes

6 med. potatoes
1/3 cup butter
2 Tbs. chopped onion
3 Tbs. flour

1 tsp. curry powder
1/2 tsp. salt
1¼ cup chicken broth
2 Tbs. vinegar

1 red apple, cored & cut in
   wedges
1/2 cup sliced celery
1/2 cup halved, grapes

Place unpared potatoes in a large saucepan. Cover with water; bring to a boil and simmer until potatoes are tender. Drain and cool slightly. Peel and cut into 1/4 inch slices.

In large skillet heat butter; add onion and cook until transparent. Blend in flour, curry powder and salt; cook, stirring constantly, for 1 or 2 minutes. Slowly stir in chicken broth and vinegar; cook, stirring constantly, until thickened. Add potatoes, apple, celery and seeded grapes. Heat 5 minutes. Serve immediately. Makes 4 to 6 servings.

Rich And Creamy Potatoes

3 Tbs. butter
1 sm. garlic clove, minced

6 cups grated raw potatoes
1¼ to 1½ cups light cream

salt and pepper
1 cup grated Swiss cheese

Melt butter in a large skillet, and saute the garlic until golden. Add the potatoes and cream, and saute for 2-3 minutes. Transfer the mixture to a greased 9x13 inch baking dish and sprinkle with salt and pepper. Sprinkle the cheese on top.

Bake the potatoes for 30 minutes in a 325 degree oven, or until golden brown on top. Cut into squares and serve. Makes 6 to 8 servings.

PATTIES, PUFFS, SKINS, FRIED & FRIES:

"Look Ruff, we could make our own fries."

Potato Patties

2 cups cold mashed potatoes	1/4 cup chopped onion	salt and pepper
1 beaten egg	1/4 cup chopped celery	2 Tbs. melted butter

In mixing bowl, combine mashed potatoes, beaten egg, finely chopped onion, finely chopped celery, salt, and pepper to taste. Mix well. Measure about 1/3 cup of the potato mixture into well-oiled hamburger press, or form by hand making a uniform patty. Repeat to make 5 more patties.

In large skillet, brown patties slowly in butter or margarine about 5 minutes or until golden brown on each side. Makes 6 patties.

Potato Rutabaga Cake

4 cup rutabagas or turnips	1/2 cup minced onion	2 Tbs. vegetable oil
2 cups grated potatoes	2 Tbs. butter	Salt and pepper

Mix the grated rutabagas, potatoes, and onion. Melt 1 tablespoon butter and 1 tablespoon oil in a large cast iron or non-stick frying pan. Spoon in the vegetable mixture; flatten it evenly in the pan, and sprinkle with salt and pepper.

Turn the heat to medium low; cover the pan, and fry the cake until it is golden brown on the bottom, 10 to 15 minutes. To turn the cake slip it out of the pan onto a plate. Place another plate on top of the cake and invert it.

Add the remaining 1 tablespoon butter and 1 tablespoon oil to the pan and heat. Slip the cake back into the pan to brown the second side. Fry uncovered until browned. Slice into wedges to serve. Makes 6 servings.

Sicilian Potatoes

1 small orange	1/2 cup butter	1 Tb. butter
pinch of baking soda	2 shallots, finely chopped	1 egg yolk (optional)
3-4 medium potatoes	salt and pepper	

Put orange in pan of water with pinch of baking soda; cover, boil 45-50 minutes. Peel potatoes; cook in boiling salted water 15-20 minutes or until tender; drain thoroughly. Mash them with a potato masher, blender or work through a sieve, and transfer to a bowl. Set oven at 400 degrees. Drain orange; cut in quarters and remove all seeds. Chop the quarters, including the rind, very finely.

Melt half the butter in small saucepan; add the shallots; cook until lightly browned. Add the chopped orange; cook, uncovered, for several minutes until fairly dry. Stir mixture into potatoes with a fork; season with salt and pepper and beat in 1 tablespoon of butter and the egg yolk, if used. Melt remaining butter; brush 2 baking sheets with it.

Shape the potato mixture into balls the size of walnuts. Arrange these on the baking sheets, allowing space between each one, and flatten each potato ball with a fork to 1/4 inch thickness. Bake in heated oven for 10-15 minutes or until well browned.

Remove baking sheets from oven and slip spatula under potato cakes to loosen. Serve Sicilian potatoes, overlapping, on a hot platter with the browned, almost caramelized, underside on top. These crisp potato cakes also make good cocktail hors d'oeuvre.

Potatoes 'N Eggs

1/2 cup salad oil	2 eggs, well beaten	paprika
4 potatoes, peeled, sliced	salt and pepper	

Heat oil in large skillet, place potatoes in skillet and cook on low, covered, until potatoes are soft but not brown. Drain off all but 1 tablespoon of oil. Pour eggs over potatoes; add salt and pepper to taste; sprinkle with paprika. Cook on low, lifting edges to allow uncooked egg to flow to bottom. Eat hot or cold for sandwiches. Makes 4 servings.

Baked Potato Rosettes

2 lbs. mashing potatoes	2/3 cup butter	dash of nutmeg
dash of salt	3 eggs	

Wash potatoes; peel. Boil in saltwater until tender. Drain the water; let the steam out and mash the potatoes. Blend in the butter; gradually add the eggs and season with nutmeg. The mixture has to be smooth and glossy. Preheat the oven to 400 degrees. Lightly grease the baking sheet. Spoon the potato mixture onto the sheet or squirt out small rosettes with a decorating gun. Bake until golden yellow for 10-15 minutes and serve immediately. Makes 8 servings.

Browned Potatoes

4 med. potatoes, peeled	1/2 tsp. salt; dash of pepper	1 cup middle-aged Gouda
4 Tbs. butter	dash of oregano	1 bunch chives
2 med onions, sliced	4 peeled tomatoes	

Cut potatoes into thin slices, and blot dry. Melt butter in frying pan; add the potatoes. Cut onions into rings or half-moons; arrange over potatoes; lightly salt. Cook potatoes until light-yellow in color. Cover; let simmer for 5 more minutes. Flip over with spatula; let other side turn golden yellow and crispy. Season with oregano and pepper. Cut tomatoes into eighths and cheese into small squares; lay over potatoes. Cook 3-4 minutes; blend carefully and serve with diced chives.

Swiss Frosted Potatoes

This is a good recipe for left over potato pulp.
Mash **5 cups mashed potatoes**; add **3/4 cup milk, 1/4 cup butter or margarine, 1/2 tsp. salt and dash pepper**. Place in buttered, shallow 2-quart baking dish. Whip **1/2 cup heavy cream** until soft peaks form. Fold **1 cup shredded Swiss cheese** and **2 tablespoons chopped green onion** into whipped cream; **salt and pepper** to taste. Spread mixture over potatoes. Bake at 350 degrees about 45 min. or until golden brown. Serves 6-8.

Westphalian Potato Cakes

2 lbs. potatoes	salt and black pepper	lard or oil for frying
2-3 eggs	flour	chopped parsley
1/2 lb. aged cheese		

Boil potatoes until tender; drain; mash well (potatoes must be as dry as possible). Beat the eggs; stir with grated cheese, into potatoes. Season to taste with salt and pepper; knead mixture to make stiff dough; adding flour if necessary. Shape a heaping tablespoon full into flat round cakes; dip into flour; deep fry until golden brown. Drain cakes on paper towels; sprinkle with chopped parsley. Alternately, the parsley can be stirred into the dough before frying.

Potato Croquettes

3 medium potatoes	salt & nutmeg	1 Tbs. flour
1 ½-oz. butter	grated rind of 1 lemon	parsley
2 eggs, separated	1 ½-oz. aged cheese	bread crumbs

Cook potatoes in boiling salted water; drain and rub through a sieve, or ricer. Stir in butter, beaten egg yolks, salt, nutmeg, grated lemon rinds, grated cheese, flour and chopped parsley.
Shape into croquettes using 2 spoons; dip into lightly beaten egg white, and roll in bread crumbs. (Repeat twice.) Deep fry the croquettes until golden brown.

Side Dishes

Carrot Fritter Puffs

4 cups diced carrots (2 cups puree)   2 cups grated sharp Cheddar cheese
4 cups diced potatoes (or 2 cups mashed) 2 cups diced onion
3 eggs slightly beaten   2 Tbs. butter or vegetable oil
1 cup all-purpose unbleached flour   1 tsp. salt & 1 tsp. pepper
1 cup bread crumbs   oil for deep frying

Cook carrots and potatoes together in water to cover until soft, about 20 minutes. Drain; mash together. Add the eggs, flour, bread crumbs, and cheese.

Saute the onion in the butter until browned and add to the batter with the salt and pepper.

Heat the oil to 375 degrees. Drop the batter in oil by the teaspoon and fry for 1 minute or until golden brown; turning once to brown the other side. Drain on a paper towel and serve warm. Makes 6 servings.

Potato Skin Snacks

The skin of the potato has many nutrients and is often tossed away. Instead, when you peel potatoes for another purpose, peel 1/8" thick and retain the peelings for fried snacks. Be sure the skins are washed clean before peeling. These can be cooked in the oven by brushing the skins inside and out with melted butter, placing them side by side on a baking sheet. Bake 500 degrees until crisp, about 12 minutes. Dip them in your favorite dip or sprinkle with a seasoning salt and enjoy.

Variation #1: Add 1 tsp. soy sauce to the butter; brush the mixture onto the skins.

Variation #2: Combine 1 teaspoon minced onion, 1/2 cup mayonnaise and 2 tablespoons Parmesan cheese; mix well; set aside. Brush skins lightly with melted butter; bake 10 minutes or until crispy. Add a topping of the set aside mixture over the skins. Place under broiler 2 to 3 minutes or until topping is golden.

Or if you prefer: In a deep heavy container and over high heat, or in an electric deep fryer; add salad oil to cover potatoes (2" in pan on stove, more in the fryer). Heat to about 400 degrees. Add potato skins, about 6 at a time and fry until crisp and golden, about one minute. Lift from oil with slotted spoon or rack and drain on paper towels. Add salt if so desired.

Or if you prefer: Dip in seasoned flour, shaking off excess. Deep fry in oil heated to 375 degree for 2 minutes or until lightly browned. Drain on paper towels; sprinkle with seasoned salt.

Potato-Cheese Puffs

1⅓ cups water	1/4 cup Idahoan® Mashed	3 eggs at room temperature
1/4 cup butter	Potatoes (dry flakes)	1/2 cup grated Parmesan
1/2 tsp. salt	1 cup coarsely grated	cheese
3/4 cup flour	Swiss cheese	

In a 3-quart saucepan bring water, butter and salt to a boil. Remove from heat. Mix potato flakes and flour and add to saucepan. Return to medium heat and stir vigorously until dough forms a ball and leaves the sides of the pan. Remove from heat; add eggs one at a time. Beat until the dough is glossy and stiff. (This step may be done in the food processor.) Stir in Swiss cheese. Place 1/4 cup of dough on greased baking sheet, 2 inches apart.

Sprinkle tops with Parmesan cheese and bake for about 30 minutes or until golden. Puffs will be slightly creamy inside.

Perfect Home Fries
(crispy outside, soft inside, with sweet, nearly burnt onions)

Parboil **6 cups cubed (1" pieces) potatoes** 5 minutes, until just tender. Drain. Heat **2 Tbs. vegetable oil** in heavy frying pan: saute **2 cups diced onions** until limp, 3-5 minutes. Add the potatoes and continue cooking. Rather than stir, flip frequently with a spatula so potatoes brown evenly. The onions will get quite browned, which makes the flavor sweeter. Season to taste with **salt and pepper.** Makes 6-8 servings.

Deep-Fat French Fried Potatoes

4 to 6 oven-sized potatoes from Idaho	deep fat	salt

Square off ends and sides of **potatoes**; cut into 1/2" thick slices, then into thick sticks. Soak in **cold water** for about 30 minutes and drain. Wrap in a cloth, or in paper towels, and leave 20-30 minutes. Heat **fat** and then dip frying basket in it (this prevents potatoes from sticking to it). Lift basket out of fat, put potatoes in; when fat reaches the right temperature 350 degrees, carefully lower basket into it.

Fry gently until potatoes are just soft (pierce with point of sharp knife to test). Lift out and drain. They can be left like this for a short time while fat is being increased to 360 to 375 degrees. Carefully lower basket of potatoes into fat; fry until a deep golden brown. Drain French fries well on paper towels; turn into a hot serving bowl and sprinkle with salt.

Variation: These can also be fried on top of the stove by putting enough oil into a heavy pan to immerse a small batch of potatoes. Test the oil's temperature by touching the end of a raw potato to it. If the potato sizzles, the oil is hot enough for frying. Place just enough potatoes in the pan to cover the bottom and cook until lightly browned. Keep moving potatoes while cooking. Drain and place on absorbent paper. Sprinkle with salt or seasoned salt and serve hot.

Deep Fry--Fries
on top of the stove

Use mealy **baking potatoes** (from Idaho), which are best suited for frying. Peel and cut into long strips 1/4" to 1/2" thick. Rinse in cold water to remove surface starch. Drain well and dry between paper towels. Put enough **fat or oil** into heavy pan on the stove burner, to immerse a small batch of potatoes. Test the fat's temperature by touching the end of a raw potato to it. If the potato sizzles, the fat is hot enough for frying. Place just enough potatoes in frying basket to cover bottom. Immerse in hot fat and cook until lightly browned. Keep moving potatoes while cooking. Drain and place on absorbent paper. Sprinkle with salt or seasoned salt and serve hot.

Rancher's Potatoes

Brown five strips of bacon; set aside. In drippings, brown hash browns, chopped onion and chopped green pepper. Beat four eggs and add 1/4 cup milk, salt and pepper. Pour over hash browns. As the mixture sets, crumble bacon on top, then Cheddar cheese. It's ready to eat when the cheese has melted.

Vaughn's Potatoes

If you substitute instant mashed potatoes for fresh potatoes, prepare the mix according to package directions (omitting the salt and butter) to make 1¾ cups.

3 med. potatoes, peeled, quartered	2½ tsp. dried instant onion soup mix
1/4 cup grated Parmesan cheese	dash pepper
1-oz. cream cheese	dash bottled hot pepper sauce
1 Tbs. butter	milk
1 Tb. chopped onion	1 beaten egg
	1½ cups corn flakes, coarsely crushed

In saucepan cook potatoes in boiling unsalted water about 20 minutes or until tender. Drain and mash. Stir in Parmesan cheese, cream cheese, butter or margarine, green onion, onion soup mix, pepper, and hot pepper sauce (optional). Mix well. Add 1 to 2 tablespoons milk if mixture is dry. Shape mixture into 8 balls. Dip in beaten egg; roll in corn flakes. Place on greased baking sheet; bake in 400 degrees oven for 10 to 15 minutes or until hot and crisp. Makes 4 servings.

Breaded Potato Sticks

1/2 cup bread crumbs	1/4 tsp. dried oregano	1/4 tsp. dried thyme
2 Tbs. Parmesan cheese	1/4 tsp. salt; 1/8 tsp. pepper	1/4 tsp. dried basil
2 Tbs. vegetable oil	3-4 cups 1/2" raw potato sticks	

Heat the oven to 400 degrees. Mix the bread crumbs, grated Parmesan cheese, herbs, salt, and pepper. Dip each potato stick into the oil, scraping off the excess oil on the side of the dish. Coat the sticks with the bread crumb mixture and place on a greased or non-stick baking sheet. Bake for 20-30 minutes or until potatoes are tender. Serve hot. Makes 6-8 servings.

Prime Time Hash Browns

5½-oz. Idaho dehydrated hash brown potatoes	1/3 cup yellow cornmeal 1/2 tsp. seasoned salt 1/4 tsp. pepper	1/3 cup butter 1 cup sliced scallions or green onions

In medium bowl, rehydrate potatoes according to package directions; drain. Stir in cornmeal, seasoned salt and pepper. In large skillet melt butter; cook potatoes over medium-high heat 10-12 minutes or until lightly browned. Add scallions; cook 2 to 3 minutes longer. Makes 6 servings.

Oven Fried Potatoes

4 med. potatoes, peeled, sliced 1 Tbs. instant onion flakes	1/2 cup butter, melted 1/4 cup water garlic bread seasoning	Romano cheese paprika

Generously butter bottom and sides of baking pan. Stir potatoes, onion, butter and water in pan. Sprinkle generously with garlic bread seasoning. Bake at 325-350 degrees for about 1 hour. Remove cover last few minutes and sprinkle lightly with cheese and paprika. Continue baking until done. Makes 4 servings.

Crispy New Potatoes

Fry **4 bacon slices** until crisp but not dry; remove slices. To hot bacon fat; add **sliced, washed, unpared new potatoes**. Cook, covered, a few minutes, to steam. Uncover; season with **salt and pepper**; cook very slowly, stirring and turning frequently, until tender and flecked with crusty golden-brown bits---about 20 minutes. Crumble crisp bacon over top.

Smothered Potatoes And Turnips

1 cup vegetable oil	1/2 cup finely chopped celery
1 cup pork or chicken stock	2 tsp. salt; 1/4 tsp. black pepper
10 cups potatoes, peeled, cut in 1" cubes	1 tsp. cayenne pepper
4 cups cubed, peeled turnips	1 cup chopped green onions also tops
1/2 cup fine chopped onion	1/4 cup chopped fresh parsley

In a 7½ quart cast-iron pan, combine the oil, 3/4 cup of the stock, potatoes, turnips, onions, celery, salt and peppers. Place over high heat and cook about 10 minutes; stirring occasionally. Cover pan and cook until potatoes and turnips are just tender, about 25 minutes; stirring occasionally at first, then almost constantly during second half of cooking time, and scraping pan bottom well each time.

Note: Let it stick, but not scorch, each time before you stir. The browned matter makes this dish good. If necessary add a little more meat stock or water to scrape clean the sticking areas. When vegetables are tender, stir in green onions, parsley and 1/4 cup stock or water. Reduce heat to low and cook 3 minutes more; stir constantly and scraping the pan bottom as clean as possible. Remove from heat and serve immediately. The finished dish should be lumpy, with lots of brown parts.

Fried Potatoes

Fry **4 slices bacon crisp**, but do not overcook. Set aside. **Peel and grate 4 heaping cups raw potatoes**. Peel and **thinly slice 1 cup onion**. Add potatoes and onions to bacon fat, **salt and pepper** to taste. **Cayenne** may also be used as seasoning. Cover and saute over low heat 15 minutes, uncover; turn heat up slightly and saute 10 minutes or until brown and crispy on underside. Turn over a small section at a time. Add a little more oil and brown the other side. Put in serving dish and top with **crumbled bacon pieces** and **parsley.** Makes 4 servings.

Variation: When potatoes are browned on both sides, break 2 eggs in dish and break yolk and slightly mix yolks and whites together; pour over potatoes; stir and keep on low heat until eggs are cooked.

CASSEROLE DISHES:

"Your mother gave me one of your favorite recipes."

Irish Potato Bake

4 cup Corn Chex crushed to 2 cups	1/2 tsp. onion powder
Tbs. melted butter	1/4 tsp seasoned salt, dash pepper
3 cups stiff hot mashed potatoes	1 pkg. frozen, cooked broccoli drained
1/2 cup dairy sour cream	1 cup shredded processed Am. cheese

Use Pam to coat shallow baking dish. Combine Corn Chex crumbs and butter. Set aside. Season potatoes and add sour cream, and broccoli. Stir gently until mixed.

Turn half of mixture into baking dish; sprinkle with half of cheese, then half of crumbs. Repeat. Bake in 350 degree oven 20-25 minutes or until crumbs are golden. Makes 4 servings.

Fresh Potato Onion Puff

4 med.potatoes, pared, cubed	1/2 cup chopped fresh onions	3/4 cup milk
1 tsp. salt; dash of pepper	1/4 cup melted butter	2 eggs, separated

Cook potatoes with 1/2 teaspoon salt in covered saucepan in small amount of boiling water until just tender. Drain well. Saute onions in butter or margarine until tender. Mash potatoes. Beat onions, milk, 1/2 teaspoon salt and pepper into potatoes. Add egg yolks; beat well.

Beat egg whites until stiff; fold into potato mixture. Pile into buttered 6 cup casserole. Bake in 375 degree oven 30 minutes or until lightly browned. Serve immediately. Makes 4 to 6 servings

Variation: Cook a 10-oz. package of frozen spinach as directed on package; drain well and add to the potatoes.

Casserole Of Vegetables

1 C. uncooked brown rice	1 cup tomatoes	1 cup peas
1 onion, sliced thin	1 tsp. chopped parsley	basil & oregano
4 med. potatoes, sliced thin	4 cups stock or additional tomatoes	

Put all ingredients into casserole with 4 cups of stock. Cover and bake in slow oven 300 degrees for about 1 hour or until rice is tender. Makes 4-6 servings.

Variation: Use 5 cups of tomatoes and omit the stock.

Cabbage-Topped Tarragon Potatoes

1 ½ cups peeled potatoes	1 Tbs. flour	1/2 cup Cheddar cheese
1/2 cup shredded cabbage	1 tsp. minced dried onion	1/8 tsp. garlic powder
2 beaten eggs	1/4 tsp. salt; 1/8 tsp. pepper	snipped chives
2 Tbs. butter	1/8 tsp.crushed dry tarragon	plain yogurt

Cook cut-up potatoes, covered, in boiling salted water until tender; drain and mash (should have about 1⅓ cups). Cook cabbage, covered, in small amount boiling water 5 minutes or until tender; drain.

In bowl combine eggs, butter or margarine, flour, onion and seasonings. Add potatoes; beat until smooth. Generously grease four 6-ounce custard cups; spoon 1/3 cup mixture into each. Top with cabbage and shredded cheese. Bake in 350 degree oven 30 minutes. Serve with yogurt and chives. Makes 4 servings.

Variation: Instead of putting mixture into custard cups, put in a casserole dish. The eggs can be omitted if you so choose.

Savory Bacon Potatoes

1 can Cream Celery Soup	4 tsp. minced onion	3 med.potatoes, peeled, cut-up
4 Tbs. water	pinch pepper	1 Tbs. bacon flavored bits

In saucepan, combine soup, water, onion, and pepper. Cook this mixture over low heat for 5-10 minutes, stirring occasionally. Add cooked potatoes, continue to heat thoroughly. Serve potatoes garnished with bacon-flavored bits. (Of course, freshly cooked, crumbled bacon will give a better flavor.)

Variation: Replace Cream of Celery Soup with Cream of Chicken Soup. Add another potato, 1/2 cup sour cream and grated cheese.

Green Bean Casserole

1 small chopped onion	2 cups medium white sauce
1/2 cup sharp grated cheese	3 cans green beans, drained
1 sm. can mushrooms with liquid	1 small bag barbecued potato chips
1 tsp. Worcestershire sauce	or shoestring potatoes

White sauce: In saucepan melt 2 tablespoons butter or margarine; add 2 heaping tablespoons flour and stir. Add 2 cups milk; cook to desired thickness.
Add onion, cheese, mushrooms with liquid and Worcestershire sauce to white sauce.

Combine sauce and greens beans in casserole dish; sprinkle barbecued potato chips over top. Bake at 350 degrees about 30 minutes, or until bubbling hot. Makes 10 servings.

TIP: For an easy cheese sauce for vegetables, mix any type cream soup with cheese. Heat until cheese melts, stirring occasionally. I like Cream of Mushroom, Cream of Chicken or Onion Soup best.

Potatoes Baked In Cheese Sauce

3 Tbs. shortening	1/3 cup grated cheese	1 tsp. salt
3 Tbs. flour	1/4 tsp. paprika	2 Tbs. chopped green peppers
1/2 cup powdered milk	4 med. potatoes peeled,	1/4 tsp Tabasco sauce
2 cups water	thinly sliced	

Melt shortening; stir in flour. Dissolve milk in 2 cups water; add to shortening and flour mixture. Cook, stirring constantly until mixture thickens and is smooth. Add cheese and seasoning; remove from heat. Place potato slices in casserole and sprinkle with green pepper. Stir tabasco sauce into cheese sauce and pour over potatoes. Bake 45 minutes in 350 degree oven. Uncover; bake 45 minutes longer.

Hash Potato Casserole

12 medium potatoes	1 pint sour cream	2 cups Corn Flakes, crushed
1 cube butter, melted	1/2 cup chopped grn. onions	salt and pepper to taste
2 cans Cr. of Chicken Soup	3 Tbs. butter, melted	

Boil potatoes with skins and whole. Peel off the thin skin and place potatoes in fridge overnight. (They shred better cool). Shred potatoes. Put half the shredded potatoes into baking dish. Pour half the sauce over potatoes; place remaining potatoes on top of sauce; pour remaining sauce over potatoes. Melt 3 tablespoons butter; add Corn Flakes, mix together. Pour over top of potato mixture. Bake at 350 degrees 30 minutes. Makes about 12 servings.

For Sauce: Combine melted cube of butter or margarine, soup, sour cream and chopped onions.

Variation: Replace grated potatoes with 1 pound package hash brown potatoes

Yummy Potato Casserole

6 med. potatoes, boiled	1/3 C. chopped green onions	2 Tbs. melted butter
1/4 cup butter	1 ½ cups sharp ched. cheese	3-4 hard-boiled, eggs
1 can Cream Chicken Soup	1/3 C. Corn Flakes, crushed	paprika
1 pint dairy sour cream		

Boil potatoes until tender; cool; peel and shred or grate (coarsely). Heat 1/4 cup butter with soup until melted and blended. Blend sour cream, onion and grated cheese into soup mixture. Mix well. (If you desire more moisture use 2 cans chicken soup or 1 can Cream chicken soup and 1 can Cream mushroom soup.) Mix with the shredded potatoes and place in a casserole dish.
Combine corn flakes and 2 tablespoons melted butter; sprinkle over casserole. Bake at 350 degrees for 45 minutes. Arrange the sliced boiled eggs over the top and sprinkle with paprika 5 minutes before cooking time is completed. Makes 6-8 servings.

Variation #1: Hash browns or french fries, can substitute for shredded potatoes.

Variation #2: Reduce the sour cream to 1 ½ pints (3 cups) and add 4-oz. softened cream cheese with 1 tablespoon chopped chives mixed in.

Potato Tomato Pot

2 med. potatoes, cut up	1 med. onion, sliced	dash pepper
1 med. tomato, cut up	3/4 tsp. salt	1 Tb. olive oil

In small baking dish, toss vegetables, salt and pepper with oil. Cover and bake at 350 degrees for 30 minutes. Uncover and bake 30 minutes more or until potatoes are tender. Makes 4 servings.

Potato-Cabbage Casserole

1/3 cup minced onion	1/2 C. grated Ched. cheese	2 lg. potatoes, cooked, sliced
2 Tbs. butter	1 tsp.salt; 1/4 tsp.pepper	2-3 cups thinly sliced cabbage
1 can Cr. Mushrm. Soup	dash garlic salt	1 cup fresh bread crumbs
.3/4 cup milk	1/4 tsp. marjoram	2 Tbs. melted butter

Preheat oven to 350 degrees. Grease a 2-quart casserole. In skillet saute onion in 2 tablespoons butter until tender. Add soup and milk; stirring until blended; gradually stir in cheese until thoroughly combined. Add salt, pepper, garlic salt, and marjoram or rosemary.

In casserole, arrange half the potatoes, cabbage, & cheese sauce; repeat; top with crumbs, and 2 Tbs. melted butter. Bake 25-30 minutes. Makes 6 servings.

Variation: Replace cabbage with equal amount of lightly steamed sliced carrots or raw grated carrots.

Kohlrabi Ham Souffle

2 cups diced potatoes	1 Tb. minced parsley	1/2 tsp. Worcestershire sauce
3 cups diced kohlrabi	1/4 tsp. paprika	6 eggs, separated
4 bacon slices, crumbled	1/8 tsp. cayenne	2 Tbs. flour
1 cup finely-diced ham	1/2 tsp dried savory	1/2 cup Cheddar cheese
2 Tbs.minced scallion	pinch thyme	1/2 tsp. salt; pepper

Parboil the potatoes until just tender, about 10 minutes. Blanch or steam the kohlrabi until just tender, about 5 minutes. In the meantime, saute bacon until browned and remove it from the pan. Pour off all but 2 tablespoons of bacon grease, and saute the ham, diced scallion or green onions, parsley, and herbs for 2 minutes. Stir in the Worcestershire sauce.

In a large bowl, combine the kohlrabi, potatoes, bacon, and ham and vegetable mixture. Whisk together the 6 eggs yolks and the flour and mix with the kohlrabi mixture. Mix in grated cheese, salt, and pepper to taste.

Beat the egg whites until stiff. Fold into the kohlrabi mixture. Spoon into a greased, shallow 1 ½ quart baking dish. Bake at 325 degrees for 40 to 50 minutes or until the top is golden. Serve hot. Makes 6 servings.

Okra Pilaf

4 slices bacon	2 tomatoes, peeled, chopped	salt and pepper
1 onion, chopped	or 8 ½-oz. can tomatoes	Tater Tots
1/2 grn. pepper, chopped	1 cup thinly sliced okra	

Dice bacon; fry in skillet until crisp. Take out and reserve. Fry onion and pepper in fat; add tomatoes and okra; cook, stirring occasionally, until soft and the liquid has evaporated. Season with salt and pepper. Line a pan with tater tots; pour mixture oven them. Cover; cook in oven for 15-20 minutes until the Tater Tots are thoroughly flavored with the tomato. Sprinkle with the bacon just before serving. If you desire to do so, tater tots can also be placed on top of the tomato mixture.

Potato And Mushroom Casserole

1 ½ lb. new potatoes	2 Tbs. flour	1-2 Tbs. heavy cream
2 cups mushrms. (1/2 lb.)	2 ½ cups milk	pinch nutmeg
2 Tbs. butter	salt and pepper	

This dish is best made with small new potatoes, but regular potatoes can be substituted. Peel potatoes, or scrape, if large cut in quarters, trimming the cut edges with a potato peeler. Cook the potatoes in boiling, salted water for 10-15 minutes or until almost tender. Drain; let stand over a gentle heat to dry; cover and set aside.

Wipe mushrooms with a damp cloth and trim each stem level with the base of the cap. Be careful not to pull out the whole stems or the mushrooms will shrink and lose their form during cooking. The little piece of remaining stem keeps the mushroom in shape.

Melt butter; add mushrooms, and toss over a high heat until soft. Stir in the flour; remove from heat; add milk and seasonings; then cook, stirring constantly, until mixture boils. Add potatoes; cover, and simmer 10 minutes. Shortly before serving stir in the cream and a pinch of nutmeg.

BAKED & STUFFED POTATOES

"The perfect recipe: Salad, baked potatoes and candle light with you."

Golden Baked Potatoes

Prick potato skin with fork. Bake in 350 to 375 degree oven for about one hour. Gently squeeze the potato; if soft it is done.

For a golden skin coloring brush milk or butter on the potato before baking. Do not use foil, this is a baked potato.

Side Dishes

Sliced Baked Potatoes

4 med. potatoes	4 Tbs. grated hard cheese
1 tsp. salt	2-3 Tbs. chopped fresh assortment of herbs such
2-3 Tbs. melted butter	as parsley, chives, thyme or sage and 2-3 tsp.
1½ tsp. Parmesan cheese	dried herbs of your choice

Peel potatoes if the skin is tough, otherwise just scrub and rinse them. Cut potatoes into thin slices but not all the way through. Use the handle of a wooden spoon, lying along side the potato, and cut until the knife hits the spoon. This is a fast way to cut yet avoid cutting all the way through the potato. Put potatoes in a baking dish, fan them (spreading the top out) slightly. Sprinkle with salt and drizzle with butter. Sprinkle with herbs.

Bake potatoes at 425 degrees for about 50 minutes. Remove from oven. Sprinkle with cheeses. Bake for another 10 to 15 minutes until lightly browned, cheeses are melted and potatoes are soft inside. Check with a fork. Garnish with a green herb of your choice, dill, parsley or maybe even mint. You may use caraway seeds or cumin in place of herbs, if desired. Use about 1½ teaspoon for 4 large potatoes.

Creamy Stuffed Potatoes

4 Idaho baking potatoes	pepper & paprika
1 tsp. butter-flavored salt	1 tsp. freeze-dried chives
2 egg whites	1/2 to 3/4 cups milk
pinch of cream of tarter	3 Tbs. grated, sharp Cheddar cheese

Bake potatoes (not in foil), and carefully slice them in half, lengthwise. Combine the salt, egg whites, and cream of tartar in bowl. Using electric mixer, whip egg whites until stiff peaks form. Add pepper and chives; whip, adding a little milk at a time until they are fluffy. Carefully scoop out the pulp of the potatoes, place them in another bowl.

Fold egg white mixture into the potatoes pulp and mix together. Pile the mixture back into the potato skins. Sprinkle the top with grated cheese and paprika, return potatoes to oven; bake 424 degrees until cheese is melted and potatoes are hot. Makes 8 servings.

Tater-Stuffed Mushrooms

1 lb. lg. mushrooms (about 30)	2 Tbs. dehydrated onion soup mix
3/4 cups mashed potatoes	1/4 cup cottage cheese
	1/2 tsp. butter

Wash mushrooms, carefully removing stems. Set aside tops. Chop stems. Combine chopped stems with remaining ingredients except butter. Spoon into mushroom tops.

With butter, grease bottom of jelly-roll pan. Arrange mushrooms on pan. Bake at 375 degrees for 10-15 minutes or until hot and bubbly. Serve immediately. Makes 30 stuffed caps.

Carrot-Stuffed Potato Supreme

4 Idaho potatoes
1/4 cup butter
1 cup chopped onion

1 ½ cup shredded carrot
1/4 cup milk
4 tsp. lemon juice

1 tsp. prepared mustard
1/4 cup chopped parsley
salt and pepper

Scrub potatoes; dry and prick with a fork. Bake in 425 degree oven 55-65 minutes, until soft. Reduce oven temperature to 350 degrees. Cut a slice from top of each potato. Carefully scoop out pulp without breaking skin. Set skins aside. Meanwhile in medium saucepan melt butter; saute onion and carrot until soft. In large bowl whip potatoes. Add milk, lemon juice, mustard, salt & pepper to taste; beat until smooth. Stir in sauteed vegetables and parsley. Spoon potato mixture into reserved potato skins. Bake in a 350 degree oven 20-30 minutes, until potatoes are heated through. Makes 4 servings.

Spicy Twice-Baked Potatoes

6 large Idaho potatoes
2 tsp. Worcestershire
1 Tb. minced onion
1/2 pkg. dehydrated
   onion soup mix

3 Tbs. Russian dressing
1/2 cup milk or buttermilk
6 Tbs. skim milk
2 tsp. salt, dash pepper

1 cup cottage cheese
1 tsp. baking powder
paprika
dried parsley flakes

Pierce each potato in several places with tines of fork. Bake at 400 degrees for 45 minutes or until tender. Cut hot potatoes in half lengthwise. Scoop out potato, leaving skins intact for re-stuffing. Beat potato pulp with remaining ingredients except paprika and parsley flakes until fluffy. Pile mixture back into skins. Sprinkle with paprika and parsley flakes. Bake 10 minutes more or until just golden. Makes 12 servings.

MASHED POTATOES & MORE:

"Mon says leftovers are good for me....sometimes they are great....like potatoes."

Mashed Potato Patties

A Leftover Mashed Potatoes Recipe:
Mix **3 cups mashed potatoes** and **1½ cups grated cheese (Swiss, Cheddar, or Monterey jack)**. Season to taste with **salt and pepper**. Form the mixture into patties; butter on both sides. To vary the recipe, coat patties with **bread crumbs** or wheat germ before frying or add **minced herbs** to the patties; or shape the potato mixture into logs about 3 inches long and 1/2 inch in diameter. Roll the logs in ground nuts instead of bread crumbs.

Potato Triangles

A leftover Mashed Potato Recipe:

3 cups mashed potatoes	2 tsp. Dijon-style mustard	Salt and pepper
1 egg, beaten	1/4 cup chopped fresh chives	1 cup bread crumbs
		4 Tbs. butter

Mix the potatoes, egg, mustard, and chives. Season to taste with salt and pepper. Shape the potato mixture into triangles 1 ½ inches long and 3/4 inch thick. (This will be easier to do if you keep your hands wet.) Or press the mixture flat and then cut into triangles. Dip the triangles into bread crumbs to coat. Fry in butter until golden brown. Serve hot. Makes 6-8 servings.

Cheesy Potato Cups

A Leftover Mashed Potatoes Recipe:

5 Tbs. butter	3 cups mashed potatoes	2/3 cup Parmesan cheese
1 cup diced onion	2 eggs, beaten	salt and pepper

Preheat the oven to 400 degrees. Melt 1 tablespoon of the butter in a small saute pan; saute onion until limp, 3 to 5 minutes. In a bowl, combine onion, mashed potatoes, eggs, and grated cheese. Season to taste with salt and pepper. Melt the remaining 4 tablespoons butter. Brush 1 dozen non-stick muffin cups with butter. Press the mashed potatoes into the cups, making the sides and bottom 1/4 inch thick. Brush the potato cups with melted butter. Bake the potato cups for 20-30 minutes or until golden brown. The potato cups will slip out of the muffin tin easily. Fill the cups with hot vegetables and serve immediately. Makes 6 servings (2 per person).

Variation: Fill cup with egg salad or tuna salad and turn this side dish into a main dish.

Left over Potato Ideas

#1) Mix grated cheese with mashed potatoes; add salt and pepper. Form in patties and fry on both sides in butter.

#2) Form in balls; roll in dry bread crumbs and deep fry until brown.

#3) Press leftover potatoes in pie plate; fill with ground beef or hash and bake for a main dish pie.

#4) Mix cold potatoes with egg yolks and pipe around tops of casseroles for duchess potatoes.

#5) Make a potato souffle by beating 2 egg yolks with 2 cups mashed potatoes and 1/2 to 1 cup shredded Cheddar cheese. Beat 2 egg whites stiff; fold in. Turn into a souffle dish; bake at 350 degrees. Makes a main dish out of used mashed potatoes.

#6) Shape cold mashed potatoes into flat cakes. Dust on both sides with grated Parmesan cheese. Then saute in butter, margarine, bacon fat, or salad oil until brown on both sides.

Mashed Potatoes And Mushrooms

While **6 potatoes boil, wash 1/2 pound mushrooms** and cut them in two. Using a heavy fryer or dutch oven, heat it hot, add **2 tablespoons cooking oil**, add **sliced onion and mushrooms**. Cover tightly; set the heat to moderate and the mushrooms will make their own cooking water. Boil them about 10 minutes; season with **sea kelp** and boil another 10 minutes; stirring frequently, until water is absorbed back into the mushrooms and they are lightly browned.

Mash potatoes with their own liquid. Serve the mushrooms spooned over the mashed potatoes. Makes 4 servings.

First-Rate Spuds

4 Id. potatoes, unpared, cut in 1/2" cubes	3/4 cup warm milk	2 Tbs. fresh chives
	3 Tbs. butter	2 Tb. finely chopped grn. onion
1/2 cup carrot cut-up	1/2 minced green pepper	1/2 tsp. salt; 1/8 tsp. pepper grated cheese

Place potatoes and carrot in large saucepan with 1 inch salted water. Cover. Bring to a boil. Reduce heat; simmer 15-20 minutes, until potatoes are tender. Drain. Mash or beat with electric mixer until potatoes are smooth. Add milk, butter, minced green pepper, finely chopped chives, onion, salt and pepper. Beat until potato mixture is light and fluffy. Place hot mixture in a serving bowl. Sprinkle grated cheese on top. This will be a little chewy with the raw onions, chives and peppers. Makes 4 servings.

Apple Potatoes

Peel several potatoes and cut into small squares; bring to boil in water, then add **peeled apple chunks or slices**, and cook together until soft. Press through a ricer or mash, add **salt and sugar** to taste. Mix in the mixing bowl until light and airy and serve with fried, **crumbled bacon** and **sauted onions**.

Bacon Cheese Nibbles

3 Tbs. sesame seeds	1 egg slightly beaten	5-6 slices bacon, crispy
1 envelope (5 ser.) Idaho Mashed Potato Granules	1/4 cup mayonnaise	paprika
	1/2 cup Cheddar cheese	

Spread sesame seeds in shallow pan. Toast in 350 degree oven 5 to 8 min., stirring occasionally, until golden brown. Prepare mashed potatoes as directed on package, except decrease water to 2/3 cup. (Potatoes will be very stiff.) Stir in egg, mayonnaise, shredded cheese, and the crumbled bacon. Shape into small balls, using a rounded teaspoonful for each. Roll in toasted sesame seed; sprinkle with paprika. Arrange on greased baking sheet. Bake in 400 degree oven 10 to 15 minutes, until golden brown. Serve hot as hors d'oeuvres. Makes 4 to 5 dozen.

Ukrainian Petehair

4 lg. potatoes	1 ½ to 2 cups flour	1/2 cup cottage cheese
1-2 Tbs. oil	1 tsp. salt	1/2 C.sour cream with chives
3 egg	1/2 cup sauted onion	

Peel and boil potatoes. Stir together oil and egg, then add flour and salt. Let dough rest 15 minutes; roll out to 1/8" thickness and cut into 2 inch squares.

Mash cooked potatoes well and stir in chopped sauted onion and cottage cheese. Fill dough squares with potato mixture. Fold corner to corner forming a triangle. Seal edges well. Boil in salted water for 3 minutes. Rinse in cold water so doughs will not stick together. Toss lightly with browned chopped onions. Serve with a thick sour cream with chives mixture.

To use as a leftover: Melt butter in skillet; add dough and fry until hot. Serve with the cottage cheese and sour cream with chives mixture.

Minted Potatoes

Boil **6 cups quartered and sliced new potatoes** until tender, about 10 minutes; drain. In a large saute pan, melt **3 tablespoon butter** and add **1/2 cup minced fresh mint** and **1 tablespoon lemon juice**. Saute for 1 minute. Add the potatoes and toss to coat. Reheat and serve immediately. Make 4-6 servings.

Browned Mushrooms In Potato Wreath

1 ½ lbs. fresh mushrooms	Instant mashed potatoes (4 servings)
3 Tbs. butter	2 Tbs. butter
pinch of salt & white pepper	2 eggs
2-3 Tbs. lemon juice	1/2 cup grated Gouda cheese

Wash mushrooms; cut into halves. Heat butter; add mushrooms with seasonings and lemon juice; stew for 5-8 minutes. Prepare the mashed potatoes as directed; blend in butter and whole eggs. In greased, heat-resistant pan, form a wreath of mashed potatoes or make a wreath with a decorating gun. Put mushrooms in center and sprinkle with grated Gouda cheese. Let it bake until golden yellow in 400 degrees oven for 10-15 minutes.

TIP: Mushrooms don't keep well in plastic bags. Loosely wrap them in paper towels and store in the refrigerator crisper.

Potato Balls

6 medium potatoes	2 tsp. butter	1/4 cup plus 2 Tbs. flour
2 slices white bread	1 egg	salt

Pare; cook potatoes; mash while hot; cool. Cut bread into small cubes and toast in butter, melted in skillet, until golden brown. When potatoes are cool, blend in egg, flour, and salt to taste. Form potato mixture into 8 to 10 balls. Place 3 cubes of toasted bread in center of each ball. Gently place the balls in boiling salted water and simmer 10 to 15 minutes. Makes 8 to 10 potato balls.

POTATOES & OTHER VEGETABLE DISHES:

"Real men eat potatoes."

Green Beans With Potatoes/Onions

9-oz. pkg frozen cut green beans	8-oz. can peeled, sm. whole, stewed
1/2 tsp. dried, crushed marjoram leaves	onions, drained
1 Tbs. butter or margarine	1 sm. can potatoes or 3 or 4 small new
	potatoes

Cook beans according to pkg. directions; add marjoram to cooking liquid. Halve onions and potatoes; add to beans a few minutes before beans are cooked. Continue cooking until onions and potatoes are heated through. Drain thoroughly; stir in butter or margarine. Turn vegetables into serving dish. Makes 6 servings.

Green And White Potatoes

7 or 8 small new potatoes	1 scallion or green onion	salt & fresh ground pepper
3 Tbs. chopped cucumber	1/4 cup plain yogurt	1½ tsp. milk

Scrub potatoes, but do not peel. Cook in water to cover, in covered pot, 15 to 20 minutes, depending on size of potatoes. Drain. Do not peel. Peel cucumber, if waxed; chop cucumber. Chop scallion. Add cucumber, scallion, yogurt, milk, salt and black pepper to potatoes; cover and keep warm.

Double-Deck Potatoes And Carrots

2 med.potatoes,cut in 1/2" slices	1 tsp. salt
1/2 cup boiling water	1 tsp. milk
2 med. carrots, cut into sticks	1/3 cup grated American cheese

Place potatoes in boiling water in covered saucepan; place carrots on top of potatoes. Sprinkle with salt; cover; cook over medium heat 5 minutes. Reduce heat; simmer 20 to 25 minutes (add more water if needed.) When potatoes and carrots are tender, drain and add milk; sprinkle with grated cheese. Replace cover; turn off heat and allow cheese to melt. Makes 2 servings.

Potato Zucchini Curry

The spice blend of turmeric, cumin, and coriander give this dish its curry flavor.

1/4 cup butter	3/4 tsp. ground cumin	1/4 tsp.red pepper
1 tsp. dry mustard	3/4 tsp. ground coriander	3 lg. potatoes, peeled, cubed
1 tsp. ground turmeric	1/2 tsp.salt	2 C. zucchini, sliced/shredded
		1 med.tomato,seeded,chopped

In 10 inch skillet melt butter or margarine. Stir in mustard, turmeric, cumin, coriander, salt, and red pepper. Cook and stir over low heat for 5 minutes. Stir in potatoes. Cover and cook over medium-low heat for 10 to 15 minutes or until tender; stirring occasionally. Stir in zucchini. Cover and cook 4 minutes or until vegetables are tender. Stir in tomato; heat through. Makes 6-8 servings.

Variation: Replace zucchini with cooked, well drained spinach.

Creamed Corn And Potatoes

Quarter or chunk in bite-size pieces, and boil **4 medium potatoes**. Leave potatoes in bite-size pieces or mash quartered potatoes, whichever is to your liking and place in a serving container. Meanwhile, in a sauce pan empty **1 can creamed corn, 1/2 cup half & half or evaporated milk, 1/2 cup regular milk, salt, pepper and cayenne pepper** to taste. Heat. Put in serving container to spoon over potatoes on dinner plates.

Saucy Potatoes And Green Beans

3 med. potatoes, peeled	1/4 tsp. oregano	9-oz. pkg. frozen French
1 tsp. salt	2 tsp. cornstarch	style green beans

Cover and cook cubed potatoes with salt and oregano in 1 inch water for 15 minutes. Add green beans and cook 5 to 10 minutes or more until vegetables are tender. Drain; reserving 3/4 cup cooking liquid. In cup, blend cornstarch with 1 tablespoon cold water; stir into reserved liquid. Cook, stirring, until thickened, about 2 minutes. Add vegetables; reheat. Makes 4 servings.

Prima Donna Pesto Potatoes

5½-oz. pkg. dehydrated hash brown potatoes	1 lb. clove garlic, minced	1/3 cup olive oil
1 cup chopped fresh parsley	1 Tb. dried basil	3 Tbs. butter
1/2 cup Parmesan cheese	1/4 tsp. salt	1 tomato cut into wedges
	1/4 tsp. hot pepper sauce	1 tsp. dried basil

Rehydrate potatoes according to package directions. Drain. In container of electric blender combine parsley, cheese, garlic, basil, salt and hot pepper sauce; cover and process until mixture is smooth. Gradually add olive oil, and process at low speed. Mixture should resemble creamed butter when all of the oil is added, and is called pesto sauce.

In a large skillet melt butter; add rehydrated potatoes. Cook 3 minutes. Stir in pesto sauce. Heat through. Garnish with tomato wedges and **1 teaspoon basil**. (2 tablespoons chopped fresh basil can be used instead of the dry basil. Makes 4 servings.

Variegated Vegetable Platter

4 ser. instant mashed potatoes	4 tomatoes	pinch of sugar
1 egg	1-oz. grated aged Gounda	10-oz. pkg. frozen peas
1/4 C. grated, aged Gouda	2 Tbs. butter	10-oz. frozen green beans
	salt and pepper	1/2 bunch parsley

Cover a cookie sheet with a layer of aluminum foil. Prepare mashed potatoes as directed on package; blend in egg and 1/4 cup cheese. With decorating gun, dollop small rosettes onto the baking sheet with the mixture. Wash the tomatoes and dry. Cut slits crosswise several times into each tomato being careful not to cut all the way through. Pull the sections open, place cheese in the open area. Set on the cookie sheet next to the rosettes.

Add butter and seasoning to peas and beans, wrap each in aluminum foil, leaving top uncovered; place them onto cookie sheet with tomatoes and rosettes. Set cookie sheet in pre-heated oven, bake at 350 degrees for 25-30 minutes.

Arrange on serving dish with rosettes around the outer edge, tomatoes in the center, beans between rosettes and tomatoes on 1/2 of the dish and the peas on the other half. Sprinkle peas with chopped parsley. Makes 4 servings.

Lemon Mustard Potatoes

Boil **4 cups sliced or diced potatoes** until just tender, about 10 min. Drain. In a large saute pan, melt **3 tablespoons butter**, and add **2 tablespoons lemon juice, 2 teaspoons grated lemon rind, and 1½ teaspoons Dijon-style mustard**. Add the potatoes and stir to mix and heat. Season to taste with **salt and pepper**. Makes 4-6 servings.

Potato Dumplings

1 ½ cups boiling water
1/2 tsp. salt
1/2 cup cold milk
2 Tbs. butter

2 cups dry potato flakes
or about 4 cups mashed
1 ½ cup biscuit mix

1/2 tsp. baking powder
1 egg lightly beaten
5 cups simmering salted water

In large mixing bowl combine water, salt, milk and butter, gently stir in potatoes just to moisten; let sit for 1 minute, or use fresh mashed potatoes.

In a separate bowl mix together biscuit mix, (or make your own from scratch), baking powder and egg; add to potato mixture; blend well. Roll into walnut size balls. Drop into the simmering salted water. When batter floats, cover and simmer for 5 minutes. Serve immediately. Makes 8 to 10 dumplings.

Variations: Use in beef and chicken stews or broths. Add fruit to dough and top with vanilla or lemon sauce.

Dipping Potatoes

8 tiny new potatoes or 6 larger ones with eatable skins, like red bliss
1 cup plain yogurt
1 tsp. chopped fresh dill

2 tsp. chop'd scallion or grn. onions
2 tsp. red caviar (optional)

Scrub potatoes and bring to boil in water to cover. Depending on size, cook 15 to 20 minutes, until tender but not mushy. Drain. Don't run under cold water. Combine 1/4 cup yogurt with dill; combine 1/2 cup yogurt with scallion; combine remaining 1/4 cup yogurt with caviar. (If you choose not to use caviar, just chop another teaspoon of dill or scallion and combine with the remaining yogurt.)

Cut large potatoes into quarters (bite-sized). Do not peel. Either leave the tiny new potatoes whole or cut in half. Dip the potato piece into the yogurt mixtures. (Forget about toothpicks. They just make things more difficult.) The potatoes are best served warm or room temperature.

Potato Chips & Green Goddess Dip

1 bag potato chips
1 clove garlic, grated
2 Tbs. anchovy paste
3 Tbs. chopped chives

1 Tb. lemon juice
1 Tb. tarragon wine vinegar
1/2 cup heavy sour cream
1 cup mayonnaise

1/3 cup finely chopped parsley
coarsely ground blk. pepper
coarse salt

Combine ingredients in order give, except potato chips. Pour in serving bowl and chill. Canned whole anchovies may be chopped fine and substituted for the anchovy paste. Serve with your favorite brand of regular potato chips.

Note: Coarse salt may be purchased in pound containers.

Garlic-Flavored Potato Chips & Peanuts

Quarter 2 cloves garlic. Insert toothpick into each of the eight pieces. In tightly covered container, place 1 quart potato chips and 1/2 pound salted peanuts, then garlic. Let stand several hours; occasionally shaking and turning container. Remove garlic before serving. (The garlic is still suitable to use in other recipes.)

Dressed-Up Party Potato Chips

Spread potato chips on cookie sheet and sprinkle with 1/2 cup shredded processed American cheese. Sprinkle lightly with ground thyme, basil, or marjoram. Heat in 350 degree oven for 5 minutes, or until cheese melts. Serve while hot. Good stuff!

Mashed Potato Stuffing

3 med. potatoes, mashed   1 tsp. salt   Tb. butter, melted
dash pepper   1 med. onion, minced   dash garlic powder
                                               2 Tbs. chopped parsley

In large bowl combine all ingredients. Use stuffing to stuff chicken, turkey or boned leg of lamb roast, or, place in non-stick baking dish. Bake at 375 degrees for 40 minutes. Makes 2½ cups stuffing.

Minty Apple Stuffing

2 med. potatoes, cooked, diced   1 Tb. butter
1 cup diced apples   1 tsp. crushed mint leaves
1/4 cup diced cherries   1 tsp. salt

In bowl combine all ingredients. Use this stuffing to stuff chicken, turkey, or boned leg of lamb roasts, or place in non-stick baking dish. Bake at 375 degrees for 40 minutes. Makes 2½ cups stuffing.

* *
GOOD CHARACTER, LIKE GOOD FOOD,
IS USUALLY HOMEMADE.
       *

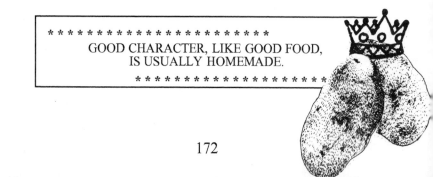

POTATO TOPPINGS

Said a potato to a turkey - "Hey--What do you say.
Shall we hang out together at the "Topper Pot" today?"
Said the turkey to the potato - "I'm glad you ask me true.
I'd rather be a "Topper" than be in a turkey stew!"
___by Carol Fielding McCabe

Information & Tips

There is no vegetable like the Idaho potato; the heart of a menu, solid, satisfying; the anchor food high in solids, cooks fluffy, not watery or waxy; has an oval shape, few and shallow eyes, net-textured skin and russet brown color. Of course the Russet potato, the most popular potato grown in Idaho, is a perfect baker. Add cheese, meat and vegetables for a full potato meal.

Buy firm-textured potatoes that have no cuts, cracks, bruises or discoloration. When you buy all-purpose potatoes, sort them, select the bakers and set them in another container. Pound-for-pound a baking potato is more expensive, but you can usually find 5 or 6 good bakers in a 5 pound bag of all-purpose potatoes.

Bake that potato right; do not wrapp it in foil. That's called steaming. Scrub the potatoes, pierce the skins with a fork and bake on an oven rack at 375 degrees for an hour. (The fork holes serve as an escape vent for steam that builds up inside the baking potato, often causing it to burst.) If you want a soft skinned potato, rub a little vegetable oil on the skin. If you want it crusty, just put it in the oven and turn it once during the cooking time.

Ever wondered why some baked potatoes look and taste better than others? It may be the way they are cut. You can use a knife and cut the potato in half. This tends to flatten the surface and compress the potato pulp. Or you can do a procedure called "Blossom". You blossom a potato with a fork. Press the tines of the fork deep into, but not all the way through the potato, like a large X. Pressing the ends toward the center, lifting and fluffing the meat of the potato. Then eat the spud, the whole spud. If you do not eat the delicious skins you're leaving a lot behind. Vitamins are concentrated near the skin, and the skin itself provides valuable roughage (fiber) to aid your health.

A leftover baked potato can be re-baked if you dip it in water and bake in a 350 degree oven for about 20 minutes.

To test the doneness of a baked potato, squeeze using a pad to protect your hand. If the potato yields to pressure, it is cooked through. Gently roll the potato on a counter to crumble the flesh inside. Then just before serving "blossom" the potato.

It's not necessary to preheat the oven for baking potatoes. It wastes some of the heat. Just put the potatoes in the oven and turn on the heat.

NON-MEAT TOPPINGS:

A 'tater popsicle!
Oh, how wonderful.
Thank you, sweetie.

Potato Bar Toppings

For a special party set out quartered baked potatoes, and offer two or three per person so that guests can mix and match toppings as they desire.

Topping #1 -- Heavenly Dip:
One cup mayonnaise, 1 cup sour cream, 1 teaspoon dill weed, and 1 teaspoon Bon Apetite (spice). Mix together well. Refrigerate overnight.

Topping #2 -- Sour Cream & Onion Dip:
One cup sour cream, 1/2 cup cottage cheese, 1/4 cup finely chopped fresh green onions, finely chopped fresh chives, 1/4 cup finely grated Cheddar cheese. Mix together well. Refrigerate 2 or 3 hours until flavors blend.

Topping #3 -- Avocado Dip:
Two ripe chopped avocadoes, 1 small package creamed cheese, 1/2 tomato-peeled, seeded, and finely chopped. Chop very finely 1 teaspoon each of the following: onion, green pepper, bacon. Blend avocadoes and creamed cheese in blender until smooth, add, but do not blend, the remaining ingredients, and 1 tablespoon lemon juice. Mix well.

Topping #4 -- Creamed Corn: One can cream style corn. Slowly mix
about 1/4 cup evaporated milk and 1/4 cup whole milk to the corn. Do not add too much milk as this should be a semi-thick topping. Add small chunks of cooked meat, such as ham, bacon, Spam, luncheon meats, etc., and 2 chopped, hard-cooked eggs. Add a touch of Oil and Vinegar type Italian dressing for a tangy taste.

Topping #5 -- Fix Your Own Topping:
Prepare separate bowls of the following ingredients for guests to spoon onto a hot baked potato quarter. Place on table or tray: Pats of butter, chopped chives and/or onions, grated Cheddar cheese, sprouts, sauteed mushrooms, avocado chunks, chopped tomatoes, black olives, sour cream, cottage cheese, and anything else you would like to add. Don't forget salt, pepper, cayenne pepper and a few other special herbs and spices.

On A Diet? Toppings

Try some of these on baked, boiled, steamed, and mashed potatoes:

- Toasted sesame seeds.
- Whipped butter and a dash of poppy seeds.
- A mound of slivered pimento and green pepper.
- A spoonful of stewed tomatoes and coarsely-grated Cheddar cheese.
- Melted butter thinned with lemon juice.
- Sliced mushrooms marinated in low-calorie dressing.
- A mix of dried herbs: parsley, chives, basil, dill or others.
- Hot skim milk or chicken broth seasoned with herbs.
- Grated Parmesan cheese.
- Mock sour cream: cottage cheese and lemon juice, whipped in blender.
- Chopped onion with coarsely-ground black pepper.
- Chive-spiked cottage cheese or yogurt.

The Cheesiest Topping

1 sm. pkg.Velvetta cheese	1 sm. can olives, chopped	hot blossomed potato
2-3 Tbs. evap. milk/cream	1 sm. can chilies, chopped	dash cayenne pepper
8-oz. pkg. Philadelphia cream cheese	1/2 cup grated hard cheese	parsley sprigs

Add milk to Velvetta cheese and heat in double boiler or micro-wave until melted, stirring often. Add Philadelphia cheese and cream together until well mixed. Mix the olives, chilies and grated hard cheese together in a separate container.

Spoon Velvetta cheese mixture over hot, blossomed potato and top with grated cheese mixture. Add a dash of cayenne pepper and a sprig of parsley. Serve hot.

Meal In A Spud

8-oz. can stewed tomatoes, drained	few drops hot pepper sauce	2 lg. eggs, poached
1/8 tsp.dried leaf oregano	1 med/lg. Idaho potato	1/4 cup shredded Cheddar cheese

In a small saucepan combine tomatoes, crumbled oregano and hot pepper sauce, breaking up tomatoes with back of spoon; heat to boiling. Split baked potato in half lengthwise with a fork. Top each half with a poached egg, tomato mixture and cheese. Makes 1 serving.

Tomato Topping

2 lg. tomatoes, cut fine	1 sm. onion, chopped fine	1 med. finely chopped
2 carrots, grated	1/2 cup cottage cheese	dill pickle
1/2 tsp. salt	2 Tbs. chopped parsley	4 baked, potatoes, blossomed

Cut tomatoes in small chunks; place in sieve to drain, pushing spoon against them to help squeeze out excessive liquid. Combine tomatoes, carrots, salt, onion, and cottage cheese, parsley and pickle; mixing well. Spoon mixture over hot, blossomed potatoes.

Slim-Trim Potatoes With Tomato Sauce

4 baking potatoes	1 Tb. chopped parsley	1/8 tsp. salt or to taste
1 tsp. butter	1 cup chopped peeled	1/4 tsp. dried oregano
2 Tbs. chopped onion	fresh tomato	1/8 tsp. pepper

Scrub potatoes, dry and prick with fork. Bake in 425 degree oven 50 to 60 minutes, until soft. While potatoes are baking, melt butter in small saucepan; add onion and cook until tender. Add remaining ingredients; simmer 10 min. Keep warm until potatoes are cooked.

When potatoes are cooked, remove from oven, cut an X in tops with a fork, and fluff some of the potato with slight pressure of fingers on sides and ends. Spoon 1/4 cup sauce over each potato.

Dilled Green Beans

2 beef bouillon cubes	2 Tbs. chopped onion	1/2 tsp. dill seed
1 cup water	1/2 C. chopped grn. pepper	2 9-oz. pkg. frozen cut green beans

Dissolve bouillon cubes in water in saucepan. Add onions, pepper and dill seed. Cook several minutes. Add beans and cook, covered, for 8-10 minutes until the beans are tender. Make a thickening with flour and water, add to mixture, cook stirring constantly until thickened. Spoon over baked potatoes.

Variation: Replace green beans with fresh or canned spinach.

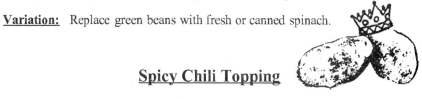

Spicy Chili Topping

Heat a 15-ounce can of hot chili without beans in a small saucepan. Serve with thinly sliced green onions, sliced avocado, and shredded cheddar cheese. Spoon generously over half of baked potato. Makes four 1/2 cup servings.

Bake Mine Vegetarian

1 ½ cup chopped onion	3/4 C. peeled,cut eggplant	1 tsp. basil
1/8 cup olive oil	2 cups frozen French-cut	3/4 C. Parmesan cheese
2 cloves garlic, crushed	green beans,thawed	8 Idaho baked potatoes
1 can peeled tomatoes,	1 tsp. dried thyme,	4-oz. smoked mozzarella,
undrained	1 ½ Tbs. parsley, chopped	cheese, shredded

In large heavy saucepan heat oil over medium heat; saute onion and garlic 3 minutes. Add tomatoes, cut-up eggplant, green beans, crushed leaf thyme, parsley and basil. Cook 20 minutes. Add grated Parmesan cheese, stir to combine. Cook 1 minute longer. Spoon over baked, blossomed potatoes. Sprinkle with mozzarella, if desired. Makes 8 servings.

Chinese Broccoli And Almonds

Very colorful and crisp taste appeal, this dish is low in calories, easy to make and easy on your budget.

3 Tbs. peanut or veg. oil	1 ½ cups chicken broth	1/3 cup slivered
1 med. chopped onion	1 tsp. vinegar	almonds toasted
1 clove garlic, mashed	1 Tb. cornstarch	1/4 cup chopped pimento
10-oz. pkg frozen broccoli	1 Tb. soy sauce	4 Idaho baked potatoes

In large skillet, heat oil; saute onion and garlic until onion is transparent. Add broccoli, chicken broth and vinegar. Mix cornstarch with soy sauce, stir into skillet; bring to a boil, boil 1 minute. Just before serving stir in toasted almonds and pimento. Spoon topping over each blossomed potato. Makes 4 servings.

Elegant Broccoli-Sauced Potatoes

1/3 to 1/2 C. chopped onion	1 tsp. poppy seeds	about 3 cups broccoli (fresh
2 Tbs. butter	1 tsp. paprika (optional)	or frozen) separated into
2 cups sour cream	1/4 tsp salt	small flowerettes, &
4 tsp. vinegar	6 hot baked potatoes	diced stems

Saute onion in butter until golden. Gently stir together remaining ingredients, except broccoli. Add to sauteed onion, stirring gently to mix. Add broccoli, mixing gently. Heat very gently until desired serving temperature. Do NOT boil, or sauce will separate. Using fork, make an X in potatoes, fluff insides. Spoon sauce over potatoes.

Guacamole Topped Potatoes

4 Idaho potatoes, baked
6-oz. pkg. cream cheese
1 ripe avocado, peeled,
1 Tb. finely chopped onion

1/2 med. tomato, mashed,
  peeled, chopped
1 ½ tsp. lemon juice
dash of hot sauce

dash of garlic salt
4 slices bacon, cooked
2 sm. tomatoes, cut into
  wedges

Beat softened cheese with mixer until smooth; add avocado, beating until smooth. Stir in tomato, onion, lemon juice, hot sauce, and garlic salt. Allow potatoes to cool to the touch. Split potatoes lengthwise, and fluff flesh with a fork. Spoon topping over potato; sprinkle with bacon and top with tomato wedges. Makes 4 servings.

COTTAGE CHEESE, SOUR CREAM OR YOGURT TOPPINGS:

"A potato a day will keep us doctors away, and we can play golf."

Sauerkraut/Sour Cream Topping

Bake an **Idaho potato**, cut in half, fluff pulp with a fork, and add **1 teaspoon butter** to each half; letting it melt into the pulp. To each half add a layer of **sour cream, sauerkraut**, and top with **grated Cheddar cheese**. Sprinkle with **onion greens or fresh chives**.

Baked Potatoes With Mock Sour Cream

1 cup cottage cheese
about 1 ½ tsp. mustard
2 Tbs. milk
salt, to taste

dash hot pepper sauce
1 tsp. lemon juice
3-4 hot baked potatoes
paprika (optional)

grated Caraway or Cheddar
  cheese
cherry tomatoes (optional)
parsley sprig (optional)

In blender, at low speed, puree cottage cheese, prepared mustard to taste, milk, salt, hot pepper sauce and lemon juice until smooth. Split baked potatoes and top with mock sour cream (cottage cheese mixture). Sprinkle a little grated cheese and paprika over the mock sour cream. Return sour cream-topped potatoes to 400 degree oven for 5 minutes. Arrange on plates; garnish with cherry tomatoes and parsley.

Sour Cream Delight

1/4 cup sour cream
2 Tbs. soft butter

1/2 cup shredded sharp cheese
1 Tb. chopped chives

Combine sour cream, butter, cheese, and chives in small bowl. Spoon over hot baked, blossomed potatoes. Makes 2 servings.

Mushroom Sauce For Potatoes

4½-oz. can mushrooms
2 cups stock
1½-oz. butter

1 to 1½-oz. flour
salt
some lemon juice

2 Tbs. cream
parsley

In a blender add drained mushrooms and stock, blend until smooth. Melt butter and stir in flour until golden yellow. Add the blended mushrooms, cook 5-10 minutes, season with salt, add lemon juice, and cream and serve with finely chopped parsley over baked or cut up potatoes.

Creamy Cottage Cheese Potato Topping

1 cup low-fat cottage cheese

1/3 cup buttermilk

Mix in a blender on medium speed until smooth and creamy. More buttermilk may be added for a thinner topping.

Variations:
#1. Blue Cheese: Add 1 Tb. blue cheese, and salt and pepper to taste.

#2. Horseradish: Add 1 to 2 tablespoons of grated horseradish.

#3. Dill-weed: Add 1/2 to 1 teaspoon of dried dill-weed, or 1 tablespoon of chopped fresh dill-weed.

#4. Green Goddess: Add 3 anchovies, 1 teaspoon chopped green onion, 1 tablespoon chopped green parsley, and tarragon to taste.

Herbal Yogurt Topping

2 tsp. lemon juice
1/2 C. plain low-fat yogurt
1 to 2 tsp. minced onion

dash tabasco
1/8 tsp. garlic powder
1 tsp. minced parsley

1 Tb. oil
1/2 tsp. paprika
1/2 tsp. salt

Mix all ingredients together in a blender on medium speed for 5 seconds. Spoon on top baked potatoes.

178

BEEF & PREPARED MEAT TOPPINGS:

"Whaddya mean I have to share my potatoes with your mother?!"

Potato Italiano

Use your favorite pizza sauce recipe. Layer the pepperoni, sliced mushrooms and black olives over blossomed baked potato. Top with mozzarella cheese. Makes 1 servings.

Campsite Supper

Idahoans love their scenic state and spend a great deal of time in the outdoors. Rustle up this Franks and Cheese Topping to satisfy appetites revved up by the brisk country and mountain air.

4 Idaho Potatoes, baked	1/2 cup catsup	6 frankfurters, cut in 1" pieces
1¼ cups milk	2 Tbs. prepared mustard	1/2 cup Am. cheese, grated
1 cup mayonnaise		

In saucepan, combine milk, mayonnaise, catsup and mustard; blend well. Add franks and heat thoroughly. Spoon topping over each blossomed potato. Sprinkle with grated cheese.

Place potatoes under a preheated broiler, broil until cheese is melted and slightly browned. Serve immediately. Makes 4 servings.

TIP: Potatoes soaked in salt water 20 minutes before baking will bake more rapidly. For still faster baking have the water very hot.

Cowboy Corned Beef & Horseradish Topping

Won't be able to resist this topping! Makes you rarin' to get up and go explore those wide open spaces.

3 Tbs. butter	3 cups milk	1 lb. cooked corned beef,
1 med. onion, chopped	2 Tb. prepared horseradish	cut in 1 inch strips
2 Tbs. flour	1 Tb. lemon juice	4 Idaho Potatoes, baked
1/2 tsp. dried leaf thyme	1/2 tsp salt	

In large skillet melt butter; saute onion until tender. Add flour and thyme, cook 1 minute. Slowly stir in milk; bring to boiling. Add horseradish, lemon juice and salt, simmer 5 minutes. Add corned beef, heat thoroughly. Spoon topping over blossomed potatoes. Makes 4 servings.

Scandinavian Meatballs

4 Idaho Potatoes, baked	10-oz. can beef broth	1 Tb. water
1 Tb. butter	2 Tbs.Worcestershire sauce	1 Tb. cornstarch
1 lg. onion, chopped	1 tsp. dried dill weed	1/2 cup sour cream
1 lb. ground beef		

In large skillet melt butter; saute onion until tender. Remove onions from skillet. Mix half the onions with ground beef; shape into 20 meatballs. In same skillet, brown meatballs over medium heat; remove and reserve. Return remaining onions to skillet; add condensed beef broth, Worcestershire sauce and dill weed. Blend cornstarch with water; add to skillet, bring to boiling, cook 1 minute. Reduce heat to low, stir in sour cream. **DO NOT BOIL.** Spoon over blossomed potato. Serve immediately. Makes 4 servings.

Baked Potatoes Rio Grande

16 med. Potatoes, baked	4 cloves garlic, minced	1 cup chopped, hot green
3 Tbs. vegetable oil	1 qt. chili sauce	chili peppers, drained
4 lbs. ground beef	2 cups catsup	1 tsp. hot pepper sauce
1 ½ qts. sliced onions	3 Tbs. vinegar cider	

In a deep skillet heat oil over medium heat; brown beef. Remove meat from skillet; reserve. In same skillet saute onion and garlic 2 minutes. Add chili sauce, catsup, vinegar, chili peppers and hot pepper sauce. Return meat to skillet, heat through. Spoon over baked, blossomed potatoes. Yield; 2 ½ quarts; 16 servings; about 1/2 cup sauce per portion.

Baked Reuben Potatoes

2 cups diced cooked corned beef,
  or 1 can corned beef, shredded
about 2 cups sauerkraut, drained
3/4 to 1 cup grated Swiss Cheese

1/2 cup grated Cheddar cheese
1/4 tsp. caraway seed
1/2 cup crumpled cooked bacon
4 hot baked potatoes

Combine all ingredients but the bacon and baked potatoes. Split open potatoes and pile some of mixture on each half. Broil 5 to 10 minutes, or until cheese melts slightly. Sprinkle bacon atop just before serving.

Baked Potato Shanghai

1 cup soy sauce
1/4 cup sesame oil
1/4 cup honey
1 ½ tsp. ground ginger
2 cloves garlic, crushed

1 ½ lb.skirt steak, trimmed
3 cups beef broth
1 ¼ qts.broccoli flowerets
8 scallions, julienned
salt and pepper

1 lb. red bell peppers,
  julienned
1/8 cup cornstarch
8 med.large Idaho
  baked potatoes

In shallow dish, combine soy sauce, sesame oil, honey, ginger and garlic; mix well. Add steak to marinade. Cover. Let stand 1 hour. Drain meat, reserving 2 cups marinade. Heat skillet over medium-high heat; saute steak on both sides 2 minutes. Remove from pan and slice thinly; set aside. Add broth to skillet; stir to dissolve brown bits. Add broccoli, scallions or green onions, red bell peppers, salt, pepper and cornstarch. Simmer 1 or more minutes, until slightly thickened. Season to taste. Add meat. Spoon over baked, blossomed potatoes. Makes 8 servings.

Chili-Cheddar Topper

Saute **1 medium-sized chopped onion, 1/2 cup finely chopped sweet green pepper** and **1 clove garlic, crushed,** in **2 tablespoons butter** in large heavy skillet for 5 minutes or until softened. Add **1 pound ground round;** saute, breaking up clumps with wooden spoon, for 5 minutes or until no longer pink. Stir in **2 tablespoons chili powder.** Add **1 teaspoon leaf thyme, crumbled.** Cook, stirring, 2 to 3 minutes. Stir in **15-oz. can tomato sauce, 2 tablespoons catsup, 1/4 teaspoon salt and 1/8 teaspoon liquid red-pepper seasoning.** Cover and let mixture simmer until potatoes are finished baking. To serve, blossom an Idaho baked potato, and ladle mixture over potatoes. Sprinkle generously with 1 ½ cups shredded sharp Cheddar cheese.

Scalloped Ground Beef Topping

Cook **1/2 lb. ground beef, 1/2 chopped onion, 1/2 chopped green or sweet red pepper, 1/4 cup finely chopped celery and 1/2 cup chopped mushrooms** together until meat is cooked and vegetables are soft. Add **1 can Cream Chicken and Mushroom Soup** and **1/2 to 1 soup can milk** (only enough to make a medium thick gravy). Spread atop baked potatoes and sprinkle with **cheese.**

Taco Potatoes

1 lb. lean ground beef	1 tsp. ground cumin	sour cream to taste
1/2 cup chopped onion	4-6 hot baked potatoes	1 chopped tomato
1 cup taco sauce(mild to	about 1½ to 2 cups grated	chopped green chilies
hot, as desired)	cheddar cheese	(optional)

Saute ground beef and onion in medium size skillet until meat is browned. Drain off excess fat. Add sauce & cumin mixing well. Simmer until hot, stirring occasionally, until mixture is desired thickness for spooning over baked potatoes.

Using fork, make an X in the potatoes; fluff insides. Spoon mixture over potatoes. Top with grated cheese, then a dab of sour cream. Sprinkle chopped tomato and a little chopped green chili if desired, over the sour cream.

Note: Grated cheese and/or sour cream can be eliminated if you prefer, but they add great flavor. Makes 4-6 servings.

Nacho Potatoes

2 hot baked potatoes	1 sm. 22-oz. can sliced	chopped green onion
1 cup grated sharp	ripe olives, drained	tomatoes
Cheddar cheese	bacon, cooked, crumbled	sour cream (optional)
2 Tbs. chopped green chilies		

Combine cheese, chilies and ripe olives in small mixing bowl. Use mixture to top potatoes, place them under the broiler until topping melts. Serve with bacon, onion, tomato and sour cream.

Beef, Mushroom & Sour Cream Topping

1/2 cup onion, chopped	2 Tb. flour	1 can Cr. Mushroom Soup
2 tsp. garlic powder	1 tsp. salt	few slivered mushrooms
1 Tb. butter	1/4 tsp. pepper	1 cup sour cream
1 lb lean ground beef	1/4 tsp. paprika	4-6 baked potatoes

Saute onions and garlic powder in butter or margarine; stir in meat, flour, and seasoning. Saute 5 minutes or until meat loses color; drain if necessary. Add mushrooms and soup; simmer for 8-10 minutes. Blend in sour cream; do not bring to boil. Serve over hot baked potatoes. Makes 4-6 servings.

TIP: Bake potatoes in muffin tins. Makes it easy to turn the potatoes and to remove them from a hot oven. Use also for apples and peppers.

CHICKEN & SEAFOOD TOPPINGS:

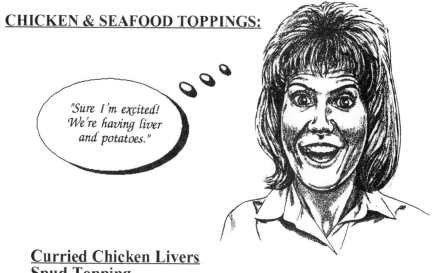

"Sure I'm excited! We're having liver and potatoes."

Curried Chicken Livers Spud Topping

1/2 cup chicken broth	1 tsp. vegetable oil	1/4 cup onion, chopped
1/2 tsp. cornstarch	1/4 lb. chicken livers	1/4 cup red pepper, chopped
1/4 tsp curry powder	1/4 C. grn. pepper, chop'd	1 med/large ld. baked potato
1/8 tsp.salt;dash red pepper	1 sm. clove garlic, minced	

In bowl, mix chicken broth, cornstarch, curry powder, salt and red pepper. In skillet heat oil; add quartered livers (free of fat), green pepper, garlic and onion. Cook 3 to 5 minutes until livers are browned, but slightly pink in the center and vegetables are tender. Stir cornstarch mixture and add to pan. Bring to boil; boil one minute, stirring constantly. Spoon over hot baked potatoes. Makes 1 serving.

Chicken & Broccoli With Mushroom Sauce

10-oz. pkg frozen broccoli	4-oz. can mushroom slices, with liquid
3 Tbs. butter	1 lb. cooked chicken, or turkey, sliced
3 Tbs. flour	2 Tbs. chopped parsley
1 cup chicken broth	2 Tbs. bread crumbs

Preheat oven 375 degrees; cook broccoli according to pkg. directions. Mix butter and flour together in saucepan. Cook briefly over med. heat. Blend in chicken broth, stirring constantly until thickened and smooth. Stir in mushrooms and their liquid. Season to taste. Place broccoli pieces in shallow pan. Cover with sliced chicken and pour mushroom sauce over all. Add bread crumbs. Mix together. Bake uncovered, 15-25 minutes, or until bubbly, and brown on top.

Spoon over the top of a baked potato. Garnish with parsley.

183

Chicken A`La King

3 Tbs. oil	1/3 cup nonfat dry milk	1/4 cup chopped pimento
4 Tbs. flour	1/2 lb. sliced mushrooms	4 tsp. sherry (optional)
3 cups chicken stock	2 cups cooked chicken	potatoes
salt & pepper to taste	1/4 cup diced grn. pepper	1 Tb. chopped parsley

Heat oil in a saucepan, add flour, and cook briefly, stirring. Pour in chicken stock, stirring constantly until thick and smooth. Season and stir in nonfat dry milk. Cook 1 minute.

Saute sliced mushrooms and add to sauce, along with chicken, green pepper and pimento. Heat through, then add sherry. Adjust seasoning, spoon on top a baked, halved potato, and garnish with parsley.

Chicken Parmigiana Spuds

4 Idaho Potatoes, baked	1/2 cup water
1 Tb. olive oil	1 Tb. sugar
1/2 cup onion, chopped	1 tsp. dried leaf oregano
1 clove garlic, mashed	3 cups cooked, boned, diced chicken
28-oz. can whole tomatoes in	2 Tbs. grated Parmesan cheese
tomato puree, coarsely chopped	4-oz. sliced Mozzarella cheese

In large skillet heat olive oil over medium-high heat; saute onion and garlic until transparent. Add tomatoes and puree, water, sugar and oregano; cook 20 minutes. Add chicken, cook 5 minutes longer. Spoon topping over each blossomed potato. Sprinkle with Parmesan cheese. Place 1 slice Mozzarella cheese over each potato, place under pre-heated broiler until cheese melts and browns slightly. Serve immediately. Makes 4 servings.

Idaho Potatoes With Moroccan Chicken Topping

4 Idaho potatoes	1 lb. boneless, chicken breasts	1 tsp. paprika
1/4 cup vegetable oil	or thighs, cut in strips	1 tsp. ground cinnamon
1/2 cup slivered almonds	2 Tbs. flour	1/2 tsp. salt
1 cup onion, chopped	1¼ cups chicken broth	1/2 tsp. hot pepper sauce
2 cloves garlic, chopped	3 Tbs. lemon juice	1/2 cup raisins

Scrub potatoes, dry and prick with a fork. Bake in a 425 degree oven 55 to 65 minutes, until soft. In large skillet heat oil, saute almonds until golden brown. Add onion and garlic; saute until tender. Add chicken; cook, stirring until chicken turns white. Sprinkle with flour; mix well.

Combine broth, lemon juice, paprika, cinnamon, salt & pepper sauce. Add to chicken mixture, stirring constantly, until mixture boils & thickens; add raisins; simmer 3 minutes. Spoon evenly over blossomed potatoes. Makes 4 servings.

Baked Potatoes A La Madison

8 large Idaho baked potatoes	1 ¼ Tbs. cornstarch
1/4 cup butter	1/4 cup water
2 lbs. chicken livers,	1/2 cup red currant jelly
1/2 C. Armagnac or Cognac (brandy)	1/4 cup tomato paste
3 cup chicken broth	3/4 tsp. salt; 1/4 tsp. pepper
1 cup Madeira wine.	

In large skillet melt butter over medium-high heat; brown livers quickly on each side, remove from skillet and reserve. Add brandy to skillet scraping bottom of pan to loosen brown bits. Add broth and wine. Simmer 2 minutes.

In small bowl combine cornstarch and water. Add to skillet, stirring until smooth. Add jelly, tomato paste, salt and pepper. Bring to boiling; boil 1 minute. Return livers to pan and heat through. Correct seasoning. Spoon over baked, blossomed potatoes. Serves 8.

Potatoes & Chicken With Mushroom Sauce

3 Tbs. butter	3 Tbs. flour	1/8 tsp. ground nutmeg
1/3 cup chopped grn.onions	1 cup chicken broth	2 C.diced cooked chicken
4-oz. chopped mushrooms	1/2 cup milk or cream	4-6 baked potatoes, split
	salt & freshly ground pepper to taste	

Melt butter in skillet; saute green onions until tender. Add mushrooms and cook about 2 min. longer. Sprinkle with flour; cook and stir another 2 minutes. Remove from heat and gradually stir in broth and milk. Return to heat and bring sauce to boil, stirring until sauce thickens. Season with salt and black pepper to taste, and ground nutmeg. Add chicken and bring to serving temperature. Serve over baked potatoes. Makes 2 ½ to 3 cups sauce, enough for 4-6 potatoes.

Variation: Add 1/4 to 1/2 cup slivered almonds.

Turkey Topper

4 Idaho Potatoes, baked	2 Tbs. flour	3/4 lb. turkey, cooked, diced
3 Tbs. butter	2 cups low-fat milk	1/4 tsp. hot pepper sauce
1 cup onion, chopped	1/4 cup Parmesan cheese	2 Tbs. dry sherry (optional
1 cup mushrooms, sliced		

In medium saucepan, melt butter; saute onion until tender. Add mushrooms and cook 3 minutes. Sprinkle in flour and cook, stirring over moderate heat, 2 minutes. Remove from heat. Gradually stir in milk; return to heat, bring to boiling. Stir in grated Parmesan cheese. Reduce heat; simmer 10 min. Add turkey, sherry (optional), and hot pepper sauce; heat thoroughly. Spoon evenly over blossomed potatoes. Serve immediately. Makes 4 servings.

Yummy Tuna Topping

4 Idaho Potatoes, baked	1 med. onion, chopped	2 cups frozen,
1 Tb. olive oil	little minced garlic	spinach,
1 Tb. butter	1 cup tomatoes, drained	7-oz. can tuna,drained

Heat olive oil and butter in large skillet; saute onion and garlic until tender. Add tomatoes; bring to a boil. Add thawed, drained spinach; cook 20 minutes. Blend flaked tuna into mixture just before serving, heat through. Spoon topping over each blossomed potato. Makes 4 servings.

Note: I feel this has too much tuna. I like it best with 1/2 the amount of tuna.

Variation: Leave out the tuna. It's still good! Also you can replace the tuna with chicken flakes.

Baked Potato With Topping From The Sea

16 Idaho Potatoes, baked	1 qt. dry vermouth
4 lbs.boned monkfish,cut 1"pieces	1 cup heavy cream
3/4 cup cornstarch, divided	2 tsp. white pepper & 1 Tb. salt
1/4 cup butter	1 qt. julienned carrots, blanched,
1/4 cup shallots, chopped	drained
4 clove garlic, minced	1 qt. snow peas cut in 1" pieces,
5 cups bottled clam juice, divided	blanched, drained

Dust fish with 1/4 cup cornstarch. In large skillet melt butter over medium heat; brown fish lightly on all sides, remove from skillet. Add shallots and garlic to skillet; saute 1 minute. Add 4 cups clam juice and vermouth.

In large bowl combine remaining 1/2 cup cornstarch with remaining 1 cup clam juice; whisk into skillet, stirring until sauce boils and thickens. Boil 1 minute. Add heavy cream, salt and pepper. Add carrots and snow peas, simmer 2 minutes. Return monkfish and heat through. Spoon over baked, blossomed, potatoes. Yield: 4 quarts topping; 16 servings; about 1 cup sauce per portion.

TIP: Any dish containing fish should not be left setting out any longer than necessary. Refrigerate any left-overs immediately. To reheat for another meal, use the microwave. It's fast and will give you a fresher, better flavor.

PORK & LAMB TOPPINGS:

*"You ate every one....
and didn't even leave
me a smell?"*

Western Pork Barbecue Supper

Enjoy the barbecue flavor all year round with this dish.

6 Idaho Potatoes, baked
1 Tb. butter
1 ½ lbs. boneless pork
   shoulder strips
1 large onion, sliced

1 tsp. dried leaf basil
1 ½ cup beef broth
1/4 cup cider vinegar
1/4 cup sugar

1/4 cup catsup
1 tsp. salt
1 tsp. pickling spice
3 oranges, sliced

In large skillet melt butter; stir pork over medium-high heat until well browned. Add onion slices and basil; saute until onion is tender. Add beef broth, bring to boiling; stir in vinegar, sugar, catsup, salt, pickling spices, and orange slices. Simmer 1 hour or until pork is tender. Spoon topping over each blossomed potato.

Idaho Sunset spuds

4 Idaho Potatoes, baked
2 Tbs. butter
1 lg. chopped onion
2 Tbs flour

1 ½ cups milk
14-oz. can pineapple,
   drained, save juice
2 tsp. vinegar

1/2 tsp. hot pepper sauce
1/4 tsp. salt
3/4 lb. (2 cups) cooked ham,
   diced

In large skillet melt butter; saute onions until tender. Add flour; cook, stirring for 2 minutes. Remove from heat, gradually stir in milk, bring to boiling. Combine reserved pineapple juice with vinegar, add to skillet with hot pepper sauce and salt. Simmer 3 minutes; add ham and pineapple chunks and heat thoroughly. Spoon over blossomed potatoes. Serve immediately. Makes 4 servings.

187

Baked Potatoes With Bacon & Eggs

4 Idaho Potatoes, baked	3 Tbs. flour	1/2 tsp. dry mustard
1/4 lb. bacon, in pieces	2 cups milk	6 hard-cooked eggs, sliced
1/4 cup onion, chopped	1/2 tsp.salt; 1/4 tsp.pepper	1/4 cup parsley, chopped

In medium saucepan, cook bacon until crisp. Remove bacon and crumble, leaving 3 Tbs. bacon drippings. Add onion to dripping and cook until onion is tender, about 5 minutes. Blend in flour. Stir in milk, salt, pepper and dry mustard

Cook over medium heat, stirring constantly, until sauce comes to a boil and thickens. Add sliced hard-cooked eggs, parsley and reserved bacon. Spoon topping over blossomed potato. Makes 4 servings.

Curried Lamb Sunday Supper

4 Idaho Potatoes, baked	1 clove garlic, mashed	1 apple, pared, cored, cubed
2 Tbs. olive oil	1 Tbs. curry powder	1/2 cup shredded coconut
1 lb. lamb shoulder, cubed	3 Tbs. flour	1/4 tsp. salt
1 large onion, chopped	1¾ cups chicken broth	1 Tb. sugar

In skillet heat oil; add lamb and brown on all sides. Add onion, garlic, and curry powder, cook 5 minutes. Stir in flour. Slowly stir in chicken broth, bring to boiling. Add apple, coconut, salt and pepper. Simmer 1 hour or until lamb is tender. Spoon over blossomed potato. Serve immediately. Makes 4 servings.

Potato, Meat & Cheese Topping

1 lg.baking potato	salt & pepper to taste	1 Tb. shredded Swiss cheese
1 egg	1 Tb. shredded or chopped	1 Tb. other cheese of your
1 tsp. butter	cooked ham or chicken	choice

Pierce potato in several spots with a fork. Bake in preheated 375 degree oven until done, 40-50 minutes. Make a cross about 2x1 1/2 inches in center top of potato. Fluff up potato with a fork and make a well in center large enough to hold one egg. Break egg into well. Top with butter, salt and pepper. Bake at 375 degree until white is set and yolk is soft and creamy.

Sprinkle meat over egg, after egg has baked for about 10 minutes. (Bake 5 minutes more, then check to see if desired consistency; add cheeses; bake longer if necessary to melt cheeses.) Makes 1 serving.

* *
A kindness done today is the surest way
To a brighter tomorrow.
* *

BREAD, ROLLS, CAKES, COOKIES, CANDY & DESSERTS

I shared a homemade loaf of bread with a neighbor one fine day.
She smiled at me so sweetly then she started in to say,
A "thank you for your kindness", but her words were choked with tears.
No one had ever done that before, in all her many years.
--by Carol Fielding McCabe

Information & Tips

Grains are known as the "Staff of Life". If we were cut-off from being able to obtain food for an extended period of time for some reason or another, we could survive on grains. If we use wisdom in their use, and learn to sprout most of them, especially wheat and if we have access to water, we could truly survive for many months. Now add a potato a day and you could fare quite well. (Another reason to store some potatoes.) Consider a variety of grains and have a big, big bag or two of Idaho potatoes on hand for those rainy days or those truck strikes, etc. One, never knows when one will have to survive on whatever is in our own food pantry.

When cooking bread, place a pan of water in the bottom of the oven and also when you allow bread to raise in the oven. It gives the moisture needed to keep the loaves of bread from splitting on the sides and drying out. Cut your bread raising time in half by using a heating pad to raise the loaves of bread. Cover the heating pad with a kitchen towel, set the pans on the towel, and cover the loaves with a damp cloth. Turn the heating pad on medium heat. The bread should raise in 10 to 15 minutes.

Add dry yeast directly to the flour mixture when making bread. No need to put it in warm water first. It works just as well as if put in a water mixture.

When a recipe calls for oil and honey, measure oil first and then the honey. This makes the honey slide out easily.

The potato, like the zucchini, is a bland tasting food. The flavors are not strong and will mix with many foods. They go especially well where flour is used as in cakes or puddings. So! Get out some of your zucchini recipes and try potatoes instead or try half potatoes and half zucchini. You may be in for quite a surprise.

In Idaho Falls, a dairy makes potato ice cream and it's good. Sorry, I tried but couldn't get the recipe for my book. I'm guessing the potato was used as a thickening agent???

If I have boiled or steam boiled potatoes and I am going to bake bread, I will use the potato water. I like using all those nutrients found in the potato water.

BREADS, ROLLS & BISCUITS:

"Come on! Tell me who helped you make the bread."

White bread

1 cup milk	2 pkg. dry or cake yeast	3/4 C. Idahoan® Mashed
3 Tbs. sugar	1/2 cup warm water	Potato (dry flakes)
2 tsp. salt	(110-115 degrees)	flour
3 Tbs. shortening		

Scald milk; stir in sugar, salt, shortening and potato flakes. Cool to lukewarm. In bowl dissolve yeast in warm water; stir into potato mixture. Add 3 cups flour; beat until smooth. Add additional flour to form soft dough. Turn out onto lightly floured board; knead until smooth and elastic, about 8-10 min. Place in greased bowl. Cover; let rise until doubled in bulk, about 1 hour. Punch down; form into two loaves. Place in greased 9x5x3" loaf pans; cover and let rise until doubled. Preheat oven to 400. Bake 10 minutes; then reduce heat to 375 degrees and bake for 30 minutes. Remove bread from pans and cool on racks.

50% Wheat Bread

Must use a bread mixer with this recipe. Doing it by hand causes too much flour to be used, thus making a dry and crumbly product. This is a moist bread. The loaves must be handled carefully after they have raised as the loaves may fall slightly. This does not effect the taste.

1 Tb. yeast	1 cup scalded milk	1 cup mashed potatoes
1/4 cup warm water	2 Tbs. shortening	2-3 cups whole wheat flour
2 Tbs. sugar	1 Tb. salt	2-3 cups white flour
1 cup hot water	1 cup cooked oatmeal	1/4 cup gluten flour

Dissolve yeast in warm water and sugar. Put hot milk and water in mixer; add shortening, salt, oatmeal and potatoes. Blend in 1 cup wheat flour and 1 cup white flour. Add gluten flour and yeast. (Try your health food store for the gluten flour.)

Add remaining flour until dough pulls from bowl, watching it close as to avoid adding too much flour. Let raise to double, punch down. Grease pans. Form 2 loaves. Let raise until it mounds above tins. Bake 350 degrees for 35-45 minutes.

Whole Wheat Potato Bread

6 cups hot water	2 eggs	2/3 cup potato flakes
2/3 cup cooking oil	2/3 cup powdered milk	1/2 cup gluten flour
2/3 cup honey	(add with 1 cup	13 cups whole wheat flour
3 Tbs. salt	whole wheat flour)	2 Tbs. yeast

2   This bread is best if made with a bread maker. Combine in mixer bowl, hot water, cooking oil, honey, salt, eggs, potato flakes, powdered milk, gluten flour and 7 cups whole wheat flour; blend; add dry yeast; blend; add 6 or 7 more cups whole wheat flour and knead at bread speed 10 minutes. Form into loaves. Place in bread pans and let rise until double in bulk.

Bake at 400 degrees for 15 minutes then 350 degrees for 30 minutes. This gives a crispier crust.

Potato Bread

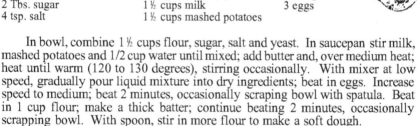

7½ to 8½ cups flour	2 pkg. active dry yeast	1/4 cup butter
2 Tbs. sugar	1½ cups milk	3 eggs
4 tsp. salt	1½ cups mashed potatoes	

In bowl, combine 1½ cups flour, sugar, salt and yeast. In saucepan stir milk, mashed potatoes and 1/2 cup water until mixed; add butter and, over medium heat; heat until warm (120 to 130 degrees), stirring occasionally. With mixer at low speed, gradually pour liquid mixture into dry ingredients; beat in eggs. Increase speed to medium; beat 2 minutes, occasionally scraping bowl with spatula. Beat in 1 cup flour; make a thick batter; continue beating 2 minutes, occasionally scrapping bowl. With spoon, stir in more flour to make a soft dough.

Turn dough onto well-floured surface; knead about 10 minutes, until smooth and elastic, working in about 1½ cups flour while kneading. (Dough will be soft.) Shape dough into a ball and place in greased large bowl, turning dough over so top is greased. Cover with towel; let rise in warm place (80 to 85 degrees), away from draft, until doubled, about 1½ hours. (Dough is doubled when two fingers pressed lightly into dough leave a dent.)

Punch down dough; turn onto lightly floured surface; knead lightly; cover with bowl or towel for 15 minutes and let dough rest.

Grease two 9x5 inch loaf pans. Cut dough in half; form loaves, and put in pans; cover with towel; let rise in warm place until doubled, about 1 hour.

Heat oven to 400; carefully brush tops of loaves with milk if you like. Bake loaves 40 minutes or until well browned, and loaves sound hollow when tapped with fingers. Remove from pans immediately and cool completely on wire racks.

Ranch Bread

Boil:
1 cup water
1/3 cup sugar
1 cup ground beef
1 cup raisins

Soak:
2 pkg. yeast
1 tsp. sugar
1/2 cup warm water

Mix the following and let rise 10 minutes:

1 cup All-Bran
3 Tbs. melted butter
2 cups white flour

1 ½ cups warm
    potato water
yeast mixture

1 Tb. molasses
2 cups graham flour

Add:
3 tsp. salt
cooled beef mixture

1/2 cup chopped nuts
2 to 3 cups white flour

Make a soft dough. Knead. Rest 10 minutes and knead again. Cover and let rise until double. Punch down and raise 20 minutes. Shape into 3 loaves, let rise. Bake 350 degrees for 40 minutes.

Potato-Bacon Bread

1 cup mashed potatoes
1 Tb. butter
2 cups all-purpose flour

1 tsp. salt
1 pkg. active dry yeast
2 Tbs. sugar

1 egg
3 Tbs. bacon bits or 6 slices
    crumbled cooked bacon

In small saucepan, heat mashed potatoes with butter and 1/4 cup water until very warm, stirring frequently. In large bowl, combine 1 cup flour, sugar, salt and yeast. Add egg and mashed potato mixture; with mixer at medium speed, beat 2 minutes, occasionally scraping bowl. With spoon, stir in bacon, then remaining 1 cup flour.

Cover bowl with towel; let rise in warm place, away from draft, until doubled, about 1 hour and 15 minutes.

Grease a deep 1 ½ quart casserole or souffle dish. With spoon, stir down dough. Place dough in casserole, shaping so that center is slightly higher than the sides. Cover with towel; let rise in warm place, away from draft, until doubled, about 1 hour and 15 minutes.

Heat oven to 350 degrees. Bake bread 30 to 40 minutes until golden, and bread sounds hollow when lightly tapped with fingers. With spatula, loosen bread from sides of casserole; remove from casserole and cool on wire rack. Makes 1 loaf.

Sourdough Potato Bread

1 pkg. dry yeast	instant mashed potatoes	1 cup sourdough starter (below)
6 cups flour	3/4 cup milk	1 egg white
1/4 cup sugar	1/4 cup melted butter	2 Tbs. water
2 tsp. salt	2 eggs	sesame seeds

In large mixer bowl combine yeast, 2 cups flour, sugar and salt; set aside. Prepare 2 servings mashed potatoes according to package directions, or use leftover potatoes. Stir in milk, butter, eggs and starter; blend. Add potato mixture to dry ingredients; beat for 2 minutes on medium speed. Add 1½ cups of the flour; beat 2 minutes more. With heavy spoon stir in enough remaining flour to form a stiff dough. Turn dough out on a flour coated board; knead until smooth, about 8 minutes. Add more flour if needed to prevent sticking. Place in greased bowl, turning to grease other side. Cover; let rise in warm place until double in bulk, about 2 minutes. Punch down; divide in half; shape and put in pans.

Let rise in warm place for 45 minutes. With razor blade or sharp knife, cut 1/2 inch slashes in top of loaf. Brush loaves with mixture of egg white and 2 tablespoons water. Sprinkle with seeds. Bake at 350 degrees about 35 minutes.

Bread may be shaped into 2 round loaves and placed on a baking sheet instead of bread pans if desired.

Sourdough Starter:

For best results, use glass or pottery (never metal) containers.

This starter has a clean sour milk odor. The liquid will separate from the batter when it stands several days but this does not matter. If replenished every few days with flour and water, the starter keeps fresh and can last for years. If the starter is not to be used for several weeks, freeze or dry to keep it from spoiling. To carry it to camp, etc., add enough flour to shape it into a ball and place it in a sack of flour. (This is drying it.) In the dry form, the yeast goes into a spore stage which will keep for a long time. Water and warmth bring the activity back into the yeast.

Mix well: 2 cups flour   2 cups water   1 Tb. yeast

Place in a warm spot overnight or longer. It will ferment and grow during this time. In the morning put 1 cup of the batter in a jar with a lid and store in the refrigerator. This is a sourdough starter for future use. The remaining batter can be used for baking items immediately.

Hints: In growing, the yeast gives off a carbon dioxide gas which forms bubbles in the dough. The bacteria changes the starch and sugar to lactic acid, giving the dough a sour odor. Soda is added to react with the acid to form more gas, which makes the product lighter. If too little soda is added, the product is more sour in taste. Never add yeast directly to the starter as it kills the yeast. Care should be taken in the amount of flour used. It is better to have dough a little soft than too stiff

Sourdough Basic Batter:
For any recipe which calls for basic batter (or Starter) do as follows: The evening before you bake or cook an item, place starter, 2 cups hot water and 2 cups flour in a bowl. Mix thoroughly. This mixture may be lumpy but it will thin down during the night. Cover bowl (not air tight); set in warm place. It is important to keep batter warm so it will ferment. Always remember to take 1 cup from starter and keep in covered jar in fridge until you are going to make more basic batter.

Wheat-Potato Batter Buns

1 med. potato, peeled, cubed	1 ¼ cups white flour	1/4 cup cooking oil
1 ¼ cups water	1 pkg. active dry yeast	1 slightly beaten egg
1 ½ cups whl. wheat flour	1/4 cup sugar	1 Tb. water
	2 tsp. salt	sesame seed

In saucepan cook potato, covered, in 1 ¼ cups water 12 to 15 minutes or until tender; do not drain. Mash potato in cooking liquid. Add enough water to make 1 ½ cups potato mixture. Cool to room temperature. In large mixer bowl combine whole wheat flour, 1/4 cup white flour, yeast, sugar, and salt. Add potato mixture and oil. Beat at low speed of mixer for 1/2 minute, scraping sides of bowl frequently. Beat 3 minutes at high speed. By hand, stir in remaining flour. Cover and let rise in warm place until double (about 1 hour). Stir down batter; let rest 5 minutes.

Divide batter among 12 greased muffin cups. Cover; let rise until nearly double (about 30 minutes). Stir together egg and 1 tablespoon water; brush over rolls. Sprinkle with sesame seed. Bake in 400 degree oven about 18 minutes or until done. Remove from pans; cool on racks. Makes 12 buns.

Brown-And-Serve Potato Rolls

5 to 5 ½ cups flour	1/3 cup cooking oil	1/4 cup sugar
1 pkg. active dry yeast	1 ½ cups warm water	1 tsp. salt
1/2 cup mashed potatoes		

Advanced Preparation: In mixer bowl combine 2 cups flour and yeast. Combine potatoes, oil, sugar, 1 ½ cups warm water (110-115 degrees), and 1 teaspoon salt. Add to dry ingredients in mixer bowl.

Beat at low speed for 1/2 min., scraping sides of bowl frequently. Beat 3 min. at high speed; by hand stir in enough flour to make a moderately stiff dough. Turn out on lightly floured surface; knead until smooth, 5 to 8 minutes. Shape into ball. Place in greased bowl; turn once. Cover; let rise in warm place until almost double. Punch down; turn out on lightly floured surface.

Cover; let rest 10 minutes. Shape into 24 rolls. Place on greased baking sheet or in greased muffin pans. Cover; let rise until almost double. Bake at 325 degrees for 10 to 12 minutes; do not brown. Remove from pan; cool. Wrap; freeze.

Before Serving: Unwrap slightly. Thaw at room temperature 10-15 minutes. Unwrap. Bake on ungreased baking sheet at 450 degrees until golden, 5 to 10 minutes. Makes 24 rolls.

__Potato Refrigerator Rolls__

1 cup mashed potatoes	1 tsp. salt	1/2 cup lukewarm water
2/3 cup shortening	2 eggs	1 cup scalded milk
1/2 cup sugar	1 yeast cake	6-8 cups flour

Add shortening, sugar, salt and eggs to mashed potatoes and cream well. Dissolve yeast in warm water, add to lukewarm milk, then add to potato mixture. Add sifted flour to make a stiff dough.

Toss on floured board and knead well. Put into large bowl and let rise to double in bulk. Knead lightly, rub over top with melted butter, cover and refrigerate until ready to use. About 1 ½ hour before baking, pinch off dough; shape; raise then bake in 400 degrees oven for 15-20 minutes.

__Parker House Potato Rolls__

By using mashed potatoes these rolls are feathery and moist. The dough can be kept in the fridge several days. Take out what you want; punch it down; shape; let it rise and bake at 400 degrees for 15 minutes. Makes about 5 ½ dozen rolls.

2 pkg. active dry yeast	9 cups sifted flour, more	2 eggs, room temperature
1 ½ cups very warm water	or less as needed	1 ½ tsp. salt
2/3 cup sugar	1 C.firmly packed, warm	1/4 cup butter
2/3 C.vegetable shortening	unseasoned mashed potatoes	

Sprinkle yeast over 1/2 cup warm water in small bowl. Stir gently to dissolve; let stand until bubbly, about 10 minutes.

Beat together sugar, shortening, remaining 1 cup warm water and 2 cups of flour in large mixer bowl. Mix on low speed until smooth. Mix in mashed potatoes, yeast mixture, eggs and salt, beating until smooth. Mix in flour; 1 cup at a time, to form a very soft but manageable dough. Unless you have a heavy duty mixer with a dough hook, you will have to knead in the final flour by hand on a floured surface. Continue to knead until smooth and elastic, 1 to 2 minutes by hand, or about 2 minutes with mixer with dough hook.

Shape dough into ball with buttered hands. Place in well-buttered bowl; turn to coat. Cover loosely with dry cloth. Let rise in warm place away from drafts until doubled in bulk, about 1 hour.

Punch dough down; divide in half. Cover half the dough. Turn out other half on floured board. Knead 1 minute; roll out to 3/8" thickness. Cut into circles with floured 2¾" biscuit cutter. Brush center of each circle with melted butter. Fold upper two-thirds of each circle down over bottom third; pinch edges together to seal. Place rolls 1" apart on ungreased cookie sheets. Roll, cut and shape remaining dough in same manner. Cover loosely with dry cloth. Let rise in warm place away from drafts until double in bulk, 25 to 30 minutes.

194

Refrigerator Dough

Mix together: **1½ cups water, 2/3 cup sugar, 1½ teaspoon salt** and **1 cake yeast**

Then add: **2 eggs, 2/3 cup soft shortening** and **4 cups flour.** Mix well. Let set for about 10 minutes.

Add more flour, about 3 to 3 ½ cups or until dough is soft, but not sticky. Let dough rise once. Roll out; cut into several pieces. Let raise again for 1 to 3 hours.

Dough can be made days before you need it. After making dough refrigerate it. The first day make doughnuts, the next day scones or rolls. It's great to have on hand in the fridge for a busy day.

Note: Using instant potatoes, instead of fresh mashed potatoes makes a finer dough.

Potato Biscuits

1 med.potato,peeled,cooked	1 Tbs. baking powder	1 Tb. butter
3/4 cup flour	1 tsp. salt	6 Tbs. milk

Put potato through ricer or mash. Set aside. In large bowl, stir together flour, baking powder and salt. With pastry cutter or two knives used scissor-fashion, cut in butter or margarine. Stir in potato, then milk, blending lightly with fork. Spoon into twelve mounds on non-stick cookie sheet. Bake at 400 degrees for 15-20 minutes or until golden brown. Makes 12 biscuits.

Potato Corn Cakes

These cakes are wonderful with fruit, such as applesauce and yogurt. (For a lunch meal, try cottage cheese and peaches.) Grated or riced potatoes and grated onions in this recipe makes much lighter pancakes.

4 med. potatoes, scrubbed with skins	1 Tbs. brewer's yeast (opt.)	milk powder for 1 cup milk
	1 tsp. salt	2 cups corn, fresh, frozen
1 lg. onion	2 Tbs. whole wheat flour	or drained canned corn
2 eggs, beaten	1 Tb. soy grits	

Grate the potatoes and the onions (leave the potato skins on); stir in the eggs, brewer's yeast, salt, flour, and soy grits. Carefully add the milk powder so that it doesn't lump too much. Stir in the corn, and your cakes are ready to fry. Fry on an oiled griddle, browning them well on each side. These cakes are high in usable protein as well as rich in the B vitamins and fibre.

Grandma's Longjohns

1 Tb. instant dry yeast
  in 1/4 cup warm water
1/2 cup sugar

1 C.warm mashed potatoes
2 eggs. beaten
1 cup scalded milk, cooled

1 tsp. salt
3 Tbs. melted butter

Mix together all ingredients then add enough **white flour** to make a stiff dough. Knead about 10 minutes. Place in an oiled bowl and let rise to double bulk. Turn out on floured board and roll to about 1/2 inch thick. Cut into bars. Let rise again until double in bulk. Fry in deep fat until golden brown. Drain on brown paper. Frost with butter frosting flavored with maple. Cover with chopped nuts.

Scones

1 cup mashed potatoes
1/2 cup sugar

3/4 cup lard or shortening

2 tsp. salt

Mix together the above and add **2 beaten eggs, 1 cup scalded milk, 1 teaspoon yeast** which has been dissolved in **1 cup luke warm water**. Add enough **flour** for a soft dough. Raise to double; punch down; pinch off to divide into egg-size pieces. Stretch out to desired size and thickness; fry in hot oil about 350 degrees, turning once until golden on both sides. Drain on paper towels.

SPUDNUTS & DOUGHNUTS:

"There's potatoes in this...You've gotta be kidding!"

Spudnuts

1 Tb. yeast
1 cup mashed potatoes
1/2 cup sugar

2 cups scalded milk
1 tsp. salt
6-7 cups flour

1/2 cup warm water
2 beaten eggs
2/3 cup shortening

Mix together; let rise 45 minutes. Roll and cut into doughnuts. Let rise 20 minutes. Cook in hot oil; dip in glaze as soon as spudnuts have been taken out of oil.

Spudnut Glaze: Mix warm milk or cream with powdered sugar (thin and runny). Dip tops of spudnuts into glaze or drizzle glaze over top in zig-zag lines.

Marj's Spudnuts

Mix. together:
1/2 cup instant warm mashed potatoes and 1/2 cup sugar. Dissolve 1 tablespoon active dry yeast into 1/2 cup warm water; set aside.

1 pt. scalded, cooled milk	1/3 cup soft shortening
2 beaten eggs	about 5 cups flour

Add milk, small amount of flour, salt, potato mixture, egg, yeast mixture, and shortening; mix well. Let set a few minutes then add the remainder of the flour or until a soft dough is formed. Let it raise; roll out to 1/4 inch thickness. Cut with a doughnut cutter or use a canning jar ring for spudnut and a small pill bottle for the center cutter. Place a little flour on a cloth; put cut out circles on cloth and let it raise. When spudnuts have raised fry in hot oil. Makes about 30 spudnuts.

Spudnuts For Large Groups

2 cups mashed potatoes	4 Tbs. salt	1 ½ cups sugar
4 cups scalded milk	11 eggs	3 tsp. nutmeg
6 yeast cakes	1 cup potato water	14 Tbs. vegetable shortening
		15 cups flour

Boil potatoes. Save 1 cup cooking liquid. Scald milk and cool. Dissolve yeast in potato water. Mash potatoes. Mix ingredients together; knead well. Let raise twice; roll out and shape; let raise again. Fry in hot oil. 85 large spudnuts.

Idaho Potato Doughnuts

2 pkg. active dry or	3/4 cups shortening	2 C.milk, scalded, cooled
cake yeast	1 ½ C.prepared Idahoan®	to lukewarm
1/2 cup warm water	Mashed Potatoes,cold	6 to 8 cups sifted flour
1 cup sugar	3 eggs, well beaten	1 Tb. salt

Doughnut Glaze:

Boiling water	1 Tb. vanilla extract	1 lb. powdered sugar

Dissolve yeast in warm water; set aside. Cream sugar and shortening. Beat in cold potatoes, eggs, cooled milk, yeast water, salt and lemon extract. Mix in just enough flour to make a soft dough. Knead well. Place dough in greased bowl; cover and let rise in warm place until double in bulk. Roll out dough to 1/2 inch thickness.

Cut with a well-floured cutter. Let rise uncovered about 30 minutes. Deep-fry in heated oil (375 degree). Drain on paper towel. Makes 4 dozen.

To make glaze, gradually add enough boiling water to powdered sugar and vanilla to make a thin glaze. Drizzle over doughnuts.

SWEET ROLLS & BARS:

"You'd rather me cook than clean?!"

Potato Mints

1 cup mashed potatoes   2½ cups powdered sugar

Put in all the powdered sugar the potatoes will take and be smooth. Color pink or green with food coloring. Add a few drops of mint flavoring. Mix well. Roll and cut or spoon into small pieces or chunks. Chill.

Cinnamon Pinwheels

2 pkg. active dry yeast
2/3 cup warm water
2 cups milk scalded,
   cooled to lukewarm
1⅓ cups sugar
2 eggs, well beaten

1/2 cup butter, soft
2 tsp. salt
1½ cups potatoes,
   6-8 cups sifted flour
   mashed, cold
6 Tbs. melted butter

cinnamon
1/2 cup brown sugar
1/2 cup raisins
1/2 cup chopped nuts
2 cups powdered sugar,
   mixed with
   2-4 Tbs. water

Dissolve yeast in warm water. Blend in milk, sugar, eggs, butter, salt and potatoes. Add enough flour to make a soft dough; knead well. Place in a greased bowl. Cover and let rise until double in bulk. Roll out dough in a rectangle about 1/4 inch thick. Spread with melted butter and sprinkle with cinnamon, brown sugar, raisins and/or chopped nuts. Roll up dough lengthwise and cut into 3/4 inch slices. Place on greased cookie sheet. Cover and let rise until double in bulk. Bake in preheated 400 degree oven for 20-30 minutes. Ice with powdered sugar mixture while still warm. Makes 3 dozen.

Note: Using dental floss instead of a knife to cut rolled dough will prevent flattening of roll.

Southern Oatmeal Bars

1/2 cup butter	1 cup quick-cooking	2 Tbs. wheat germ
1/2 C. packed brown sugar	rolled oats	1/4 tsp. salt
1/2 tsp. vanilla	3/4 cup flour	1/4 tsp. baking soda
1 slightly beaten egg	1/4 cup mashed potatoes	1/2 tsp. finely shredded
3/4 cup cooked, mashed	2/3 C. sweetened cond. milk	orange peel
sweet potatoes	1 tsp. pumpkin pie spice	1/4 cup chopped walnuts

In mixer bowl beat butter, brown sugar, and vanilla until light. Combine rolled oats, flour, wheat germ, salt, and baking soda; stir into butter mixture until crumbly. Pat about 1 ½ cups of mixture into bottom of 9x9x2 inch baking pan. Bake at 350 degrees for 10 minutes.

Meanwhile in medium bowl beat together egg, sweet potatoes, mashed potatoes, sweetened condensed milk, pumpkin pie spice, and orange peel; pour over baked layer in pan. Combine nuts with remaining crumbs; sprinkle over top. Bake in 350 degree oven for 25 to 30 minutes or until golden. Cool; cut into bars. Makes about 1 ½ dozen.

Spud Bars

2 Tbs. butter	1 tsp. baking soda	1 egg
3/4 C. granulated sugar	1/4 tsp. salt	1 tsp. vanilla extract
1/4 C. packed brown sugar	1/4 tsp. cinnamon	1/2 cup potato buds
1/2 cup flour		

In large bowl, with electric mixer at medium-high speed, cream together butter or margarine, granulated sugar, and brown sugar. Beat in flour, baking soda, salt and cinnamon until well blended. With spatula, stir in egg and vanilla, then potato buds. Pour batter into non-stick 8 inch square baking pan. Bake at 350 degrees for 20 minutes. Cut and remove from pan while still slightly warm. Makes 16 2-inch bars.

Do you know where the word "spud" came from? It's an acronym, S.P.U.D. It came about in Ireland a long time ago. It seems a group of concerned citizens were sure potatoes were not food for humans. They formed an organization to fight the use of potatoes. They called themselves the "Society for the Prevention of Unhealthy Diets". S.P.U.D.

Potato-Peanut Candy Pinwheels

America's pioneer women's candy recipe. Makes about 5 ½ dozen pinwheels.

1/3 cup cold mashed potatoes	1 tsp. vanilla	1 cup chunk-style peanut
1/2 stick butter	abt. 5 cups confectioners	butter
	sugar	

Blend mashed potatoes, butter and vanilla in large bowl with electric mixer on high speed. Add sugar, 1 cup at a time, and mix until stiff enough to shape; mixture should be slightly tacky to the touch. (When you first begin adding the sugar, mixture will liquefy. But continue adding sugar, and mixture will stiffen. Do not attempt to make this recipe in rainy or humid weather because the candy will not harden properly.

Roll out candy between two sheets of wax paper into a rectangle, about 18 inches long, 10 inches wide and 3/8 inches thick. Remove top piece of wax paper. spread evenly with peanut butter. Roll up from a long side, jelly-roll fashion, using the wax paper as a guide.

Cut roll in half crosswise to form two 9 inch long rolls. Wrap each snugly in wax paper. Chill 2 to 3 hours or until firm enough to slice. To serve, cut rolls into 1/4 to 3/8 inch thick slices. Serve immediately.

Note: Amount of powdered sugar used will vary depending on humidity in kitchen and wetness or dryness of mashed potatoes.

Moravian Sugar Cake

1 pkg. active dry yeast	1/2 tsp. salt	2 cups sifted flour
1/2 cup very warm water	1 egg beaten	1/2 to 3/4 cup packed
1/3 cup sugar	1/2 C.hot mashed potatoes	light-brown sugar
	2/3 cup melted butter	1 tsp. cinnamon

Sprinkle yeast on water; set a few minutes, then stir until dissolved. Stir sugar and salt into egg; blend with potato. Stir in 1/3 cup butter and yeast mixture. Slowly add flour (the dough should be soft). Knead lightly on floured board 2 to 3 minutes, or until smooth and springy. Put in greased bowl and grease top. Cover with towel; let rise in warm spot 1 to 1 ½ hours, or until doubled. Press into greased 9x13x2 inch pan or two 8 inch square pans. Dough should be no thicker than 3/4 inch. Butter top, cover and let rise 30 minutes, or until doubled and puff looking. With thumb, make holes in rows about 2 inches apart.

Using a course sieve, sift brown sugar and cinnamon evenly over dough and drizzle with rest of butter. Bake in hot oven 400 degrees 20 minutes, or until browned and bubbly-looking. serve warm, cut in squares or fingers.

CAKES & CUP-CAKES:

*"That's Daddy's little girl....
learning to cook....and
I'm gonna have to eat it!"*

Apple/Potato Walnut Cake

3 cups flour	1 ½ cup sugar	3 eggs
2 ½ tsp. baking powder	3/4 cup shortening	vanilla
1 ½ tsp. cinnamon	3/4 cup applesauce	1 cup raw apple, chopped
1/2 tsp. allspice	3/4 cup mashed potatoes	2/3 cup walnuts, chopped
1/4 tsp. cloves		

Combine dry ingredients except sugar and set aside. Beat sugar and shortening until light. Beat in applesauce, potatoes, eggs and vanilla. Stir in flour mixture. When well blended, stir in raw apple and nuts. Bake at 350 degrees for 1 hour and 20 minutes in a 10" tube pan or bundt pan. Cool 10 minutes before removing from pan.

Potato Chocolate Cake Or Cupcakes

2 cups sifted flour	2 cups sugar	1 tsp. vanilla extract
1 tsp. baking soda	4 eggs	1 cup mashed potatoes, cold
1 tsp. salt	2 squares unsweetened	3/4 cup sour milk or
1 cup butter	choc., melted	buttermilk

Heat oven to 375 degrees. Sift flour, soda and salt. Cream together butter and sugar. Add eggs one at a time; beat thoroughly after each addition. Add melted chocolate, vanilla and mashed potatoes; mix well. Add flour mixture alternately with sour milk, blending well after each addition.

Grease and flour baking pans. Bake in two 8 inch round pans for 55 minutes, 9 inch tube pan for 1 hour, 9x13x2 inch pan for 45 minutes. Inserted toothpick will come out clean when cake is done.

Variation: For Chocolate Spice Cake add 1 teaspoon each cinnamon and allspice to sifted dry ingredients. One cup raisins and/or 1 cup chopped nuts may be added. Makes 12 servings.

Chocolate-Potato Cake

2 med potatoes, peeled and cubed	1 tsp. vanilla	1/2 cup unsweetened cocoa
1 cup butter	4 egg yolks	3/4 cup milk
2 cups sugar	2 cups all-purpose flour	4 egg whites
	1 Tb. baking powder	1 recipe Rum Glaze (below)

Cook potatoes, covered, in boiling salted water for 12 to 15 minutes; drain and mash (no butter or seasonings). Measure 1 cup mashed potatoes; cool. In mixer bowl beat butter, sugar, and vanilla on medium speed of mixer until well combined. Add egg yolks, one at a time, beating well after each addition.

Add potatoes; mix well. Stir together flour, baking powder and cocoa. Add to potato mixture alternately with milk, beating just until combined. Wash beaters thoroughly. Beat egg whites until stiff peaks form; fold into flour mixture. Turn into greased and floured 10 inch tube pan. Bake in a 350 degree oven 1 to 1¼ hours. Cool in pan 10 minutes. Invert on wire rack; cool. Frost with Rum Glaze.

Variation: For a special flavor add 1 teaspoon nutmeg and 1 teaspoon cinnamon.

Rum Glaze: Combine **2 cups sifted powdered sugar, 1/4 teaspoon vanilla or rum extract**, and **dash salt**. Add **about 4 tablespoons milk** to make icing of drizzling consistency. Garnish with **walnut halves**, if desired.

Dutch Chocolate Cake

1 ½ cups sifted cake flour	1/2 tsp. cloves	1 ½ cups sugar
2 tsp. baking powder	3 sq. unsweetened choc.	4 eggs separated
1/4 tsp. salt	3/4 cup chopped walnuts	3/4 C cooked potato, chilled
1/2 tsp. cinnamon	3/4 cup butter	1/2 cup milk
		Rum-Glaze (above)

Sift together flour, baking powder, salt and spices. Mix with grated chocolate and finely chopped walnuts. Beat butter and sugar together until creamy and light. Beat in egg yolks one at a time. Stir in peeled, grated, cooked potato. On low speed of mixer, blend dry mixture alternately with milk. Beat after each addition until smooth. Beat egg whites until stiff but not dry and fold into batter. Turn into greased lightly floured 9" tube pan or two 9" round cake pans.

Bake tube cake in moderate oven 350 degrees 1 hour, layers at 375 degrees, 25 to 30 minutes. Cool on wire racks and spread with rum icing. This is usually served as a single tube cake or thick layer cake with the thin rum icing poured over top and allowed to run down sides. If you prefer, you may use a favorite vanilla or chocolate filling between layers.

Potato Coffee Cake

Bake at 375 degrees for 40 minutes. Makes 10 serving.

1/2 cup warm water	1 ½ tsp. salt	1 cup coarsely chopped golden
1 tsp. sugar	1 cup mashed potatoes	and dark raisins
2 pkg. active dry yeast	cooked, unseasoned	1/2 cup chopped pecans
1 cup milk	2 eggs lightly beaten	1 cup sugar
1/2 cup sugar	about 6 C. all-purpose flour	1 tsp. ground cinnamon
1/2 C. veg. shortening	1 stick butter, softened	1 egg white slightly beaten

Combine warm water, 1 teaspoon sugar and yeast in cup; stir to dissolve yeast. Let stand in a warm place until bubbly, about 10 minutes. Heat milk, 1/2 cup sugar, shortening and salt in saucepan until warm; pour into large bowl. Stir in yeast mixture, potatoes and eggs.

Beat in 3 cups flour, then stir enough additional flour to make a soft dough. Turn dough out onto floured surface. Knead 8 to 10 minutes or until dough is smooth and elastic, adding only enough of the flour to keep dough from sticking.

Press dough into buttered bowl; turn dough over to bring buttered side up. Cover loosely; refrigerate overnight.

Turn dough onto lightly floured surface. Roll out to a rectangle 1/2 or 3/4 inch thick. Spread with the softened butter. Scatter raisins and pecans evenly over. Combine remaining sugar and cinnamon; sprinkle over fruit and nuts. Roll up, jelly-roll style, starting with one of the short sides. Press edges to seal. Join ends; place in a 10x4 inch angel food tube pan.

Brush top with egg white. Let rise in a warm place, away from drafts, until double in bulk, about 1 hour. Bake in moderate 375 degrees oven for 40 minutes or until ring sounds hollow when tapped with fingers. Remove from pan; cool on wire rack.

Banana/Potato Bread

1 tsp. soda	2 eggs separated	2 cups flour
1 Tbs. sour milk	2 large bananas	1 tsp. Salt
1 cup sugar	1/2 cup mashed potato	1/2 cup nuts
1/2 cup shortening		

Dissolve soda in sour milk; mix sugar and shortening; add egg yolks, mashed bananas, and potatoes. Mix well; stir in soda, flour and salt. Fold in whipped egg whites and nuts. Bake in 2 loaf pans, at 350 degrees for 40 minutes or until done.

Fruit & Vegetable Cake

2¼ cups unsifted flour	2 cups sugar	1/2 cup raw grated potato
2½ tsp. baking soda	3 eggs	1 sm. mashed banana
1½ tsp. cinnamon	8-oz. crushed pineapple	1½ cup flake coconut
1 tsp. salt	1½ cup grated carrots	1/2 cup chopped nuts
1 cup oil		

Mix dry ingredients, except sugar, and flour. Beat oil, sugar and eggs well. Add flour; beat smooth. Add pineapple, carrots, potatoes, banana, coconut, and nuts. Grease and flour pan. Bake 50-60 minutes at 350 degrees. Good warm with whipped cream, or use one of the frosting recipes on page 226.

Variation: Chopped or whole raisins could also be added to this cake.

Carrot Potato Cake

2 cups flour	1¼ cups oil	1 tsp. baking powder
4 eggs	2 cups sugar	3 cups carrots, shredded
1 tsp. salt	1 cup potatoes, shredded	1 tsp. soda
sm. can crushed, pineapple	1/2 cup chopped nuts	1 tsp. cinnamon

Mix all ingredients together; pour in a greased 9"x13" pan; bake at 350 degrees for 40-45 minutes.

Cream Cheese Frosting:

8-oz. r. cheese, softened	1/2 to 1 tsp. vanilla	3-4 cups powdered sugar
1/2 cup butter	1 Tb. cream	

Blend softened cream cheese and butter. Add vanilla and cream. Add enough powdered sugar to reach desired consistency.

Frosting:

1 cup sugar	1/2 cup buttermilk	1 tsp. corn syrup
1/2 tsp. soda	1 cube butter	1 tsp. vanilla

Mix all ingredients together except vanilla. Bring to a boil; boil 5 minutes; remove from heat and stir in vanilla. Pour over hot cake. Make frosting about 10 minutes before cake has finished baking.

> *TIP: To keep cakes or cookies from burning use shinny pans. The darker the pan, the quicker your baked dishes will burn.*

Almond-Potato Torte

6-oz. blanched almonds,
   prepared ahead & dried
2 med. Id. bakers, cooked,
   unpeeled & chilled

8 eggs, separated
1 cup sugar
rind & 3 Tbs. juice
   of 1 lemon

1/2 tsp. mace
1 Tb. rum
2 Tbs. fine dry bread crumbs
   or grated almonds

Put dry almonds in blender. Whiz on low a few seconds, then on high a few seconds to grind. Do not grind so fine they become oily and compact. Peel potatoes and grate. Beat egg yolks and sugar together until mixture is light, satiny and the color of cream. Stir in almonds, potato and flavorings. Blend lightly. Beat egg whites until stiff and fold quickly into first mixture. Butter 9" springfoam pan and sprinkle with crumbs. Turn batter into pan.

Bake in slow oven 325 degrees 1 hour and 15 minutes, or until cake shrinks slightly from sides of pan. Remove and cool overnight, if possible. It will sink slightly in the middle. Remove springform rim and put torte on serving plate. Cut in small wedges with serrated knife.

Potato Zucchini Cake

4 eggs
2 cups sugar
1 cup vegetable oil
2 cups flour
2 tsp. cinnamon

1 tsp. baking soda
2 tsp. baking powder
1 tsp. salt
sm. can drained, crushed
   pineapple

1 cup walnuts, chopped
1 ½ cups grated raw
   zucchini or other squash
1/2 cup grated raw
   potatoes.
2 tsp. vanilla

In large bowl, beat eggs and sugar until lemon colored. Add oil; blend. In separate bowl, sift flour, cinnamon, baking powder, soda and salt. Add dry ingredients to creamed mixture; beat 2 minutes. Stir in pineapple, walnuts, zucchini, potatoes, and vanilla. (Squeeze zucchini in paper towel to remove excess moisture). Mix thoroughly. Pour batter into well-greased, floured 10 inch tube pan.

Bake at 350 for 1 hour. Cool on rack 30 min. and remove from pan. Glaze with 1 cup powdered sugar mixed with 1 tablespoon milk, if desired.

TIP: As you take a cake from the oven, place the pan on a cold damp cloth for a very few moments. It should turn out easily without sticking to the pan.

PUDDINGS & DESERTS:

I bet I can have some pudding if I don't get all wet in the rain today."

Potato Custard

1 heaping cup Idahoan Hash **Brown Potatoes** (dry shredded)	1/4 cup sugar	2 egg yolks
	1/2 tsp. salt	1 tsp. each, grated orange,
	1/2 tsp. ground nutmeg	lemon rind
2 lg. eggs beaten	3/4 cup milk	1½ Tbs. luke-warm water

Heat oven to 350. Butter 8 custard cups. Prepare potatoes according to Cooked Shredded Potato recipe on back of box; using 1/2 ingredients called for; set aside. In large bowl, beat eggs and sugar until sugar is dissolved; add salt, nutmeg, milk, egg yolks and grated rinds; beat well. Divide potatoes evenly among custard cups. Pour custard over potatoes; sprinkle with lukewarm water. Place cups in large baking dish and fill dish halfway with hot, not boiling water.

Bake for 30 minutes or until custard is set. Custard mixture may be prepared early and refrigerated. Let sit at room temperature for 1 hour before baking. Recipe may easily be doubled or tripled. Makes 8 servings.

Carrot Pudding

1/2 cup shortening	1 C. grated raw carrots	1¼ cups flour
1/2 cup brown or white sugar	1 cup unpeeled potatoes	1/2 tsp. salt
	1 cup raisins	1/2 tsp. nutmeg
1 egg	2 tsp. grated lemon rind	1/2 tsp. cinnamon
1 Tb. water	1 cup nuts	1 tsp. soda

Cream sugar and shortening; add eggs and water. Add raw unpeeled, grated carrots and potatoes. Add raisins, lemon rind and nuts. Add dry ingredients, adding soda last. Put in bread tins or cans. Cover air tight with foil. Put these in pan with about 2 inches water. Boil about 1 hour. You may need to add more water. Pudding will rise like a cake and feel firm when done. Don't peek while cooking. Makes about 1 pound or 5 to 6 servings. Can be made ahead and kept in fridge for a few days.

Variation: Add 1 mashed banana and/or 1/2 small can well drained crushed pineapple. Increase flour to 1½ cups if batter is too thin.

206

BREAKFAST DISHES

To live right is to eat right!
A good breakfast is like unto a strong foundation,
It helps us stand straighter and stonger
And be brighter and wiser throughout our day.
--by Carol Fielding McCabe

Information & Tips

Potatoes Are Nourishing: And do you know how good they are for you? And how modest in calories and price? If you've heard that potatoes are high in calories, it's just another "old wives' tale". The truth is there are only 90 to 110 calories in a medium sized Idaho baked potato, and 63 calories in one-half cup potatoes mashed with milk. In other words, it has about the same calories as a large apple or less than a half cup serving of cottage cheese.

For those that don't need to worry about the calories in food, they can enjoy potatoes with eggs, bacon, sausage, etc. For very tasty meals, the flavor of potatoes can be changed with the addition of meats, other food items and spices.

Breakfast is the most commonly <u>missed</u> meal of the day, yet it is so important you start your day with a good breakfast. Many people say there are too many calories in breakfast. That may be so if its sugared cereals, sweet rolls, fatty sausage, or hot chocolate. Add low calorie potatoes to some of your morning meals. Potatoes are also an energy food!

To save time in the busy mornings prepare the potatoes the evening before. Mashed, hash-browns, baked potatoes, can all be prepared the evening before and turned into potato cakes, fried potatoes, or a number of other tasty breakfast dishes. They are wonderful and soooo satisfying.

If an apple a day will keep the doctor away, then a potato a day will surely do the same thing. "Start your day the potato way."

"Start the day out right from the very first bite." Serve your family breakfasts featuring genuine Idaho potatoes. Observe. Next time you offer your family an entree with a side dish of Idaho potatoes, you'll notice that nine times out of ten they'll take a bite of the potatoes first. Why? Because you know and they know that the great taste, light and fluffy texture of Idaho potatoes are irresistible. It's always "love at first bite".

Remember that only potatoes grown in Idaho can be called Idaho. To make sure you're buying genuine Idaho potatoes, look for the "Grown in Idaho" seal on the bag.

PANCAKES & BREAKFAST CAKES:

"Boy, that great breakfast makes me feel like skipping."

Potato Pancakes

Potato Pancakes can be served as a breakfast dish or as a side dish or main dish along with apple sauce, sour cream, or yogurt.

4 cups grated raw potatoes	1/3 cup minced parsley	1 ½ tsp. salt
1 cup grated raw onion	(optional)	1/4 tsp. pepper
3 eggs, beaten	1/3 cup flour	Oil for frying

Mix the potatoes, onion, parsley, eggs, flour, salt and pepper. Heat a small amount of oil in a frying pan and spoon in 1/4 cup potato mixture for each pancake. Gently flatten the pancakes with a spatula.

Fry over medium heat until golden brown on both sides. Keep the pancakes warm in the oven. Makes 6 servings.

Variations:

German-Style Potato Pancakes: Add 1 cup grated carrots and 1 tablespoon caraway seeds to the batter.

Herbed Potato Pancakes: Add 1/2 cup fresh dill or 2 tablespoons minced fresh basil to the batter.

Indian-Style Potato Pancakes: Season the batter with 1/4 teaspoon each of turmeric, curry powder, ground cumin, and coriander.

Cheese Lovers-Style Potato Pancakes: After turning the pancakes and while they are cooking on the other side, smother with grated cheese.

Herb-Breakfast Potatoes

8 med. potatoes, cut as	1 cup cream	crushed herbs; your choosing
French fries	grated American cheese	parsley, dry or fresh

Slice potatoes; arrange in greased baking pan. Sprinkle herbs, except parsley over potatoes. Pour cream over potatoes; sprinkle as much grated cheese as you like, and sprinkle parsley on top of the cheese. Bake at 400 degrees for 35-40 minutes. Can make the night before.

Simple Hash Brown Potatoes

4 med.peeled,cooked,cold potatoes 1 Tb. grated onion	1 tsp. salt dash of pepper 3 Tbs. bacon fat	3 Tbs. butter cheese & parsley

Grate potatoes and onions, mix together with salt and pepper. In skillet, heat butter and bacon fat, add potato mixture, pressing down well with turner and shaping into a circle, leaving 1/2 inch trough of fat around edge. Saute about 20 minutes, or until crisp and brown on underside. Lift edges to test browning.

When potatoes are golden on bottom, hold skillet, with turner, cut through mixture from outer edge to center. With turner, fold these 2 cut quarters, in turn, toward you onto the un-cut half. Sprinkle a little grated cheese along the cut, tucking a little underneath and add parsley sprigs if desired.

Mashed Potato Cakes

This is an ideal recipe for left-over potatoes. Mash them; whip in some milk, butter, salt and pepper. Store refrigerated in a closed container until needed.

Shape fluffy mashed potatoes into cakes or form a roll; wrap in waxed paper; chill; slice. Dip into flour. Fry slowly in hot fat until brown. (The potatoes could be prepared and placed in the fridge the night before.)

Crispy Browned Hash

1 C. chopped cooked beef 1 onion, minced	1 Tbs. minced parsley 1 C.cubed cooked potatoes	Salt & pepper to taste 1/2 cup milk

Mix all ingredients except milk. Place a little fat in a hot heavy skillet over medium heat. When fat is very hot, spread hash evenly in skillet. The pan should be hot enough to brown the bottom of the hash quickly, 10 to 15 minutes. Add milk and mix. Cover and cook slowly until crisp, about 10 minutes more. Makes 2 servings.

Variations: You can use chopped cooked veal, lamb, ham, chicken, or turkey in place of beef.

Substitute corned beef in place of 1/2 the beef. Cut the potatoes in half instead of cubed and add chopped beef to the other half.

Potato Cakes With Corned Beef

1 onion	2 cups water	8 thin slices canned corn beef
1 bunch chives	vegetable oil	4 slices process Am. cheese
1 pkg. potato pancake batter		ketchup

Chop the onions; dice the chives finely; add to the water for making the pancake batter. Stir mixture; let it boil. Heat vegetable oil in fry pan, cook small potato pancakes and keep warm. Cover 1/2 of each pancake with a thin slice of canned corn beef and cheese. Top with a dollop of ketchup and fold over the other half of the cake.

CASSEROLE &/OR BAKED DISHES:

"Dig in...Then off to school with you."

Au Gratin Potatoes For Breakfast

Boil **8 medium potatoes** the day before needed (saves time in the busy mornings). Remove thin peelings from potatoes (optional). Slice into thin slices and put down a layer in a **buttered** baking pan until all potatoes are in the pan. Season with **salt** and **pepper** between each new layer of potatoes. Place pieces of **butter** here and there on top of the potatoes.

Cover with **3 cups of light cream**. Place in preheated oven set to 325 degrees and bake 20 minutes. Sprinkle **grated cheese** on top, return to oven and bake 10 minutes more or until cheese starts melting.

Potato And Egg Bake

1 tsp. butter	8 eggs	2 Tbs. grated Cheddar cheese
3 cups mashed potatoes	2 tsp. paprika	1 tsp. salt; 1/4 tsp. pepper

Grease baking pan with butter. Spread potatoes in bottom of pan. Make 8 evenly spaced indentations in potatoes; break an egg into each. Sprinkle potatoes and eggs with cheese, paprika, salt and pepper. Bake at 400 degrees for 10 minutes or until eggs are set and cheese melts. Makes 8 servings.

Breakfast Casserole Delight

4-oz. cream cheese	1/2 clove garlic, crushed	1/8 cup chopped chives
1/2 cup dairy sour cream	6 med. potatoes, cooked,	1 Tb. butter
1 tsp. salt; 1/8 tsp.pepper	mashed	1/4 tsp. paprika

Add cream cheese, sour cream, salt, pepper and garlic to the soft mashed potatoes in mixer. Beat at high speed until smooth and light. Stir in chopped chives. Spoon into a lightly greased baking dish; sprinkle with paprika and dot with butter or margarine. Bake in 350 degree oven for 30 minutes or until lightly golden and heated through. Makes 6 serving.

Breakfast Scalloped Bacon & Eggs

1/4 cup chopped onion	1 cup sharp process Am.	6 hard-cooked eggs, sliced
2 Tbs. butter	cheese, shredded	cooked, crumbled
2 Tbs. all-purpose flour	2 lg. boiled, cold potatoes	1 cup crushed potato chips
1½ cups milk	salt and pepper	10-12 slices bacon, crisp

Cook onion in butter or bacon fat until tender, but not brown; blend in flour. Add milk. Cook, stirring constantly, until mixture is thickened and bubbly. Add cheese; stir until melted.

Thinly slice cold boiled potatoes; using half the potatoes arrange one or two layers on bottom of a baking dish; season with salt and pepper; add half the egg slices in layers; pour half the sauce over all; then half the crumbled bacon.

Repeat with the other half of everything except potato chips. Add the crushed potato chips on top of mixture. Bake at 350 degrees for 20 minutes or until heated through. Makes 8 servings.

Olive Egg Dish

butter for frying	8 anchovy fillets	1/2 bunch parsley
4 med. boiled potatoes	1 large onion	1/2 cup med. cheddar cheese
2 sm. Vienna sausages	4 egg	
sm. jar green olives	freshly ground pepper	

Heat butter in fry pan. Slice potatoes and sausages; drain and halve the olives; separate the anchovies; cut the onion into rings, and add all into the pan. Lightly stir with spatula and flip over. Beat the eggs with pepper; blend in the chopped parsley and pour over the ingredients. Let cook on the lowest temperature for 8 minutes. Cut the cheese into strips and lay over the mixture. Cover, and let it cook for a few minutes, until the cheese begins to melt.

BREAKFAST OMELETTES:

"Won't mom and dad be surprised with our neat breakfast?"

Vegetable Omelette

1 tsp. vegetable oil	1/4 cup chopped green	dash salt & fresh
1 med. Idaho potato,	pepper	ground pepper
scrubbed, diced	2 large eggs	
1/4 C. chopped onion	2 Tbs. water	

In a skillet, heat oil; add potato, onion and green pepper. Saute over medium heat about 15 minutes or until vegetables are tender. Remove and reserve. Lightly beat together eggs, water, salt and pepper. Add to skillet. Cook over medium heat until almost set. Fill with reserved vegetables and fold omelet in half. Serve immediately. Makes one serving.

Omelette Pommes De Terre

1 Tb. butter	2 Tbs. chopped green	4 tsp. tomato paste
1 lg. potato, peeled,diced	pepper	4 eggs, slightly beaten
1/3 cup minced onion	1/2 tsp.salt; pinch pepper	

Melt butter in skillet. Add potato, onion, and green pepper; season with salt and pepper. Saute for about 20 minutes, stirring occasionally until they are tender and lightly browned. Stir in tomato paste and cook and stir for 2-3 minutes longer. Add beaten eggs. Tilt pan until eggs flow evenly through and around the potato mixture. Cook just until eggs are set. Fold the omelet in half and slide it out of the pan onto a serving dish. Makes 4 servings.

Bacon And Potato Omelette

1/2 Tbs. butter	2 med. potatoes diced sm.	salt and pepper to taste
2-3 slices bacon, diced	1 sm. onion, finely sliced	plain omelet (see next page)

Melt butter in pan; add bacon, potatoes and onion. Season; cover pan, and cook slowly for 7-8 min., until potatoes and onion are tender and browned. Stir occasionally. Make a plain omelet and spoon in the mixture before folding.

Plain Omelette:

4 eggs	2 Tbs. butter	salt
1 ½ Tbs. cold water	pepper, freshly ground	

Break eggs into a bowl and beat with a fork. When yolks and whites are broken up, add water, and seasoning.

Heat pan on medium heat; add butter in two pieces and, as soon as it is foaming, pour in egg mixture. Leave 10-15 seconds before stirring around slowly with the flat of a fork. Stir once or twice around pan, then cook for another 5-6 seconds.

Lift up the edge of omelet to let any remaining raw egg run onto the hot pan. When the egg is cooked to your liking, tilt the pan away from you and fold the omelet over to the far side. Serve at once.

Spanish Omelette

7 Tbs. olive oil	2 med. potatoes, peeled, sliced or
1/2 cup chopped small, raw ham	coarsely grated
1 lg. Bermuda or mild onion, sliced	salt and pepper to taste
1 clove garlic, crushed (optional)	8 eggs, well beaten

A true Spanish omelette is made with a base of potatoes and onion; cooked in olive oil and flavored with garlic. Another version that includes cooked mixed vegetables is a good way of using leftovers.

The consistency of omelettes should be firm but not too solid. To serve, cut into wedges like a round cake.

Heat the oil in a frying pan or skillet; add the chopped ham and fry until it starts to brown. Add onion and crushed garlic, if you like. Fry until the onion is soft, then add the potato. Season well and cook until potato is tender. Drain off any extra fat and pour beaten eggs into the pan. Stir to mix, then cook until the bottom of omelet is brown. Loosen omelette with spatula. The top of mixture will be hardly set, so put the pan under the broiler for a few moments to brown the surface.

Turn out the omelette onto a flat platter, cut into wedges and serve with pepperoni as a special treat.

> *TIP: Breakfast on the run? Prepare omelette vegetables the evening before; combine and cook in the morning; slap on a slice of bread and be off to work, school or where ever you go.*

One Potato Omelette--Serves Two

1 lg. potato, peeled, diced	1 Tb. butter	dash of pepper
1/3 cup minced onion	1/4 cup ketchup	sprinkle or two of hot sauce
2 Tbs. diced green pepper	1/2 tsp. salt	4 eggs, lightly beaten

In skillet, saute potato, onion and green pepper in butter or margarine for 20 minutes, stirring occasionally until tender and lightly browned. Stir in ketchup, salt, pepper and hot sauce, cook, stirring 2 to 3 minutes more.

Pour eggs into skillet, tilting pan so eggs flow evenly through and around potato mixture. Cook until set; loosen edges and fold in half. Slide onto a breakfast tray and serve. Makes 2 servings.

Variation: Use other vegetables such as carrots, peas and tomatoes.

Sausage And Hash Brown Omelette

1/2 lb. bulk pork sausage	1/4 C. chopped grn. pepper	1/4 cup milk
2 cups cooked potato	salt and pepper	1/2 C. shredded process
1/4 cup chopped onion	4 eggs	American cheese

In large skillet brown the sausage. Drain; reserving 1/4 cup drippings; set aside. Return reserved dripping to skillet. Combine shredded potato, onion, and green pepper; pat into skillet.

Season generously with salt; sprinkle with pepper. Cook over low heat until underside is crisp and brown. Blend eggs, milk, 1/4 teaspoon salt, and dash pepper. Pour over potatoes. Top with cheese and sausage. Cover; cook over low heat for 6 to 8 minutes. Loosen omelet; cut in wedges to serve. Makes 4 servings.

Green Pepper & Potato Omelette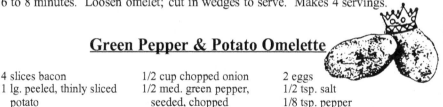

4 slices bacon	1/2 cup chopped onion	2 eggs
1 lg. peeled, thinly sliced potato	1/2 med. green pepper, seeded, chopped	1/2 tsp. salt 1/8 tsp. pepper

Cook bacon crisp; drain and crumble. Drain all but 2 Tablespoons of drippings. Add potatoes; cook at medium heat until almost tender, about 5 minutes. Add onion and green pepper; cook until potatoes are tender.

Beat eggs with salt and pepper; pour over potatoes. Sprinkle bacon over eggs. Cook over medium heat without stirring until eggs are almost set. Cover; cook a few minutes longer just until eggs are completely set. (**Don't overcook.**) Loosen omelet from pan with spatula. Fold onto warm plate. Makes 2 servings.

Potato Waffles

1 cup flour	2 tsp. baking powder	1 ½ cups milk
1/3 cup potato flakes	1/2 tsp. salt	1 Tb. salad oil
2 tsp. sugar	2 eggs	

In large bowl, and with fork, mix dry ingredients. In small bowl, beat together eggs, milk and oil. Add to dry ingredients. Mix well. Bake batter on waffle iron according to manufacturer's directions until golden brown. Makes 12-16 small waffles.

Mashed Potato Waffles

1 cup flour	1 cup leftover mashed potatoes
1 tsp. sugar	1 egg
1/2 tsp. salt	3/4 cup milk
2 tsp. baking powder	1/2 cup blueberries
	1 Tb. vegetable oil

In large bowl mix first four ingredients (dry ingredients). In small bowl, beat together the egg, milk, and vegetable oil. Blend in mashed potatoes, then the dry ingredients until mixture becomes smooth. Gently and without breaking up the berries, fold in the blueberries. The mixture should be semi-thick. The thickness will usually depend upon how much liquid has been added to the leftover mashed potatoes. If too thin add a little more flour; if too thick add a little more milk. Spoon or pour onto the waffle iron and spread out. Bake until the mixture is browned. Will make about a dozen small waffles.

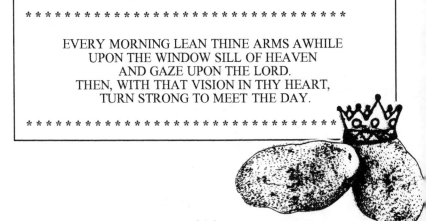

* *

EVERY MORNING LEAN THINE ARMS AWHILE
UPON THE WINDOW SILL OF HEAVEN
AND GAZE UPON THE LORD.
THEN, WITH THAT VISION IN THY HEART,
TURN STRONG TO MEET THE DAY.

* *

INDEX BY SECTIONS
AND CATEGORIES

SECTION II -- SOUPS

217

SECTION III -- MAIN DISHES

SECTION IV -- SIDE DISHES:

SECTION V – POTATO TOPPINGS:

**SECTION VI -- BREADS, ROLLS,
DESSERTS:**

SECTION VII -- BREAKFAST DISHES:

INDEX OF NON-POTATO RECIPES
(Used to Accent Potato Recipes)

228

"FABULOUS 50" MAIN DISH RECIPES" --by **Dorene Gomm** The perfect gift for yourself, for bridal showers, club prizes or the "just because" gestures, can be had in the "power-packed" **Main Dish Recipe** booklet. Fifty main dishes. A choice collection of recipes from friends and neighbors, each being the absolute family favorite main dish. This is a great assortment of tempting dishes which are sure to please the family as well as guests. Chicken dishes rank high as a favorite, ground beef came in second, and Mexican dishes took third place. This booklet is small but power-packed. It also has an 7 additional bonus recipes. For a rich variety of outstanding recipes you must have this collection.

Sink your teeth into the **Pizza** or the **Lasagna** from page 6, or drool over the **Broccoli & Chicken Casserole** from page 17. The **Tuna Ring With Cheese Sauce** from page 19 is superb. And wait until you try the **Chicken Enchiladas** from page 4. Enjoyable surprises with each recipe.

'THE FABULOUS 50'
MAIN DISH
RECIPES

From Friends & Neighbors

- by Dorene Gomm

Fabulous 50 cookbook is well organized, easy to use and indexed for ease in finding the recipes. This small cookbook has been designed with;

- ● **Slick, 2-tone durable cover.**
- ● **Simple saddle binding.**
- ● **User friendly.**
- ● **Indexed for your convenience.**
- ● **A treat on every page.**

This is not a gourmet cookbook, although many recipes could be converted into gourmet dishes with the addition of certain spices and other special effects. Many of these recipes can also be converted to dutch oven cooking.

Good basic recipes, yet elegant enough for company. Some are new, some are traditional, but all are tested and found to please. Most ingredients will already be in your kitchen. This booklet is a must to take with you when cooking away from home.

JUST $5.95

"HOT POTATOES" --by **Dorene Gomm** This spud cookbook has 551 potato recipes, and 41 supporting recipes. A delight to both the novice or experienced cook and a "must have" for cookbook collectors. This book is filled with information about this potato, its different varieties, and many helpful cooking tips." Some features of this book are:

- **Durable plastic spiral binding.**
- **Attractive 4 color cover.**
- **User friendly index.**
- **"Non meat" dishes in each section.**
- **7 sturdy divider pages with potato tips.**

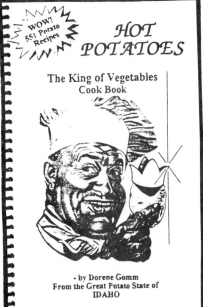

Potatoes are so versatile they can be used for all meals, even snacks. With **Hot Potatoes** as a guide, meal planning is easier and your food budget will decrease. Couple the two together for a winning combination. For outstanding dishes, try:

Chicken Chowder in Crusty Bread Bowls on pg. 78, Spoon Bread Meat Pie on pg. 105 or Apple/Potato Walnut Cake Pg. 201

Potatoes are synonymous with nutritious eating and low cost dishes. Few calories and zero fat per serving. Rich in vitamin C and B6, low sodium, high potassium, and high fiber. Potatoes are the best vegetable source of protein and usable iron found along with valuable trace minerals. The potato is truly. . . **THE KING OF VEGETABLES**

A STEAL AT $14.95

"DUTCH OVEN COOKING" --by **Colleen Sloan** A must for the beginner or experienced cook who loves outdoors and nutritious dutch oven cooking. Written by the owner of a dutch oven catering service that takes you back to those days when food was food, without additives, and nutrition wasn't compromised. People are returning in droves back to cooking out of those cast iron pots. It's such a healthy way to eat. The book is delightfully illustrated and full of useful instructions on using Dutch oven methods including seasoning of the oven and sizes that are best and why. Special features include:

- **Durable spiral binding.**
- **Will stand or hang on a branch.**
- **Sturdy section divider pages**

Other recipes are easily converted to dutch oven methods. Soups, stews, one pot meals, breads, desserts and much more can be cooked in the Dutch oven. When you learn to become a dutch oven chef your cooking will be relished at outdoor events. A perfect gift for the out-of-doors person. You'll be glad you purchased this educational cookbook.

WORTH EVERY BIT OF THE $9.95

"LOG CABIN GRUB" –by **Colleen Sloan**   A cookbook filled with 236 old recipes that brought the Mormons and other pioneers out West. Learn to cook from scratch (the more healthy way) with these basic recipes covering meats, breads,

desserts and miscellaneous.   And learn why Grandma was so creative with her **noodles, soda-crackers, mayonnaise, hore-hound candy,** and much more -- even **home-made soap**. Also old remedies and cures, and helpful hints are found throughout this book.

Colleen's refreshing sense of humnor is splashed throughout all her cookbooks. Some words of wisdom are shared, such as. . . " to keep peanut butter from sticking to the roof of your mouth, turn the sandwich upside down." This book will make you laugh, and laughing is like nutritious food... good for what ails you... good for your health.

Just $9.95

"LOG CABIN LEFT-OVERS" –by **Colleen Sloan**   "As a kid on the farm my Mom would call, 'Supper's on'.....so we came running. No matter what Mom fixed, it was special. She'd bring out the left-overs and put them on a new level. I have

tried to be as creative as mother with this book on leftovers."

Old timers were frugal. It was sinful to waste food, so new creations were made. It behooves us all to be a little more frugal with the high cost of living always increasing. It's an art to reuse foods; putting together leftovers from two or three meals to make a great meal. Only the cook knows leftovers were used.

You'll find the same features in this cookbook as are found in Colleeen's other books. In addition it is filled with ideas to add zest and new life to your leftovers. May the many recipes and stories bring back memories of the "Good Old Days", or if young, acquaint you with how to prepare left-overs. Read, use and enjoy this book, and share your talents and the wisdom you learn from it with others.

Only $9.95

OTHER BOOKS NOW IN THE MAKING BY DORENE AND COLLEEN:

"Family Treasures" --by **Dorene:** Ten excellent family cooks gathered together the best of their best for this treasured collection. These are so good the person submitting them has signed their name to their recipes.

"Log Cabin Holidays & Traditions" --by **Colleen:** It took four years of researching old traditions, games and recipes. All holidays from New Years, through Christmas are covered, including things old timers made, games they played, and lots of recipes.

ORDER FORM: For larger quanity purchases call for quotes.

SUMMIT PUBLICATIONS
1554 North 700 East Dept. 1   Shelley, Idaho 83274
For MasterCard or Visa orders: Phone (208)-357-5359   Fax (208)-357-2302

<u>Yes!</u> I want to order the following books. Please send:

_____ "Hot Potatoes" at $14.95 plus $2.25 shipping each . . . . $_____

_____ "The Fabulous 50" at $ 5.95 plus $1.25 shipping each . . . . . $_____

_____ "Dutch Oven Cooking" at $9.95 plus $1.75 shipping each . $_____

_____ "Log Cabin Grub" at $9.95 plus $1.75 shipping each . . . . . . $_____

_____ "Log Cabin Leftovers" at $9.95 plus $1.75 each . . . . $_____

_____ "Cookin' With Home Storage $14.95 plus $2.50 shipping . $_____

Think of a Friend. Buy two or more of the same title and subtract $1.50 per book.

Idaho residents add 5% sales tax . . . . $_____

Total amount enclosed for books, tax and shipping . . . . $_____

Print name and address CLEARLY for shipping.

NAME: _____

ADDRESS: _____

CITY: _____ ST. _____ ZIP _____

PHONE NUMBER: _____

Circle method of payment: Money Order Check Visa MasterCard

Name as it appears on credit card: _____

Card # _____ Expiration Date _____

For MasterCard or Visa orders: Phone (208)-357-5359   Fax (208)-357-2302

Thank you for your order. If ordering by Money Order, Visa or MasterCard, your order will be shipped immediately. Orders paid by check will be held until check clears.